Praise for
There Was a Time

"Alan Leeds was a protégé of James Brown and a true historian of the world that nurtured the great entertainer. Alan was a witness to the vibrant black music scene of the '60s and '70s whose book is both a memoir and a document of a lost world of sound."

—NELSON GEORGE

"Alan Leeds is one of those cats that absorbs the situation & can recite it back to u word for word, always on point with details & graphics. That is what drew me closer to observing him, other than his big red Afro! We all started with James Brown around the same time. I didn't know what all Alan was doing at the time, but I knew if JB hired him he had to be on 'Heel & Toe or else u got to Blow!' That was one of JB's famous expressions to me while he was laughing, but u knew he was serious. To this day, when Alan speaks about something that happened back in our JB days u can just about take it to the Bank! Thxs Mr. Leeds for helping to preserve that funky & sometimes funked up history."

—BOOTSY COLLINS

"I learned, I laughed, and I saw myself in Alan's history with my father. Alan's business and personal experiences with Dad will enrich each reader. Mr. Leeds may not be a doctor but he's a great writer!"

—DEANNA BROWN THOMAS, daughter of James Brown

"One of Alan Leeds's greatest gifts is that of a storyteller. *There Was a Time: James Brown, The Chitlin' Circuit, and Me* is one of the most entertaining, informative and gripping memoirs I've ever read. Mr. Leeds continues to inspire generations of musicians and music fans with his insights and innate hipness."

—CHRISTIAN MCBRIDE, Grammy-winning bassist & bandleader

THERE WAS A TIME

JAMES BROWN,
THE CHITLIN' CIRCUIT,
AND ME

ALAN LEEDS

Post Hill
PRESS

A POST HILL PRESS BOOK

There Was a Time:
James Brown, The Chitlin' Circuit, and Me
© 2020 by Alan Leeds
All Rights Reserved

ISBN: 978-1-64293-384-0
ISBN (eBook): 978-1-64293-385-7

Cover art by Cody Corcoran
Interior design and composition by Greg Johnson, Textbook Perfect
All interior images courtesy of the Alan Leeds Archives.

Post Hill Press
New York • Nashville
posthillpress.com

Published in the United States of America

To Gwen, Tristan, Eric & Skates

JAMES BROWN ENT.
850 SEVENTH AVE.
SUITE 703
NEW YORK N.Y.

CINCINNATI OFFICE
1540 BREWSTER AVE.
CINCINNATI, OHIO
(513) 221-4899

December 31, 1969

Hi Brothers and Sisters!

JAMES BROWN PRODUCTIONS is proud to announce that the top
name in Soul will play the top hotel...JAMES BROWN at the
sparkling INTERNATIONAL HOTEL in LAS VEGAS...opening January 9th through January 25th!!! For the first time SOUL
is on top and we're proud that JAMES BROWN put it there!

1969 has been the greatest year yet for JAMES BROWN and
as usual we have you to thank.

JAMES BROWN HONORS AND AWARDS-1969

Businessman of the Year-Memphis, Tennessee
Humanitarian Award-B'nai B'rith, Lodge of Performing Arts
Top Male Vocalist and Top Soul Vocalist-Billboard, Record
        World and Cashbox magazines
Man of the Year-Detroit, Michigan
NATRA-Artist of the Year
Mr. Brown received the keys to numerous cities throughout
        the country proclaiming JAMES BROWN DAYS.
To date JAMES BROWN has sold over 70 million single records
        and 30 million albums!!!

For all of this we thank you.

On January 9th when Mr. Brown opens the historic engagement at the International Hotel, we will all be thinking
about you, knowing that you helped put us there. It looks
like a great year for JAMES BROWN PRODUCTIONS....thanks
again and in return may we wish you the best of New Years!

Sincerely,

JAMES BROWN PRODUCTIONS
Alan M. Leeds

FOREWORD

By Ahmir "Questlove" Thompson

THIS BOOK IS ABOUT JAMES BROWN, of course, and, later, slightly about Prince, but more than anything, it's about Alan Leeds. It's about how a young white Jewish kid with a love for black music moved to Virginia in 1959 at the age of twelve and felt the world around him changing. It's about how he obtained an early foothold in the world of radio. It's about how he learned to understand and, later, to love the Chitlin' Circuit, the network of towns, venues, lodgings, and restaurants that hosted and nourished black entertainers in the 1960s. It's about the incredibly complex cultural fabric of civil rights-era America, the deaths of beloved leaders, the importance of artists, political power, Black Power, soul power, and more. It's a story with sweep and, because of that, a story where it's all the more important that the main character hold the center. Alan does.

Let's go back a step into the world of James Brown, which is where Alan's world starts to accelerate. If you grew up in America in the last part of the twentieth century, you felt the impact of James Brown. Alan felt it at close range. He met him when he was a kid, and then returned later to work for him as a concert promoter and more. For much of the '70s, Alan didn't just have a front-row seat to James Brown's life and career; he was in the ring. He watched at close range as Brown courted and alienated the press, as he hired and fired legendary musicians, as he spent lavishly and denied payment to some of his closest associates—including Alan himself.

This sounds fun. I'm sure it was fun—at times, almost too much fun to believe. But it was also grueling, and Alan shows that side too. His time in Brown's orbit, which started during the period of incendiary soul and funk hits, took on a different feel as Brown descends into idiosyncrasy. Not just that, but time was passing him by as well: other artists like Kool & the Gang and Harold Melvin & the Blue Notes rose from obscurity to mainstream success. Alan witnessed that process, tried to understand it, and sometimes even participated in it. Maybe most importantly, Brown's musical innovations, his musical DNA, and even some of his musical collaborators drifted away from him into the orbit of George Clinton and the P-Funk empire, which borrowed as much from arena rock and theatrical productions as they do from the old Chitlin' Circuit acts.

Alan's story, which didn't start with James Brown, doesn't end with James Brown either. When he eventually left the JB orbit, he went to work with the brightest and most innovative star in that new constellation: Prince. Hired to Prince's camp as a direct result of his experience with Brown, Leeds arrived just as Prince was about to ascend into the stratosphere. His presence in Prince's camp became the second act of his life, and a place where he saw several of the earlier patterns reappear. That makes Alan uniquely qualified to speak on matters of stardom, culture, and race. Standing near one genius is a life-altering experience. Standing near two is a credential.

The brilliance of Alan's book is that, even as he shows how the larger musical world shifts, he never forgets to talk about how it affected him. He's a historian, of course, and a chronicler of the time, but he's also a talented memoirist who isn't afraid to show what he learned and admit that he sometimes unlearned those same things. As a result, this memoir offers an indispensable look inside some of the most important music of our time. So please welcome Mr. Prose Prose Prose, Mr. Dynawrite, the Hardest Working Memoirist in Show Business: Alan Leeds.

INTRODUCTION

STARTING A NEW JOB IS SUPPOSED TO BE EXCITING. There might be a bit of anxiety but, overall, it ought to be an upbeat experience. But filling a new position at James Brown Productions in Cincinnati wasn't that simple. It came loaded with apprehension. For me, it was about more than just the immediacy of the gig. James Brown and his company could have easily been a metaphor for an entire culture and society I had become infatuated with through music. It was a world that most young white guys knew nothing about in 1969, but I had been dancing around its edges since my early teens, and now I was about to dive into the deep end. James Brown had pretty much invented me a position as a publicist, an attractive enough idea for me to quit college and set out for Ohio.

Set amidst a mom-and-pop industry, everything about James Brown's operation seemed impressive. He had the elite tour on the soul music circuit, and I assumed that his business was run with the efficient, military precision that guided his show. Wrong. I would discover that his touring show sometimes struggled to make payroll, that his nattily dressed promo men weren't always on top of their game, and that every horn player in the band wasn't a star-quality musician—but those were the exceptions. The biggest surprise was how his impulsiveness and ego frequently trumped his vast knowledge of the black music business into decisions that weren't always in his best interest.

What JB didn't know was that I had dreamed of working for him since we'd first met in 1965, I wanted to be part of that special something that James stood for beyond just the music. He was already renowned for cleverly and effectively thwarting the institutionalized racism in the touring, recording, and media industries. He never cowered from any obstacle and he never forgot the Jim Crow poverty that he had come from. His way of giving back could be as direct as slipping a hundred-dollar bill to a hard-working kid in a gas station, a derelict on a street corner, or an old friend down on his luck. In the wake of Dr. Martin Luther King's assassination, Brown became a go-to TV guest when talk shows needed a "black view." His social convictions were sometimes surprisingly conservative, but he spoke the language of America's black ghettoes, where his cred among youngsters was without peer (at least, until he endorsed Richard Nixon for President, but that came later).

After five years of following the James Brown tour bus, first as an R&B radio disc jockey in Richmond, Virginia, and then as a fan and a friend, I was on a first-name basis with most of the JB touring entourage. I was a veteran of Brown's legendary after-show gab fests, at which he would brazenly share his opinions and ideologies about music, race, and politics, and even sometimes hire or fire someone— such as a new publicist. It occurred to me that the people I knew in the Brown camp worked on the road, not in Cincinnati where production manager Bud Hobgood, record promoter Speedy Brown (no relation), tour director Bob Patton, and several secretary types were based. Other than Patton, none of them had a clue who I was or why I was coming.

I naively hoped that being anointed by the boss himself would enhance my welcome in the little office that was headquarters for both his recording and touring enterprises. What I did know was that job security was a rare commodity within James Brown Productions. Band members and roadies seemed to come and go at a pace beyond the normal road attrition. One time, I caught the show and one of the Famous Flames was missing. I asked about him and was told something like, "Oh, he's off getting his teeth fixed." Another time, veteran emcee Danny Ray came up missing, supposedly away somewhere in "radio school." The next time I saw the show, both were back in the saddle without explanation. While Brown went to lengths to conceal certain realities from fans or friends who might visit backstage, his tyranny was legendary on the music biz grapevine. It was said that, on any given day, he might simply grow tired of an employee and invent an issue to provoke his or her dismissal. As I got closer to Cincinnati, I wondered if my years of loyal friendship offered any immunity to JB's impulsiveness. Probably not. That impulsiveness was the very reason I had a job and an all-access pass to the world I had coveted so desperately.

This is not a James Brown biography. For those who wish to learn details about his long career, how he rose from abject poverty to an international superstar, how he reinvented black music several times over, I recommend RJ Smith's *The One*.

Nor is it a complete memoir. My years with James Brown had not been designed as the launch of a career strategy. I had no clear-cut professional goals other than to keep my gig, and foolishly spent very little time looking ahead. I had devoted myself to working my way into Brown's camp but, once inside, it *felt* like the job had come easily. I quickly learned that the fan in me was, in fact, the professional in me. My biggest gratification came when the house lights went down, the curtains opened, and the audience screamed. I soon discovered that the music business was like a club and, once accepted into the club, it wasn't difficult to find work. One job just seemed to morph into another. So, it should come as no surprise that I spent many of my prime years as a free-lance tour manager.

Some relationships were lengthy, others brief. But, over the 1970s, 1980s, and 1990s, I worked or toured with Bobby Byrd, Kool & the Gang, Harold Melvin & the Blue Notes, Bootsy's Rubber Band, George Clinton and the P-Funk All Stars, Kiss, Cameo, Morris Day and The Time, Sheila E, Barry White, Maxwell, Raphael Saadiq, and Chris Rock. Along the way were ten consecutive years working for

Prince, first as a tour manager and then as head of his Paisley Park Records, a joint venture with Warner Brothers Records. It's been a great ride full of interesting experiences of all kinds, but those wishing to hear about Prince, Kiss, and the other artists I've worked with will have to wait. Up until my retiring from the road in 2019, I was co-managing D'Angelo, who was as much a godson as he was a client.

Despite the different forms of racism still prevalent in this country, I can safely say that Americans know more about each other than they did when I joined James Brown Productions, naïve enough to think that I really knew my boss. I quickly found that I didn't. But what I learned during the next five years is the reason that I am who I am, and have the career that I have today.

Actually, I don't think anyone completely KNEW James Brown, not even his wives and children. Each of us who did know him well encountered different sides. There were many—wives, offspring, friends from his early days—who knew sides of him that I did not, but, in reminiscing with some of them, I recognize that I knew things they didn't. James Brown's extraordinary story spanned six decades and was never boring. Long after his music was defined and his performance skills aged, his off-stage escapades remained tabloid fodder. The economics of modern show business and the culture of celebrity being what they are, Brown earned more money than ever in his latter years. But the years that mattered most, the years in which he reinvented black music, the years in which he pioneered the liberation of the black artist, the penultimate years of the civil rights struggle, were the years I happened to be around. It's a taste of that era's ambition, passion, energy, hope, inventiveness, and spirit that I try to capture in this book.

1

There was never much question that I'd end up spending my life around show business. My parents' relationship with music was limited to appreciation, but there is still a DNA argument to make on my behalf. During my grade school years, an uncle, Mel Leeds, was program director of WINS Radio in New York, home of the legendary disc jockeys Alan Freed, Cousin Brucie Morrow, and Murray the K. An aunt, Florence, worked for a major song publisher, figuring in the nascent careers of Paul Simon and Quincy Jones while her husband, Phil Zolkind, was a saxophonist who spent years backing Perry Como on NBC television and briefly played in the *Tonight Show* band. These associations begot tons of free promo records and exposure to captivating trade magazines like Cash Box and Billboard. But I was too young to think about a career. I was just a kid that loved radio and records.

In fact, I had a downright fetish about records. Among my earliest memories is standing transfixed in front of the record player, staring at the needle gleefully strolling through grooves, those magical grooves that nested so much excitement and joy.

Anyone who knew me probably would have predicted I'd be a musician. I sang in the chorus at school, but so did every other kid who could carry a tune. My passion surfaced at home where I'd overturn wastebaskets and form a drum-kit, banging away until my parents screamed for me to stop. But I discovered that I had a good sense of time, so I enrolled in a fourth-grade drum class and anxiously looked forward to trading my trash cans for real drums. To my chagrin, I was given a rubber practice pad. No matter how I hit that pad, the only thing produced was a distinctly unmusical thud. Not what I had in mind. The second week, we were instructed to practice a very basic paradiddle, which I attacked with a vengeance, all the while madly tapping my foot. The instructor, whose personality was no more musical than the pad I was playing, silently but sternly shoved his hand on my knee to stop my foot tapping. Had he respected my intelligence enough to explain that tapping my foot was a bad habit I would have to break in order to develop the independence necessary to play a bass drum and hi-hat, I might be a drummer today. But all he did was clamp down on my knee, so my stubborn, anti-authority streak surfaced, sending me back to my wastebaskets until I could eventually mimic Sonny Payne's entire performance on the classic *Basie at Birdland* album. I never returned to class. Turned out my younger brother, Eric, would be the musician in the family. A remarkable saxophonist, flautist, composer, and band leader, Eric, had the patience, focus, and discipline that I lacked.

As a kid, my interests were as simple as they were enthusiastic. All I really cared about were baseball, music, and my birthplace, the city of New York. If the order of my priorities changed from time to time, my *modus operandi* did not. I was a maniac about the things I loved.

My early grade school years were spent in Milwaukee, where we first lived, just up the hill from County Stadium, the new home of the Braves. Still, I spent much of my summers back in baseball-crazy New York, the ward of a doting grandmother and the aforementioned uncles and aunt. New York had three baseball teams, and they all got love in our household. My Dad was a life-long Yankee fan, although he'd happily take me to see whatever team was around. Uncle Phil's cousin, Sid Gordon, was an outfielder for the Giants, so the Polo

Grounds was his turf. Uncle Mel cheered for the Dodgers at Ebbets Field. So did I.

Dad was convinced that Mel bought my Dodger allegiance with the gift of my first baseball glove, but there was something intriguing about the Dodgers. Having broken the color line with Jackie Robinson the year I was born, seven years later they had a league-leading number of black players—Jackie Robinson, Roy Campanella, Don Newcombe, Junior Gilliam, Joe Black, and the Cuban outfielder Sandy Amorós. All were exciting players, but so were white Dodgers like Duke Snider, Gil Hodges, and Pee Wee Reese, who I adored just as much. Maybe it was the style of play they brought from the Negro Leagues, or the fact that the black players *had* to be star-caliber players to earn their place in the dugout. Even the "liberal" Dodgers weren't interested in any bench-warming African-American journeymen. And, by the way, Dad's Yankees were one of the last teams to integrate, not fielding a black player until 1955. I asked Dad, "What took them so long?" But, none of this was really part of a seven-year-old's sensibility. Maybe my affection was as simple as the team's underdog history or their cool-looking blue uniforms. (Out of deference to Pop, I'm obligated to admit that, by the mid-1990s, the now Los Angeles Dodgers were mired in dysfunction, owned by Rupert Murdoch, and inept on the field. The Joe Torre-Derek Jeter Yankees now represented what I had loved about the BROOKLYN Dodgers as a kid. I gulped and gradually became a die-hard Yankee fan. Dad asked, "What took so long?")

New York in the 1950s was a wondrous place to be a kid. On the family's block in Jackson Heights, Queens, there was a candy store that had comic books, baseball cards, and a soda fountain with egg creams. Everything I lusted for was right there under one roof. As I got older, that sense of possibility only opened wider. Every street, every patch of sidewalk in New York seemed to hold a surprise.

Such as the rainy afternoon Uncle Phil and I took off for Colony Records in Manhattan. The shop had been in business for decades and boasted "If we don't have it, we'll find it!" I was going through a blues phase at the time, so I asked a clerk for several obscure sides by Muddy Waters and Howlin' Wolf. He brushed me off. But we weren't easily turned away. Actually, Uncle Phil probably slipped him a buck because the fella finally abruptly grunted, "Come on, kid," and led me behind the counter and down a flight of rickety wooden stairs to a grimy, dimly lit dungeon lined with dusty, ceiling-high shelves stuffed with old records. "The old blues records are over there," he gestured as he turned and went back upstairs. I was shaking at the promise of untold treasures that lay on the shelves, or maybe it was my vision of man-eating rats dancing around to the music on those same funky shelves. I lasted about five nervous minutes, long enough to locate four or five discs I wanted before making a mad break for daylight. Traumatic as it was, that afternoon confirmed that there was nothing I couldn't find in New York if I wanted it badly enough.

One Saturday evening, I was surfing the radio dial when I happened upon a song unlike anything I'd ever heard before. I had stumbled across the Camel Cigarette Rock 'n' Roll Dance Party, Alan Freed's nationally syndicated broadcast from New York. The record was Little Richard's madly rockin' "Long Tall Sally."

It's impossible to describe how it felt to hear music like that for the first time. I couldn't then, and I can't now. I wrote down the name of the record and proceeded to make my mother's life hell for a couple of days.

"MA, YOU GOTTA TAKE ME TO THE RECORD STORE...."

"MA, CAN I HAVE SEVENTY-NINE CENTS? PLEEEASE!"

I got the record. I remember thinking that even the Specialty Records label was exciting, with its bold, gaudy, yellow-and-black stripes and odd script—so unlike the sedate familiar labels like Columbia and RCA Victor. Once we brought it home, Mom wanted to know what I'd been throwing a fit about, so I played "Long Tall

Sally" for her. She looked at me like I was from outer space. Not angry or worried, just mystified. And all I could think to say was, "Ma, isn't it PRETTY?"

I don't give it a lot of thought. I'll probably never understand what drew me so specifically to black music. It wasn't just the rhythm; some *rockabilly* records were equally rhythmic (and I liked them too). Ultimately, it was something else that wrestled my focus from much of pop music and steered it towards black radio and rhythm and blues. The music was an entrée to a community made mysterious simply because I had no other access to it. It sounded like someplace I wanted to go long before I knew where it was. Or maybe it wasn't that deep. Let's face it—there was an undeniable excitement and lure to this music that stood on its own.

There were perks to having an uncle running a radio station. Once Mel recognized my interest in music, he began sending me care packages from WINS, boxes of unsorted records, duplicates, and overstock from the station's library. The grab bags always contained some of the current pop hits that I heard on Milwaukee radio, but I was more intrigued by the less familiar R&B discs on colorful labels like Atlantic, Chess, and King. Soon, Aunt Florence was sending still more records. It was like having my own radio station. In fact, I started running my own little fantasy disc jockey show from my bedroom, "broadcasting" via walkie talkie, to a captive audience, my brother Eric across the hall.

I found the contrived radio formats for rock 'n' roll and rhythm and blues confusing, as confusing as the institutionalized racism that pervaded everything in America. I soon recognized that pop stations had a quota limiting how many R&B records they aired at any given time. Those slots usually went to artists who had managed to "cross over," such as Chuck Berry, Fats Domino, and Little Richard. Black music fans who coveted a steady diet of the real thing were relegated to stations whose programming was strictly aimed at the black community.

It was 1959, less than three years since I discovered "Long Tall Sally," and the rock 'n' roll revolution was barely out of its infancy, but things were changing. Little Richard divorced Sally for Jesus; Elvis swapped his pegged pants for army khakis; Chuck Berry traded a night with an under-age southern belle for a jail cell; and a backlash against rock 'n' roll was in full swing. The stage show tours sponsored by Alan Freed and others were accused of stirring up "riots"—in reality, a few scattered melees that were magnified by white fears of all the "race-mixing" going on in the audiences.

White America, thus white radio, wasn't having it. The days of Little Richard's hard-hitting, sex-infused, black rock 'n' roll were over or, at least, banished to black radio. Almost overnight, a freshly scrubbed pop radio was emphasizing banal dance tunes and sappy love songs by the likes of Frankie Avalon and Pat Boone. The few black records that crossed over were often ballads by crooners like Brook Benton and a young Sam Cooke.

Somehow, in the middle of all this, one of Mel's care packages delivered my next epiphany: Ray Charles. Charles' "What'd I Say" was the diametric opposite to everything else on the radio, arguably the most risqué pop hit of rock's first era. It wasn't just that the lyrics, the heated call, and response between Ray and his sexy Raelettes left little to the imagination but the primitive, syncopated push and shove of the rhythms. The record was hypnotic, innovative, deceptively simple, and downright on fire. Against all odds, the disc became pop's anti-Christ, inexplicably working its way onto white radio, becoming Ray's first pop hit and the party anthem of the summer.

Now I had to track down all the previous Ray Charles records, which was not a simple matter; he had been making them for a decade and most had never left the black community. But, before I could get started, my world turned upside down.

My father, enjoying a department store career on the rise, came home one day and reported he'd taken a new job as vice president of a store in Richmond, Virginia. Yikes! Richmond? They didn't even have major league baseball! I may have yearned to be considered a New Yorker but, let's face it, Milwaukee was really home. And, by the way, it was the only home my brother ever knew and, if I liked it, he loved it. In other words, to my taste, unless we were moving to the Big Apple, we ought to just stay put. Poor Richmond didn't even have a place in my conversation.

Mom and Dad tried to assuage Eric's and my dread by touting our new home and the huge front yard that awaited us. Dad made it sound like Yankee Stadium. Great place to play baseball, he claimed, "big enough to lay out a diamond."

On the day we arrived, a torrential rain was falling. As we pulled into the driveway, a wet mongrel dog charged the car and snarled at us—my first taste of Southern hospitality. The field-of-dreams front yard had so many trees it would play more like a pinball table than a baseball field. In my eyes, those of a devout city boy, nothing was right about the place. It was a ranch-style house in a suburban development; the streets were barely paved, there were no curbs or sidewalks, and everything of any interest was too far away to safely reach by bicycle. And, even if I tried, everybody in the neighborhood seemed to have dogs that ran loose and chased bikes. The hounds sensed my fear, which didn't help matters. Soon, I was peeking through the windows for prowling canines before I ventured outside. When I did, they'd get together and follow me down the street like a gang of toughs out to snatch the new kid's lunch money. Even *they* seemed to know I was a Yankee Jew...Nazi dog bastards!

My independence was gone. When the dogs weren't around to remind me of my outsider status, there were other clues. The rudest early reminder that I wasn't in Milwaukee anymore came during my first week of school. "Now then," the teacher drawled one afternoon, "which ones of y'all aren't gonna be here tomorrow because of the Jooooeesh holiday?" I was one of two or three kids to raise my hands. After class, my locker mate stared at me. "You're Jewish?" he asked. "You don't look Jewish." The word got around, and I was viewed

7

differently after that. YOU DON'T ACT LIKE A JEW, people would say when the subject arose—hey, thanks!—but, socially, there remained a barrier I'd find difficult to cross. It didn't mean I got into fights, or even that I was taunted much; it just meant I was invisible. I could never be one of *them*.

(This is not to say that I wouldn't have faced anti-semitism had I continued to grow up in Milwaukee, hardly a bastion of liberalism. But, as a grade-schooler in the "Father Knows Best" neighborhood I lived in, being Jewish had never been a discussion, let alone an issue— at least not that I was aware of.)

OF COURSE, ONCE I GOT ADJUSTED to Richmond, I began discovering some upsides. One was the proliferation of old jukebox records for sale. Every drug store and dime store had a box of used 45s on the counter selling three or four for a buck. And, because the populations in Richmond and the surrounding counties were over 50 percent black, many of those records were late-model R&B singles. It was a terrific means to stock up on Ray Charles' back catalog as well as inexpensively explore sides by artists I had read about.

Another saving grace of Richmond was that, owing to some geographical phenomenon, it was a terrific place to pick up faraway radio stations at night.

From "high atop the Life and Casualty building in downtown Nashville, Tennessee," on any given night, half the country was groovin' to WLAC. This legendary, 50,000-watt clear-channel station broadcast news and milquetoast pop music by day, but every night about 9:00 p.m., an astonishing transformation took place. WLAC turned into something unlike anything else before or since, the closest thing possible to a national soul radio network. Their one-of-a-kind nighttime signal reached east to Bermuda, south to Cuba, west to Colorado and north to Canada. But, more importantly, they covered the entire southeast because, at night, they played nothing but black music.

WLAC's bizarre mixed format created full-fledged icons out of three white disc jockeys who loved rhythm and blues so much they became part of its very fabric. I don't know what was greater, their influence on record sales or on the hundreds of kids like me who dreamt of being on the radio. Gene Nobles, John R. (Richbourg) and Bill "Hoss" Allen probably introduced more white people to hard-core country blues, southern soul, and even gospel music than anyone on the planet.

For the smaller southern cities that lacked a local black station or, like Richmond, had a station that signed off at sundown, WLAC became their own. Several hours after local station WANT signed off the air, black Richmonders habitually reached for the radio and "put on Nashville."

As a white kid laying in bed in the suburbs, WLAC was better than dreaming. John R. and Hoss Allen had classic radio voices, that nicotine-and-alcohol-thickened octave that massages your ears. While hardly anyone outside of Nashville had any idea these slang-slinging guys were white, their voices did come from the south; where, regardless of the weather, it always sounded like a hot, sticky, sexy, soulful summer night.

It was WLAC that launched me on my next quest when I heard James Brown's "Lost Someone." Up to that point, Brown had managed to elude me. I had worn out the dime store bargain bins, so that meant I was going to have to get downtown and work up the nerve to cross Broad Street.

Broad Street is Richmond's main thoroughfare, dissecting the city from the historic Church Hill district on the east side all the way to the western suburbs. It also served as downtown Richmond's color line. On the south side of Broad sat the department stores, exclusive jewelry shops, and boutiques. The north side hosted more modest storefronts that catered to a mostly black clientele, among which must have been half a dozen mom-and-pop record shops, ranging in specialty from gospel to R&B to jazz. And there were blocks of small retailers, selling everything from clothing to furniture, usually clip joints that preyed on the poor with "easy payment plans."

My first venture across Broad Street was high on both apprehension and excitement. I was finally tip toeing into that world the music I loved had been hinting at. Once on the north side of the street, I walked through Standard Drug, a sprawling pharmacy/variety store that extended the depth of the block. A door in back opened onto a small parking lot; from inside the air-conditioned store, I swore I could see the ninety-plus degree heat rising in waves off the pavement. One step outside and I was officially in the business district of black Richmond, and I'll be damned if I couldn't hear music in the distance. It was James Brown's "Night Train," gaining in volume with every step towards Marshall Street. The summer stickiness tugged the rhythms of the Brown band into some kind of hypnotic cloud that sucked me forward. I followed it across Marshall and another half block up First Street, straight to a pair of blaring speakers framing the door of Barky's Record Shop.

There really was a Barky—actually, Everett Barksdale. Wiry, frenetic, and chatty, Barky always greeted customers with the same shtick. As soon as I passed through the doorway, he exploded, "Why, I'll be damned. Look who's walkin' in my door. Cuz, I was just thinkin' about you. Betty, wasn't I just talkin' about him a minute ago?"

Betty and the other clerks, women who wore the same beige smocks as the boss, always played along. Mind you, this was the first time I'd been anywhere near the store. Surely Barky knew that, but for the slim chance he had me confused with some other black-music-seeking white teenager. (Maybe on First Street, *we* all looked alike).

Barky's inventory was meticulously organized—to the point that Betty shot a hairy eyeball at any browser who didn't re-place records in the correct spot. From that day on, every dime I could hustle I spent at Barky's.

It was around this time that I attended my first R&B concert and my life was forever changed. It was a Sunday night show at the Mosque, a grand old theater that seated just over 3,000. Billed as the "Biggest Show of Stars" for 1962, the show included the Drifters (then featuring the amazing Rudy Lewis), Fats Domino and his New Orleans band, a young Curtis Mayfield and his Impressions, Brook Benton, and Gene Chandler.

The lights dimmed, the band hit the downbeat, the musty Mosque curtain rose, and I gasped. Emcee Harold Cromer bounced on stage as saxophonist Paul "Hucklebuck" Williams led a hard-hitting orchestra that instantaneously made me feel something I'd never experienced. Listening to records or radio was one thing, but absorbing R&B's live rhythms and funky melodies in a theater was a *physical* thing. Just as vividly, I recall being struck by the romance of the whole milieu—the mingled scent of perfume and sweat within the excited crowd as the show lights reflected off of the tight, matching spangled jackets the band wore. And then came the dancers—an ensemble called the Twisting Parkettes. Among the Parkettes were three girls with the shortest skirts and cutest legs I'd ever seen who promptly broke into the sexiest version of the twist imaginable, sexy but short of nasty. I instantly imagined that a date with a Parkette would be a night to remember but I also convinced myself that, if she put on some jeans, I could take her home to meet Mom. The show was great, but I have to admit I don't remember much about it, I couldn't get past the Twisting Parkettes! My mind was racing. Where were they as the Impressions took the stage? Backstage chillin'? Changed into their street clothes and heading for the show bus? The world those girls lived in could have been on Mars, it seemed so far removed from mine. But I couldn't help but fantasize what it was like on their tour bus. And fantasy it was, since I neither sang nor played a note of music. But then came the aha moment. It struck me that there must be some guy who organized their travel, kept the tour on its feet,

11

much less got to hang with these girls backstage every night and spend a month on a bus together. AND get paid!

As the crowd filed out after the show, people buzzed about this artist or that, but my mind was fixed on the tour bus parked behind the Mosque. I was hooked. I had no idea what contribution I could make that would earn a seat next to a Twisting Parkette, but I'll be damned if I wasn't going to get a ticket to ride.

2

My forays north of Broad Street eventually came more naturally. Maybe part of me relished the role of innocent outsider. One thing was for sure, my answer to color lines was that everyone, of any color, should have the right to ignore them.

One Saturday afternoon in the fall of 1962, I was strolling around downtown with Tom Hill, one of my boys from school and a fellow music buff. Tom happened to play tenor sax and, after he and some other kids from the suburbs formed a band called The Escorts, I had a brief notion to be their manager. They ended up managing themselves, but this particular day Tom and I were meandering down Main Street, when we stumbled upon the studio of WANT, Richmond's only black radio station. We stood on the sidewalk for a minute or two, conjuring a plausible excuse for going inside, which turned into inquiring about renting studio space for an Escorts demo recording.

The preppy young man who greeted us was nothing like what I'd stupidly imagined WANT's jive-talking DJs to be. Clayton "C.P." Brown was a college student who worked weekends at WANT. God knows why he invited us in. Maybe he just found us curious, two white teenagers without any real agenda. He led us into a cramped broadcast booth where we could continue our conversation, pausing every two or three minutes while he did commercials and announced the next record. We chatted about music, made vague noises about a demo tape, thanked him for his hospitality, and left.

About a year later, my brother and I bumped into Clayton at the take-out counter of a tiny downtown greasy spoon. To my surprise, he not only remembered me but proudly invited us to see the station's new nearby headquarters. We swapped numbers and soon WANT became my regular Saturday hang, where I befriended another part-time DJ named Ben Miles.

As I learned more about what I innocently saw as the eccentricities of black radio, the songs that had drawn my interest in the first place came to represent a larger culture. A culture that included advertisements for products unknown in the white community such as hair straighteners and skin-tone creams, stores whites didn't patronize, and for concerts and night clubs that whites didn't know existed. Black radio, and the vivid personalities of its announcers, brought that culture to life.

But it was still the music that drove my interest. With my record player, a professional microphone, and a new reel-to-reel tape recorder, the walkie-talkie shows I did for Eric in the '50s turned into a slightly more complex imaginary radio station in the '60s. I might not be a singer or have the patience to learn the drums, but it didn't take long to discover that this was something I COULD do.

Inspired by the legendary disc jockeys, like Jocko Henderson, that I grew up listening to, my template was that of a quick-tongued, often-rhyming announcer who embellished the music he or she played. In those days, it wasn't taboo to talk over the records, so I set out to master the knack of musically timing a clever rap over the intro or fading vamp of soul records. In that regard, my innate musical sense served me well because it wasn't really something you could learn. A disc jockey jive talkin', or what we called "talkin' trash," came from instinctively knowing what SOUNDS rolled off the tongue with rhythm, cadence, and syncopation while bringing out something special in the song you were playing. Anything in a song might be an inspiration, a drum beat, a guitar stroke, a flashy horn lick, or something as obvious as the singers' first verse; any highlight of the record that I could latch onto to grab the listener's attention. I preferred to believe that a DJ's job was to set up the music as excitingly as possible. As important as a DJ's style was his arsenal of devices—pre-recorded, dynamics-filled segues, cues, and "drops" (mini station IDs or time checks); everything was designed to keep the show moving and the listeners on their toes.

Pretty soon, I was playing around at home, practicing drops for WANT. A few actually got on the air. I tried to find other ways to make myself useful to Clayton and Ben, even reading brief newscasts over the air when one of them needed a bathroom break.

Clayton and I gradually became close friends, getting to know each other's families and breaking bread at each other's homes. He was four or five years older and my folks liked him enough to accept me staying over at his place on weekends. I'm sure our friendship was unusual for Richmond circa 1964, but nobody kept tabs of such things. More importantly, nothing about it felt abnormal. C. P.'s dad was a dentist. His older brother and sister were both college grads. The Browns were pretty much typical middle-class Americans, a family I had as much in common with as any of the white kids I knew from school.

C. P., Ben Miles, and I gradually became inseparable. And, when those two had dates on a Friday or Saturday night, since WANT signed off at sundown, they would let me into the radio studios to practice my DJ skills while they were out on the town. I would turn on everything but the transmitter and spend hours taping mock air shifts. I played records, read news, and followed the commercial log, just as if I were live on the air.

The three of us also became a common sight in the taverns and restaurants of black Richmond. Home base was a cafe called Abe's, that was a hang-out for students from Virginia Union, the black university both Ben and C.P. attended. Abe's had great burgers and a killer jukebox.

On one level, I was feeling myself—here I was, rolling with two older college students in a joint where white people seldom ventured; how cool was that? On another level, hanging in black Richmond quickly dispelled any lingering stereotypes. Sometimes I could sense folks checking me out, but I never felt threatened. By and large, I was accepted with little question.

This was the mid-1960s and the civil rights movement was alive and well, heady with optimism. Of course, the treacherous realities of racism always festered and could unexpectedly surface at any given moment. But my point is that the crowd at Abe's wasn't an angry or bitter bunch obsessed with white folks or the racism that was simply taken for granted. Politics and "the movement" certainly got air time, but, like any college scene, the conversations also ranged from mid-term exams to football or the upcoming school dance.

Soon, some of Clayton's other friends began acknowledging me. I got to know their girlfriends and I couldn't avoid looking at the other girls who hung out at Abe's. To my surprise, a few of them looked back. It was all innocent stuff. Other than Twisting Parkettes, my sexual fantasies had been confined to the cheerleaders at my own school, but they were all dating football players (who happened not to be Jewish). Of course, if you hang with a couple of guys long enough, and they've got girlfriends who have friends, pretty soon they figure, "we've got to get Leeds hooked up." Enter Clayton's girlfriend's roommate. You could hardly call it dating; we barely fooled around. We just hung at Abe's, played pinball, and laughed a lot. That drew a few harder looks but, since we were always part of a group that included black guys, I guess everyone assumed there was nothing seriously amiss.

Abe's was mostly an afternoon and early evening hang. At night, one of the more lucrative fringe benefits C.P. and Ben enjoyed as radio personalities was emceeing live shows at dance hall joints like the Clay Street Coliseum, Gregory's Ballroom, and the Market Inn. Inevitably, I began to tag along. I'd be lying if I said I wasn't self-conscious at first. I was not only under age, but usually the only white face in the place. That Clayton and Ben were sometimes uncomfortable didn't help. The mostly blue-collar, sometimes rowdy folks who regularly patronized these joints weren't their peer group either. But none of that mattered much because, for me, it was all about the music, and the music was alive and well in those clubs.

Eventually, I discovered that most of the clubs weren't dangerous at all. Sure, sometimes there were beefs, no different than any clubs white or black where booze, music, and women commingled. In those days, before everyone was packing a weapon, violence in the clubs wasn't serious or frequent enough to justify the label of "cut and shoot joints" that some people automatically attached to black clubs.

Clayton's and Ben's paid appearances were unabashedly in exchange for on-air hype. They also made side money hosting record hops, spinning records at parties, school dances, and church socials. Eventually, it occurred to us that these hustles would benefit from some organization. Thus, was born my first music business venture, Ben Miles Enterprises—or B.M.E.

To be honest, B.M.E. began as Clayton's and my scheme to keep ourselves attached to Ben, whose popularity was skyrocketing. Radio wasn't a career for Clayton, just a fun way to make some cash while he was in school, but Ben lived and breathed broadcasting. As a teenager, he had jerry-rigged a ham transmitter with a signal that stretched down his block. Now, with his daily drive-time slot at WANT, Ben had become a home-grown sex symbol, exciting teenage girls with his hip slang, baby face, and wild hair, straight enough that it flew in all directions when he danced. I was still the unknown, just an occasional voice on the air, but I managed our bookings and did most of the grunt work. I also tested my show biz instincts, convincing Ben and C.P. to turn their ordinary record hop into a production. The idea was to put Ben front and center, promote him as a local celebrity. I reasoned that, for Ben to be received like a star, he would have to play the role, so we would seclude him out of sight until his introduction. He didn't always enjoy that idea. Sometimes it meant sitting alone in a dressing room or his car, for an hour or two, waiting his turn to perform. I would open the show, spinning records as walk-in music to warm up the growing crowd. Then I mustered up some great hyperbole with which to bring on C.P., who did his thing for an hour or so. The climax, star time, was Ben's appearance. With a dramatic intro befitting James Brown at the Apollo, Miles would bounce towards the stage, doing the jerk or the mashed potatoes to whatever disc Clayton had blaring through the system. The kids went nuts.

Many of our gigs were in the rural counties surrounding Richmond. The poverty and isolation of those places was something completely foreign to me. Many of these kids lived in what most of us would call shacks, and went to horribly ill-equipped schools. I remember one winter gig, in a basement that passed for a school cafeteria, where the kids danced as close as they could to the wood-burning stove in the middle of the room, the only source for heat. We played churches and what passed as community centers, where dangerously exposed electrical wiring barely supported the equipment we carried. In this world, Ben and Clayton were not just radio personalities, they were *stars*—handsome, smartly dressed brothers from the city whose shows on WANT delivered a taste of a world and life beyond the one country folk knew. As much as my partners excited these kids, I baffled them. I could hold my own on the mic, so many figured me for some kind of mulatto/albino mutt, unable to fathom that a white guy would even be there. I never overtly claimed to be anything I'm not, but my thick, wavy Jewish hair added to the mystery. There wasn't a night that my hair alone didn't convince some little girl that I had to be Ben's lighter skinned brother.

Occasionally, we were hired to play a white frat party. I can't speak for my partners, but I wasn't crazy about those events. Most white kids genuinely enjoyed rhythm and blues, but I was convinced that some of them embraced the music as a license to act "black" in the ignorant and ribald terms that they imagined blackness represented. That translated to drinking an extra beer, grabbing the girlfriend a little bolder, and dancing a lot wilder. In a sense, that sounds like just about anyone who got loose on a Saturday night, but I'd been to black frat parties too, where the beer flowed just as generously but the brothers understood that the guy who stayed in control of himself and danced the COOLEST, not the herky-jerky slobbering drunk, got the girl. Somehow, that message hadn't reached the white frats. I despised the hypocrisy of white kids eagerly embracing black music with the same zealousness with which they defended Jim Crow traditions.

The white frat parties reminded me of the incongruous realities of southern racism in the '60s. Black entertainers had performed at white college functions for decades, and I eventually discovered that many performers welcomed these gigs where they might find an appreciative audience, better and more reliable paydays, and seemingly safer work environments than the rough and tumble club circuit. Of course, if those entertainers tried to join the next frat party as guests, they wouldn't get inside the door, and God forbid one of the brothers was caught paying any attention to a white girl. Those were the simple dichotomies that prevented me from relaxing and enjoying those gigs. (In light of all this, it's fair to say that my social allegiances and, in a sense, my whole identity was shifting pretty radically, but that's a whole other story beyond the realm of this book.)

Somewhere along the way, for reasons I've forgotten, WANT began referring to itself as "Tiger Radio." Around that time, our Tiger Radio record hop caravan expanded to include three mini-skirted dancing girls whom we dubbed—guess what—the Parkettes...oops, sorry, the Tigerettes! Three guys, three girls, spending nearly every Friday and Saturday night working together—what came next was inevitable. Ben hooked up with one of them first and, soon, I began flirting with another, a girl three years my senior named Georgia, or Gigi for short. She was funny and outgoing, but a fairly straight-laced girl. Then, in January 1965, thanks to one of Richmond's rare—and, therefore, paralyzing—snowstorms, our little posse found itself stranded with a pint of rum at a Holiday Inn. From that point on,

Gigi and I were a couple. Mostly, we socialized as part of the group in the relative safety of black Richmond. Often, after record hops, the six of us ended up back at the radio station, where we didn't have to look over our shoulders.

By now, I was spending nearly all my weekend time with black friends in black settings. It never seemed like there was anything terribly unusual; I was really just living a life, and too busy living it to give it much thought. To be fair, part of the reason why I didn't have to think about it was a testament to the watchful eyes of C.P. and Ben. Like any pals, we had each other's backs.

There were a lot of places in the South where my lifestyle might have put me in harm's way. It wasn't that Richmond was any less race conscious than the rest of America, but there was less mayhem and random violence than in other Southern cities. Richmond may have been the capital of the Confederacy, but it was a community where both blacks and whites valued civility. A relatively gentle colonial paternalism was the rule in race relations, and it kept the peace, so long as blacks didn't push boundaries too energetically.

Meanwhile, I was just a kid who wanted to hear music and enjoy my friends. The greatest dangers to someone like me traditionally lay on the white side of town. It wasn't black folks who blew up little girls in churches or turned dogs loose on kids wanting to attend school. Anyone who found me weird also found me harmless. One day at school, a kid I casually knew pulled me aside. He *had* to talk to me. "Is it true?" he asked with alarm. Was what true? "I heard you were dating a *nigger* girl."

Ahh, that "N" word. Something about the spewing Southern accent left a venomous echo in my ears. He didn't even wait for an answer. "Man, are you out of your mind? You really don't know what you're doing. That kind of shit can be dangerous, you know."

This went on for another minute or two before I calmed down enough to tell him to fuck off. Thing was, this kid was honestly trying to give me a heads up, save me from some horrible curse that could only lead to sin, exotic disease, and finally green kids with three eyes. A few weeks later, a more direct, man-to-man piece of advice came from a good ol' boy with a leery grin. "It's cool to screw 'em," he whispered. "But don't be seen with 'em, for God's sake." This kid didn't wait for a response; he just walked away.

Thankfully, this particular "movement" didn't gain any further steam. I suppose I was already so low on the social totem pole that I wasn't even taken seriously enough to worry about. At least now I understood why I could no longer get dates with any of the girls at school. I guess I was viewed as tainted goods, but it honestly didn't bother me as much as one would think. By then, my life was somewhere else entirely, and Gigi had proven a lot more interesting than any high school girl. Turns out we had a lot more in common than homework.

WANT, LIKE A GREAT MANY SMALL AM stations at the time, had a daytime license; at sundown, it signed off. Late in the spring of 1965, the brief late afternoon air shift opened up and Clayton and Ben recommended me for the job. I was the only white person at the station, aside from Silas Bell, the laid-back general manager who didn't involve himself in programming matters. Thankfully, Tom Mitchell, program director and our mentor, had already accepted my presence. To my everlasting gratitude, Tom took a shot and put me on the air. At age eighteen, I had my own radio show.

My first revelation was discovering that girls dug calling up and flirting with deejays while the records played. But the real gratification came from being the first to break (introduce) a new hit record, as I quickly got the chance to do with Sam & Dave's "You Don't Know Like I Know" and Otis Redding's "Respect."

One thing was always clear: For me, it wasn't really about broadcasting. I was about the music. Radio was a means to an end, and I was already plotting my next step.

First, I began emceeing club shows, another means to an end. Introducing an act on stage took all of a minute or two, and it was worth a hundred bucks from the promoters. R&B radio personalities were all woefully underpaid, my first weekly pay check was less than fifty dollars. Hustling the promoters and hyping their gigs was an industry-wide modus operandi. The whole economy of the black radio business was geared to it. Stingy station owners willingly looked the other way, recognizing that our payola opportunities kept us from demanding better pay.

WANT HAD NO LOBBY AS SUCH—just a large room divided between two office cubicles and a common space, the main broadcast booth, and a small second studio. To the receptionist's chagrin, the common area was basically a club house playing host to a cast of characters straight out of Damon Runyan: promoters, musicians, an alcoholic former announcer who suffered Korean War-inspired shell shock, and various hustlers and hangers-on who gathered to play the dozens and seek their next score.

Show business always had a place for streetwise entrepreneurs. Successful promoters shared a certain kind of flair. They were big shot operators, or wannabe big shots, with big ideas. They knew how to parlay a bankroll, theirs or somebody else's, into business ventures and a public profile that boasted of rubbing elbows with celebrities. The local scene's half dozen promoters regularly congregated at WANT to transact their business and keep tabs on each other. Aside from one who owned and operated a dry cleaners, none of them had any other visible means of support. Nor did any of them own a venue.

Competitive both by nature and necessity, they'd cautiously speak of deals in progress, debate the potential of future shows, and brag about the women they'd partied with the preceding weekend. Local band leaders would pass through hustling gigs from the promoters.

In the 1950s and 1960s, demographics and geography made Richmond a hub on the black music night train. The metro population was over 50 percent black, and the city sits smack in the middle of the I-95 corridor, just 110 miles south of Washington, D.C. Any artist whose touring was routed from the northeast—Boston, New York, Newark, Philadelphia, Baltimore—to the South had to come through Richmond. Consequently, there were always tons of shows available to keep the promoters active on a regular basis. The nature of the business dictated that they hang loosely together, sometimes sharing deals. They also maintained a loose cartel, shutting out any upstarts chasing a piece of the action.

Like several Southern states at that time, Virginia prohibited the sale of liquor by the drink—no bars and no alcohol-serving night clubs. As a result, most of the venues were basically four walls and a stage that promoters rented on a per-event basis. The building proprietors and promoters would share a concession deal, selling food and set-ups to customers who brown-bagged their own booze.

The Godfather of this scene was WANT's own Tom Mitchell. He was cut from a different cloth than the rest of the promoters. A former newspaper reporter and self-styled intellectual—a black Bohemian of sorts—Tom didn't drive but nearly always looked like he'd slept in the backseat of a car. His clothes wrinkled, his shoes worn, and usually sporting two or three days' growth of beard, his appearance belied the fact that he was one of the most respected men in black Richmond. A straight man amongst smooth hipsters, Tom's affectations consisted solely of dated slang like referring to a crony as "Buddy-ghee" and his catch-all response to any greeting, "Country's safe." His only other colloquialism was a raised hand and Dave Garroway's patented sign-off, "Peace."

Tom was a switchboard for whatever happened in black Richmond, be it politics, church functions, or society affairs. We younger guys all believed that he should have been a lawyer or a politician, but Tom liked nothing better than to read his newspapers, do his morning air shift, take a slow lunch at a soul food café, and spend the rest of the day bullshitting about the days of baseballs' Negro Leagues or the state of local government.

Tom didn't fool around much with the dance hall gigs, but he fiercely protected his interest in the major shows, the multi-act packages like the one I'd seen in 1962, that played the larger venues like the Mosque or the Richmond Arena. Mitchell's partner and front man was the veteran of the local promoters, Allen Knight. They made an odd couple. Knight was the shrewdest and boldest of hustlers. One day, he might be selling cars on the side, then fix-it-now-and-pay-forever home improvement schemes, even airtime on WANT. Allen didn't mind getting involved in things Mitchell wouldn't stoop to, like wheeling and dealing with agents, cutting corners with artists when a show wasn't selling, or playing hardball with the other promoters.

I learned a great deal about the business from Knight, the most important lesson being how to deal with people like Allen Knight. (It was rumored that he also taught James Brown in the early '60s, tipping off the singer to his manager Ben Bart's practice of silently co-promoting his appearances.) None of the other promoters had Allen's fast-talking pizazz. Or his stature. As Tom's partner, he handled many of the more prominent single-act shows that came through town, people like Brown, Sam Cooke, and Otis Redding. Allen was also the sort who would go out to sticks and rustle up gigs in places like Beckley, West Virginia, to fill open dates on an artist's itinerary. Knight's hustling ways usually worked to his benefit, but everyone watched him closely because you knew he'd be working an angle down to the last dime.

Occasionally, Knight met his match but, even then, he came out on top. One legendary tale involved Ike & Tina Turner. In the early 1960s, Knight hired Ike and Tina's revue to play an open-air gig at a makeshift venue somewhere out in the boondocks. As the story goes, before the show, Turner wanted all his money up front and Knight wouldn't give it to him. Disputes like this weren't uncommon, and promoters usually got their way.

The deck was stacked against the artist, if only because it didn't usually make sense for an artist to show up and then refuse to play; it was better to take a chance on getting paid rather than packing up and not getting paid at all. However, Ike Turner didn't see it that way. He called Allen's bluff by taking to the stage and announcing that there would be no show because the promoter had stiffed him, directing the crowd to go and get their money back. Meanwhile, Knight was several hundred yards away, beyond the P.A. system's reach and still selling tickets from his makeshift box office near the highway. Suddenly, he noticed a mob, off in the distance, racing for their cars. Allen put two and two together, grabbed the cash box, and took off on his hands and knees, shimmying through the tall grass by the roadside. He ran a quarter of a mile to a farm house, where he persuaded the lady who answered the door to let him in to "phone the auto club about his flat tire." He stayed there chatting her up for a couple of hours until the crowd had disbursed and the coast was clear.

It was the perfect payday: he had all the cash from the ticket sales and no artist to pay. None of the hundreds of people who'd been snookered out of two or three bucks knew who the promoter was, much less where to find him. And no one who knew Allen Knight had any reason to doubt the story.

3

I don't know the origin of the term "Chitlin' Circuit" but, in the music biz, it referred to just about any venue in the black community that hosted entertainment. There was a healthy but regionalized west coast scene, but the heart of the circuit radiated from two centers, the urban North and the South. In the R&B era, the circuit's "A" level consisted of theaters, the most storied of which was New York's Apollo. Artists would often be booked "around the world," their colloquialism for a series of consecutive week-long theater engagements at the Apollo, Washington D.C.'s Howard, Baltimore's Royal, Philadelphia's Uptown, and Chicago's Regal. On the next level were dance halls, like the Graystone Ballroom in Detroit and the Rockland Palace in Harlem, or clubs like Leo's Casino in Cleveland and Club Harlem in Atlantic City.

In the South, the situation was less formal. There were black theaters and clubs in cities like Atlanta and Memphis but, in smaller towns and rural areas, popular acts often performed in makeshift venues that ranged from decrepit juke joints to tobacco warehouses to open fields, just about anywhere a promoter could effectively stage an event. And I'm not talking way back in the day: A James Brown gig I attended in March 1965 took place in an unheated livestock shed on the Virginia State Fairgrounds outside Richmond. The back of Brown's equipment truck became his dressing room for the evening, and one or two jerry-rigged spotlights illuminated the unusually low-sitting stage. Despite the collective body heat of 2,000 or so fans, the temperature was barely above freezing inside that aluminum building. I remember watching dumbfounded as the band played their aptly described "warm-up" set in their overcoats.

To grasp what life on the road was like for R&B performers in the 1950s and 1960s means ignoring everything you know about the modern concert business: strategic tour scheduling, custom buses and chartered jets, sexy hotel suites and huge paydays. The word "tour" was only used to refer to block bookings, such as a month of one-nighters packaged with other attractions. Artists didn't think of what they did as "touring"; they were WORKING, staying on the road as long as they had gigs. Those fortunate enough to string together some hit singles, a James Brown, Jackie Wilson, or Otis Redding, might play a market like Richmond three or four times in a single year.

Chitlin' Circuit bookings usually followed one of three formats. The most prominent was the "package" tour, one that hit the road with as many as a dozen acts, from major stars down to one-hit wonders.

The package format dated back to the late 1940s when booking agencies like Gale, Shaw, and Universal would periodically assemble shows from their respective talent rosters of jazz and pop stars and then divvy up the dates among regional promoters, such as Virginian Eli Weinberg, Texan Howard Lewis, and Washington's Irvin Feld.

The New York agencies maintained control of their circuit until the mid-1950s when the rise of rock 'n' roll introduced a sudden stream of new artists, fly-by-night independent record labels, and upstart talent managers that held no allegiance to industry status quos. An ambitious entrepreneur like Feld spotted the opportunity to grow from promoter to producer. Instead of fronting for the agencies or limiting his investment to his own territory, he could expand to promoting an entire tour. And, by producing his own show, he could buy performers individually and steer clear of the "cigarette and toilet" acts the agencies stuffed their packages with. (Old-school vaudeville slang for a lousy performer who drove theater patrons to take cigarette or bathroom breaks.)

Few artists would refuse a month of dates with an established promoter, so the agencies had to play ball. By 1960, the package tour had become the domain of three promoter-producers: Irvin Feld, Henry Wynn, and Teddy Powell.

With offices in New York and Newark, New Jersey, Teddy Powell had the smallest operation of the three men but was probably the busiest, bankrolling any and every show that might turn a profit. The "T.P. Presents" banner might hang anywhere, outside a gospel show in a ghetto theater, a jazz festival in Atlantic City, or a concert in a huge arena. Throughout the '60s, Powell randomly packaged any promotable acts, but the one blemish in his legacy is that at least one of the performers advertised usually ended up a suspicious no-show. Although Teddy continued to promote until his health failed in the mid-'80s, he didn't comfortably adapt to the increasingly detailed demands of the modern-day touring industry.

For example, a 1977 contract for a Marvin Gaye arena show in Pittsburgh required the star's dressing room to be fully furnished and carpeted at the promoter's expense. Pittsburgh radio personality Matt Ledbetter remembers an exasperated Powell telling him, "Ain't this a bitch. I've been in this business twenty-five years, I'm paying this guy a ton of money, but I'm supposed to drop what I'm doing and become a rug merchant. This is going too far." When Gaye walked into his dressing room that night, he found a "carpet" made of newspaper taped to the floor.

Unlike Teddy Powell's smaller packages that might be booked for anywhere from a weekend to ten days, Henry Wynn's "Supersonic Attractions" and rival Irvin Feld's "Super Enterprises" both staged self-contained theatrical productions that would be routed into a busy month or two of one-nighters.

Henry Wynn's operation was based in the Atlanta offices of his Royal Peacock club, a notable stop on the Chitlin' Circuit. The

Auburn Avenue night spot first opened in 1937 as the Top Hat, featuring stars like Cab Calloway and Louis Armstrong. Wynn bought the club in October 1960, a year after forming Supersonic Attractions. One of black Atlanta's most ambitious entrepreneurs, Wynn also owned the popular Henry's Grill as well as a liquor store, a taxi company, a car wash, and was rumored to be involved in a variety of "other enterprises."

Wynn's entrée into the big leagues came quickly, thanks to lucrative relationships with stars like Sam Cooke and Jackie Wilson, and a clean reputation among agents. Jerry Brandt, a talent booker at the William Morris Agency, told author Peter Guralnick that Wynn was, "a man of honor," and that "his word was the Rock of Gibraltar."

Wynn employed a tour staff that included accountants and experienced road managers like the rough and tumble Nat Margo. In the segregated south, it paid to have a savvy white tour manager, and Margo had earned his stripes in the 1950s with the Ravens and Dinah Washington. Henry's other right-hand man was the ubiquitous Gorgeous George O'Dell, a clothes designer-turned-singing-emcee. Between tours, George worked at the Royal Peacock and lived down the street in the Forest Arms Hotel, where he sketched flashy stage wear for countless entertainers. But the gorgeous one's greatest value was as a stage manager/emcee. He patrolled backstage and made sure that shows in union venues didn't lapse into expensive overtime. Needless to say, the acts who bought his clothes got the most robust introductions.

Decked out in a shiny, sharkskin suit and sporting a platinum blond process the size of James Brown's, George would open Wynn's shows with a song or two. He'd never have made it as a singer, but that didn't discourage a stage presence that was straight out of Jackie Wilson. By the end of his short act, he had lost his jacket and tie and was rolling around the edge of the stage cajoling screaming girls in the front row into unbuttoning his shirt. On a couple tours. George carried his own guitarist, a youngster called Jimmy James who could stop a show playing funky licks behind his back and with his teeth. I've always wondered how many of the tens of thousands who saw those shows later realized they had seen a young Jimi Hendrix. (George's career didn't end in the '60s either; he spent many years in Marvin Gaye's touring entourage and can usually be found wherever Ronald Isley appears.)

Irvin Feld preferred hiring comedians as emcees, effectively filling two positions with one paycheck. Feld's concept was hardly unique, Flip Wilson, Stu Gilliam, Allen Drew, Jimmy Pelham, Bill "Winehead Willie" Murray, Irwin C. Watson, and Clay Tyson were among the veteran comics that competed for the precious few slots on the package shows and in theaters like the Apollo. Through 1962, Feld's favorite was Harold Cromer, a.k.a. "Stumpy of the vaudeville team Stump & Stumpy." Later, he hired Apollo favorite King "Mashed Potato Man" Coleman. As a Florida radio personality, in 1959 Coleman contributed vocals to the James Brown-produced hit, "(Do the) Mashed Potatoes" (issued under the name of Brown's drummer, Nat Kendrick) and earned his nickname for the entertaining gangly manner in which he performed the popular dance.

Irvin and brother Izzie Feld first formed Super Attractions to promote concerts and dances of all kinds in Washington and surrounding towns in Maryland and Virginia. Izzie's specialty was classical music, while Irvin favored pop, jazz, and rhythm and blues.

In February 1955, working closely with the Shaw agency and producer/talent-manager Lou Krefetz, Irvin successfully promoted the barnstorming "Top 10 R&B Show" that starred The Clovers and Big Joe Turner. Then he hit the jackpot with Harry Belafonte during the short-lived calypso craze. Little more was heard from Izzie's side of the office, but now Irvin could afford to produce his own packages. He signed Bill Haley & His Comets, The Platters, Lavern Baker, The Drifters, and Bo Diddley; and dubbed his caravan the "Biggest Show of Stars for 1956." Super Attractions never looked back.

By 1959, Feld was sending out four or five national tours a year. The itineraries inevitably included stops in the segregated south, cities like Chattanooga, New Orleans, Memphis, and Birmingham, where black and white entertainers were prohibited from sharing a stage. But, from the beginning, Feld dared to place white and black acts on the same bus and, somehow, he avoided the firestorm that ruined Alan Freed for doing the same thing.

As promoters go, Feld was relatively artist-friendly. His venues tended to be classier, his buses cleaner and safer, and he paid on time. A few artists, like Paul Anka, LaVern Baker, and Clyde McPhatter, grew comfortable enough to make him their manager.

(In 1967, Feld startled the amusement business when he bought the Ringling Brothers and Barnum & Bailey Circus, ironically, an institution long whispered about for its behind-the-scenes racism and anti-semitism. The new Jewish owner's first move was to hire the all-black King Charles Troupe, a specialty act from the southern carnival circuit.)

Throughout the 1960s, Feld and Wynn fielded new units every season, often competing for dates in the same venues. Feld's "Biggest Show of Stars" was usually the more polished production, smoothly backed by a skilled show band that didn't object to remaining in the background. On the other hand, Wynn's funky Upsetters band were experienced showmen. Texas saxophonists Grady Gaines and Gene Burks had formed the original Upsetters to accompany Little Richard in the mid-1950s, a gig that required as much charisma as musical skills. When Richard quit show business, the group became guns for hire, touring behind Dee Clark, Little Willie John, and then Sam Cooke. Their warm-up sets were always entertaining, but the Upsetters had a downside. Unschooled musicians, they struggled with the tricky, sophisticated arrangements common to "uptown" soul singers, such as Ben E. King or Dionne Warwick. In her autobiography, *My Life, as I See It*, Ms. Warwick remembers, "That is just what they were:

upsetting. I never once heard them play the time signature changes and melodic notes of my material during an entire tour."

Wynn was partial to straight-ahead soul singers like Jackie Wilson, Sam Cooke, and Jerry Butler, while Feld aimed at a wider audience and took his shows all over the country and into Canada. He featured every form of R&B—even the occasional token "blue-eyed soul brothers" like the Dovells or Ronnie Dove. With as many as ten different acts, the shows kept a busy pace; opening acts might do less than ten minutes, the stars thirty to forty minutes—tops. The grueling runs did their best to avoid off days, often appearing in as many as thirty cities in as many days.

The package tours were dependable work and great exposure before diverse audiences but, when they ended, the same artists had to hit the road alone, stopping anywhere a promoter offered a nights' work. A typical one-nighter kicked off with a band set for dancing and one or two local attractions, maybe a vocal group, a comic, or even an exotic dancer. The headliner closed things out with a seven- or eight-song set expected to last about thirty minutes.

The Chitlin' Circuit's wide variety of venues and formats required artists to have several acts of various lengths. For example, as a mid-level attraction on a package tour, a group like The Drifters might do a fifteen-minute four- or five-song set. If they were headlining the Apollo, they'd add a few more songs. But, if they played a club, they might be expected to do two different shows for the same audience, each a half-hour or longer. Prolific groups like The Drifters or Curtis Mayfield's Impressions had enough material to support all these scenarios, but artists with fewer hits had to flesh out their shows with whatever familiar cover tunes the back-up band already knew.

The third common format on the circuit was the self-contained, revue-style show built by and around major stars. The advantages were obvious, as the stars could assume creative control of the entire show, command a higher fee, and place their support acts on salary, which was less expensive than paying freelancers.

Louis Jordan and then Ray Charles had been pioneers of the form as it related to contemporary R&B, but the concept of carrying a pretty girl vocalist, a dance act, and a comic dated back to Cab Calloway and Duke Ellington in the 1930s. As the soul era approached, Ray Charles was at the top of the heap until he cut two astoundingly successful country and western albums. As Brother Ray crossed over into the pop realm, James Brown became the gold standard, the undisputed king of the Chitlin' Circuit revue, filling his show bus with a big band and a troupe of singers and dancers.

Throughout the rest of the 1960s, most of the successful soul men patterned after Brown's template as soon as they could afford to. Bobby "Blue" Bland, Otis Redding, Joe Tex, Sam & Dave, Chuck Jackson, and Jerry Butler all assembled self-contained revues at the peaks of their popularity, although none of them managed to sustain a complete show for more than a few years. Even with his career still on the rise, Redding had slashed his show to an inexpensive young band at the time of his tragic death in 1967. On the other hand, with the exception of a down period from the late 1970s into the early 1980s, Brown toured with a complete package for the rest of his fifty-year career.

WHATEVER THE FORMAT OF THE SHOW, the road was where performers made their living. In those days, few artists earned anything more than chump change from their records. Royalties were paid at ridiculously low rates, if they were paid at all. The real money was always in the publishing rights, and the labels did everything they could to keep that too.

The deception and creative bookkeeping that flavored the relationships between artists and their record companies goes back a long way. The system was so inbred that most record men didn't see it as wrong. After all, they'd reason, offering an artist an opportunity to record provided the route to a performing career.

James Brown and Ray Charles were the anomalies among R&B artists, having earned stunningly unique agreements that allowed them to record what, where, and when they chose to. Their bands were top notch, so they were also free to record with their own sidemen. But most R&B artists had no such say-so over their sessions. It was a routine, record company-driven process. Several times a year, they would be booked into a studio, with their label's house band or union musicians they may have never seen before, and cut three or four sides—songs usually suggested or supplied by the label's choice of songwriters. If they were lucky, they'd land a hit single or two that could keep them on the radio and in demand. Tour income was nothing like it is now but, even in the modest soul music economy, the road was where the money was.

By 1965, when I promoted my first shows, James Brown was playing the biggest halls and pulling down guarantees of $5,000 in the wake of "Papa's Got a Brand New Bag," his most successful record to date—twice the sum he had commanded less than two years earlier. Five grand was big money in the three-dollar-ticket R&B business. A lot of artists with proven track records, like Jerry Butler or the Drifters, still earned guarantees of less than $1,000 a night. Bigger stars like Jackie Wilson were lucky to get two grand. Keep in mind that most Chitlin' Circuit venues held anywhere from four hundred to fifteen hundred people, that ticket prices could not exceed two or three dollars without becoming unaffordable, and that record labels contributed nothing towards travel, lodging, or promotion. Everything came out of the singer's pocket, including payroll costs for a band and entourage. No wonder nobody—not the promoters, not the club owners, and certainly not the performers—was getting seriously rich.

It was a grueling life, but there was no point complaining. In the soul era, few black Southern artists had any kind of formal education or attractive alternatives to music—all back home had to offer was working in fields or on railroads. The slicker guys might have added, "or hustling." Actually, by the time I came on the scene in the 1960s, in lieu of any legitimate career opportunities, most of the singers and musicians I knew would have opted for hustling by default—shooting dice, playing cards, selling weed, even "sponsoring" prostitutes, whatever might pay the bills. I'm not saying these were bad guys, but that they were survivors and weren't about to tuck their heads and spend a life "working for the man."

Take Jerry Butler and Wilson Pickett, two people as different as one could imagine. Butler is a refined middle-class family man who always carried himself with a quiet dignity. He invested his money in a successful beer distributorship and got elected Cook County commissioner in Chicago. On the other hand, Pickett was a handful, a hard-drinking, womanizing, coke-snorting piece of work. But he and Butler had one thing in common beyond their rural Southern heritage—neither one of them was going to wind up picking anybody's damn cotton. In the early 1960s, no matter how tough life on the road was, it could have been much worse back home.

Back in the day, nobody on the Chitlin' Circuit referred to themselves as "artists." Despite a pride in and commitment to their art, even the biggest stars considered themselves working entertainers. James Brown referred to his bookings as "jobs" until the end of his career, and would often introduce a soloist from his group to an audience as someone who "works hard for you"—in his eyes, the highest compliment. The art aspect was irrelevant; their livelihoods depended on pleasing audiences night after night.

Actually, the performances were probably the least demanding part of the life. Prior to commonplace integration, one of the biggest hassles for touring black performers was lodging. There were thriving black hotels in major cities, the Forest Arms in Atlanta, the Sir John in Miami, the Dunbar in Los Angeles, and the fabled Theresa in Harlem, but it went downhill from there. If they were lucky, they'd find a clean rooming house like Jackson House in Tampa, but the problem with lesser hotels in other towns might be who the establishments catered to, from transient criminals and prostitutes to roaches and rodents. Many an exhausted performer risked sleepy-eyed, after-show drives rather than spend a night in a sleazy establishment.

Playing the theater circuit was another story. Engagements were usually seven days or longer, so headliners looked for the most convenient and comfortable hotel they could find. Artists playing the Apollo, for example, stayed at the Theresa or the less expensive Cecil. If they didn't mind the distance and wanted to be downtown, they ended up at the quasi-residential Gorham on 55th Street, one of the few mid-town Manhattan hotels to openly cater to black entertainers. The less expensive Alvin Hotel, behind the original Colony Records store on Broadway, was another option (Jackie Wilson and jazz legend Lester Young sometimes lived there), but it was hardly in the same class as the cleaner, safer Gorham.

It was another story for the modestly paid musicians, dancers, and lowly support acts for whom playing the theaters was both a blessing and a curse. Besides just regulating ones' body clock, staying in one place for a week presented opportunities for shopping, family visits, and getting stage clothes cleaned or altered. But these folks either shared rooms or couldn't afford hotels. They'd end up staying in rooming houses, which still cost more than they'd like to have been spending.

There were industrious landlords, such as a Washington woman fondly remembered as Ma Buford who owned a brownstone directly across "T" Street from the Howard Theater, and rented out rooms on a regular basis. "Hostesses" like Ms. Buford served home-cooked meals, and it wasn't uncommon for a musician or comedian to get a lead on their next gig from a networking conversation around the breakfast table. Word of mouth was all the advertisement these rooming houses needed.

The path from a humble rooming house to the glitter of the stage was full of potholes. To wit the long list of people who died before their time. Automobile accidents claimed the lives of Jesse Belvin,

Billy Stewart, and two friends of mine from the Impressions' band, Lenny Brown and Billy Griffin. Otis Redding and most of the original Bar-Kays died in a plane crash. Then there is Jackie Wilson, drinking and drugging his way from one performance to the next until he suffered a stroke on stage at the age of forty, leaving him a vegetable for the last ten years of his life.

Suffice it to say, the eternal boredom of highway after highway, hotel after hotel, gig after gig, always wondering if you're going to get paid fairly, raised the likelihood of personal problems. It was as bad in the theaters, just different. The Apollo shows began in the early afternoon and ran late into the night, as many as four or five performances a day. You're due on stage every three or four hours, so you can't go far between shows. The first day, you might get a haircut at the Celebrity barbershop, slip out for a steak at Frank's Restaurant, or hang out at Bobby Robinson's record shop a few doors down 125th Street. By the third day, you've lost more than you can afford in the eternal basement craps game, and run out of things to do. There's nothing left but to read a newspaper, take a nap, OR dull your senses with a nip, smoke, snort, or shot.

The list of lives fraught with substance abuse is way too long. Singer Little Willie John, a hard-living character who evidently never met a drug he wouldn't try (he introduced Sam Moore of Sam & Dave to smack), killed a man in a bar fight and ended up dying in prison at the age of twenty-eight. Rudy Lewis of the Drifters died of an overdose in a Harlem hotel room. Gene Chandler, apparently as much a dealer as a user, did time in a federal penitentiary on drug-related charges. Marvin Gaye and four of the best-known Temptations died young, mostly because of drink and drugs. Ray Charles was an all-out heroin addict for the first eighteen years of his career, and I'll never forget my own personal encounter with the monkey on Ray's back.

In December 1964, Charles was booked to play an NAACP-sponsored cabaret in the Richmond Arena. I spent the afternoon of the show lurking around the shadows of the arena, hoping to no avail that Ray might play a sound check. Around six o'clock, I heard some commotion from the dressing room area. Out came Ray Charles on the arm of a non-descript-looking character who led him across the length of the empty arena basketball floor to a phone booth just beneath the bleachers, where I was perched killing time.

Ray could barely walk; his aide was supporting him, and it took them forever to reach the phone booth. I couldn't take my eyes off Charles talking on the phone, shivering, hugging himself for warmth, nervously shifting his weight from one foot to the other. He was shaking so violently that the phone booth started wobbling and the leather coat draped over his shoulders fell to the ground. I couldn't hear his words, but Ray was urgently shouting something into the phone. Aware of his habit, my imagination went to work. Maybe somebody sold him some bad dope or maybe a connection had fallen through and he was in withdrawal. In any case, Ray eventually hobbled his way back out of sight and I sadly assumed there wouldn't be a show that night. But, apparently, I was the only one who thought so, because everything went on as scheduled. Doors opened on time, a happy crowd packed the place, Charles' big band stormed through their warm-up set and, at ten o'clock, the emcee was getting ready to introduce the "Genius." I had been promised a quick meet and greet with Brother Ray, maybe even a picture, so Tom Mitchell and I positioned ourselves by the side of the stage. The announcer called out his name, the dressing room door opened, and a grinning Ray Charles GLIDED in our direction with the smooth grace of a Michael Jordan lay-up. I still have the quick photograph we took, and I look stunned. I was. Not at meeting my long-time idol, but at the transformation I had witnessed.

Not long afterward, Charles took a year off and kicked his habit. It may be no coincidence that, once Ray was straight, he fired his long-time manager. That same guy later turned up managing Sam & Dave; I guess it's also no coincidence that Sam & Dave had drug problems. Predatory managers or mobbed up characters who "owned" artists like Jackie Wilson were another Chitlin' Circuit hazard. These guys exerted a level of control over their clients that you'd never find in a typical managerial contract.

Sobriety certainly was safer than not, but it didn't make things much easier. Artists in demand, like James Brown, were on the road constantly. Time off would have meant losing band members to other shows or digging in his pocket to make payroll. Brown wasn't having it; he took all the work he could get.

On a single Saturday late in 1964, I followed the James Brown Show to three separate gigs—a matinee at Randolph-Macon University, outside the city, an early-evening set at the University of Richmond, and a midnight show and dance at the Richmond Arena. I was already at the Arena when the bus arrived around ten thirty. The basketball nets were still in place from a high school game earlier that day and, while the show was loading in, I found myself on the court casually lofting up shots with Bobby Byrd and Bobby Bennett, two of Brown's Famous Flames. Shaking my head with disbelief, I said, "Man, I have no idea how you guys are even standing up."

"It's all right," Byrd shrugged. "We do this all the time. If we sit down, we'd probably sleep through the next show."

What's even more staggering is the itinerary that surrounded that busy day in Virginia. This particular run began Thanksgiving night in Raleigh, North Carolina, with a four-hour dance and show. The next afternoon, they opened at the Howard Theater in Washington where they'd perform thirty shows in seven days. Their last night in D.C., they had a marathon recording session before setting out for Virginia. After the Richmond show, about four in the morning, they rode 550 miles to Atlanta and immediately hit the first of three shows at the Auburn Avenue Casino. Let's go to the scorecard—in eleven days, that's a staggering total of thirty-seven shows and a recording session spread out over five cities.

By the mid-'60s, James Brown had his own Learjet and stayed in the finest hotels, but his band and entourage still traveled by bus, a standard coach with seats that only slightly reclined. Most acts on the circuit drove themselves from city to city, with their stage clothes and whatever gear they may have owned tossed in back. One afternoon while I was still earning my stripes at WANT, I went to a local club to meet the Impressions and tape some promo drops for the station. When they arrived, I was surprised to see the three of them walk in each carrying a thin Samsonite briefcase and their own garment bags slung over their shoulders. Curtis Mayfield schlepping his own wardrobe? Goodness. After our visit, they trudged off to find a cleaners that could press their stage clothes in time for the show that night.

Once they accumulated a string of hits, the Impressions hired a small band, a driver, and a road manager, but those were luxuries many R&B acts never could afford. Artists who travelled alone relied on promoters to line up a local band that could learn a half-dozen or so songs from the performers' repertoire. If they were lucky, there might be an afternoon rehearsal. But sometimes singer and band met for the first time on stage, winging their way through the set. The Drifters, one of the most durable vocal groups of the era, travelled with just a guitarist, Billy "Abdul Samad" Davis. Many a night, Abdul would stand onstage like the captain of a foundering ship, desperately shouting out chord changes to a crew of lackluster musicians he'd never seen before.

There were some killer regional bands that made a living out of effectively backing major artists on a moment's notice. Richmond had several, Stacy Henry's Majestics and Mike Harris' Imperials (including Melvin Ragin, a young guitarist who would later become a widely regarded studio musician under the name Wah Wah Watson) regularly backed shows up and down the East coast. But these bands weren't always available or affordable, so the performance levels on soul shows varied wildly. Sometimes it was simply a case of turning up the vocal mics and hoping that the singers prevailed over the stumbling sidemen. The salvations were that soul music was a singer's art and vocals were what people came to hear and, since nobody was accustomed to anything better, if the vocals were clear and audible, everyone usually went away happy.

One friend of mine, a Richmond-based drummer named Gregory (G.C.) Coleman, figured out how to make the circuit work to his own benefit. G.C. was the regular drummer for Motown's Marvelettes and, later, Otis Redding. But, when he came off the road, he and Johnny Gilliam, a guitarist from Pittsburgh, would head for the Apollo or the Howard to hustle work accompanying the entry-level acts on the bill. Doing business as "Sticks & Strings," they would arrive in time for rehearsals and wait around the theater for opportunity to knock; it always did.

The theaters had house bands full of quality musicians, but they observed a pretty rigid hierarchy. They played their asses off for head-liners—Solomon Burke, say, or Chuck Jackson, someone whose professionalism the band respected. But singers like Percy Sledge, a rookie fresh from Alabama with just one hit record, weren't going to get any favors. Predictably, the band leader would ask for the artist's charts and, almost as predictably, there'd be none. That's where G.C. and Johnny stepped in. "Hey, fella, you need some charts and musicians," they would tell the panicked newcomer. "Otherwise, you're gonna sound like shit and this audience is gonna eat you alive."

Coleman and Gilliam made a point of learning all these new artists' hits. Then they'd work with the singer to figure out a couple cover songs they all knew. *Voila*, Percy Sledge had an act; but an act that might only earn $500 for the entire week, half of which went to G.C. and Johnny. In 1966, I saw a Sam & Dave show at the Howard Theater at which Sticks & Strings backed three different acts—Sledge, Robert "Barefootin'" Parker (a one-hit wonder from New Orleans), and The Royalettes (a girl group from Baltimore). Coleman and Gilliam probably made more money that week than anyone on the show but Sam and Dave.

Despite the competition, there was a backstage camaraderie on the circuit. In his autobiography, Smokey Robinson tells about the first time the Miracles played the Apollo with Ray Charles headlining. The Miracles had just scored their first hit, "Shop Around," and didn't have arrangement one. Charles took pity and saved their butts by conjuring up some sketchy charts on the spot.

It was a common thing. James Brown saxophonist St. Clair Pinckney hastily wrote charts for Otis Redding when they toured together on one of Irvin Feld's packages in 1964.

Artists fortunate enough to put together a string of hits could afford to grow their entourage and improve their act. The first hired was usually a guitarist, someone who could rehearse and conduct pick-up bands. Second came a drummer to tighten the show and give it dynamics.

An effective show drummer knew how to accent choreography with dramatic rim shots and break-downs, while maintaining the role of time-keeper. In another setting, it might be viewed as overplaying, but R&B show drumming is an art. The best of the breed back then, like Coleman, Clayton Fillyau, John "Jabo" Starks, Bernard "Pretty" Purdie, and Leo (Idris Muhammad) Morris, were in constant demand and among the highest paid players on the circuit.

Acts that continued to prosper might next hire a bassist and some horns. The other crucial role to fill was that of road manager, someone to help drive and make sure you got paid. The best of them were street-tough, savvy guys who talked fast and carried guns.

Getting paid was often an adventure in itself, particularly if, for some reason, tickets didn't sell as expected. There was an unwritten rule that—contracts be damned—if tickets didn't sell, the artist was expected to share in the loss. Occasionally, they didn't get paid even when a date was successful—promoters simply disappeared with the box office receipts. In that case, there was little to do except complain to your booking agency. You could try chasing the promoter, but that didn't usually accomplish much. It was the promoter's town, and they only had to hide until the artist was forced to leave for their next gig. Call the police? You think the cops gave a damn about some out-of-town black singer they probably never heard of who claimed he or she had been ripped off?

Of course, running off with the money didn't bode well for promoters who wanted to keep doing business with the agencies that supplied their talent. That didn't mean they wouldn't resort to other scams. Under-counting the house was a pet trick. If the performer's contract included a share of the gate, promoters might conceal some of the ticket stubs and claim that a crowd of eleven hundred was really only eight hundred. Road managers on their game carried clickers and might actually stand at the door counting the folks who entered. Even then, a promoter might insist that a portion of the tickets had been giveaways to publicize the show.

Double-contracting was another common hustle. Promoters would buy an attraction from an agency and then re-sell it at an inflated price, maybe to a wanna-be with deep pockets or someone without any industry connections like the entertainment director of a school or community organization.

Then there were the promoters who would stoop to putting fake acts on the road.

In the days before cable TV and social media, rural audiences sometimes didn't know what some artists really looked like. So, it was as simple as hiring a local band, teaching them a few songs, and painting "The Drifters" or "The Manhattans" on the side of a station wagon before sending them "on tour" to a bunch of towns out in the sticks.

In 1955, when Little Richard went to Hollywood to sign with Specialty Records, he left behind a band and some unfulfilled bookings. A young James Brown, who shared managers with the Georgia peach, reluctantly agreed to pose as Richard for a couple weeks. According to Johnny Terry, one of Brown's original Famous Flames, it came to an end one night in Nashville when somebody—a fan, or maybe the local promoter—recognized that James was not Little Richard. After a hasty retreat in which gunshots were reportedly fired, Brown decided it might be better for his well-being to concentrate on his own career.

A handful of entertainers on the R&B circuit were very shrewd businessmen—Ray Charles, James Brown, Sam Cooke, Solomon Burke—but, for many, life on the road encouraged a loose attitude toward money. Some had families to support and dutifully saved every dime to send home, but others may not have even had a home of their own, and their money sometimes burned a hole in their pockets. There were no mentoring financial managers or accountants on the road, just singers and musicians who had grown up dirt poor and had little or no sense of how to manage their affairs.

Thankfully, as the civil rights movement's mentality spread to the R&B world, it became "cool" to appear more responsible about your business. I remember sitting backstage at the Howard Theater with Otis Redding and appreciating how much pride and pleasure he took in describing the plane he'd just bought. He even boasted of showing up James Brown, who had always patronized Otis. "Mr. Redding, you can't be me," Otis said in a spot-on impersonation of Brown. "Son, I know you're tryin' hard and doin' great things. But there's only one James Brown. You cannot be me. Be yourself, son."

"Yeah," Redding told me, "I got me a plane. But the difference with me, I'm gonna take my band on the plane and save some money. I got a big enough plane to take everybody, ain't gonna be like Brown, flyin' in a plane while my band's ridin' on a raggedy bus. That ain't right."

But most performers weren't making James Brown money, or even Otis Redding money. Sometimes that was where females entered the picture. I won't say it was typical, but it certainly wasn't uncommon for guys on the circuit—performers, band members, emcees, or road managers—to have a working girl or two hustling on their behalf. Even around the Brown organization, I encountered it more than once. There was the former Brown aide who was reputed to keep a stable of girls in Atlanta, and a mid-'60s advance man who was shot to death in Los Angeles under dubious circumstances. Years later, when I moved to Augusta, Georgia, I found myself living in a somewhat exclusive townhouse development just a few doors down from another long-time Brown associate who quietly sponsored his prostitute-girlfriend's modest operation out of his apartment.

After leaving Brown in the mid-1970s, I road managed one of the more popular R&B vocal groups of the day. Once, while we were playing a week-long stand at a club in Baltimore, I couldn't figure out why a couple of the guys insisted on driving home to Philadelphia each night after the show. Finally, someone broke it down for me: they had hookers on the street back home, and they stood to lose a lot of money (and the girls) if they weren't on the case.

The R&B world was a fast track and often intersected with the urban underworld of pimps and "players." In the 1970s, soundtrack albums for popular Blaxploitation films like *Super Fly* and *Shaft* officially brought the worlds together. But, even in the 1960s, soul singers and street players had at least one thing in common: They represented a kind of black man who had achieved a form of self-sufficient success while circumventing the "man" and the "system."

When I moved back to New York in 1970, I briefly stayed in a mid-town building on Eighth Avenue. It was one of the few decent buildings in that part of Manhattan where black tenants were welcomed, regardless of their pedigree; James Brown's wardrobe mistress, Gertrude Sanders, had an apartment there, as did a number of entertainers including both Sam (Moore) and Dave (Prater). While there were also plenty of everyday tenants, we show biz folks shared the hallways with a nightly procession of prostitutes and their pimps. Every night around 4:00 a.m., the customized Cadillac El Dorados and Lincoln Continentals would line up at the front curb, flashy-dressed pimps sitting inside waiting for their girls to get home from work. Inevitably, that business had its problems too, because it wasn't unusual to wake up to the sound of girls getting slapped around in the halls.

These denizens of the "leisure time world" might surface anywhere. One of the most renowned black music clubs on the East Coast in the early '70s was a gangster-run Boston bar called the Sugar Shack, whose boisterous clientele always included people "in the life"—gamblers, pimps, prostitutes, drug dealers, and the freakiest groupies on the circuit. Similar clubs weren't uncommon in the urban centers of cities like Detroit, Baltimore, Washington, New York, Philadelphia, and Atlantic City.

Please recognize that I am not suggesting that everyone on the Chitlin' Circuit was a conniving, irresponsible, doped-up misogynist. They were a distinct minority, but there was enough dysfunction that we all had to know how to deal with it to hold our ground. The scene was also home for some well-meaning, fair-minded agents, managers and, yes, even promoters; not to mention the countless sincere musicians and singers devoted to their craft and focused on developing their skills and their lives in general. When asked what he did to kill time between shows at the Apollo, G.C. Coleman, who had more than his share of road fun, didn't even hesitate, "I listened to the other acts. Over and over. Or, if there was a nearby club with a band, I'd leave the theater and go hear them. Sometimes I'd even jam at a club and then run back to the theater. I was always trying to learn something new from someone better than me."

The Chitlin' Circuit actually *was* the community that it served. It was only natural that, as that community changed, so did the circuit. The gestation may have been slow and gradual but, when change actually came, it came quickly. I saw it in 1968 when I visited the Howard Theater, about a month after the catastrophic riots that followed Dr. Martin Luther King's assassination. I was stunned by the devastation, a neighborhood that I had known as thriving—the commercial heart of Northwest Washington (just as 7th Avenue and 125th Street was the heart of Harlem) was utterly and forever changed. The Howard had been spared, but Sonny's barber shop at the corner, Waxie Maxies record shop, the liquor stores and cafes and other shops were all either out of business, trashed, or simply gone. I suspect that Ma Buford's rooming house had a lot of empty rooms.

Certainly, neighborhoods like this had been in long decline. By 1965, the first wave of civil rights-era integration was luring away the middle class—doctors, lawyers, teachers, and entrepreneurs—taking away the high end of the community's economics and role models. People always told me I should have seen the area in the 1940s, its glory years, but, if you didn't see it until the '60s, it was still pretty impressive. It was home to businesses and restaurants and people of all economic and educational levels, supporting all kinds of successful enterprises. But, after the riots, that version of community disappeared.

It was easy for me to see that this world I'd always wanted to be some part of was finished, at least, as I'd come to know it. At the same time, as the tumultuous '60s drew to a close, the music business was reinventing itself, and soul music had moved downtown. There was a rapidly growing circuit of new arenas and auditoriums throughout America. All these venues had dates to fill, and rock and R&B concert promoters were happy to oblige. Once a James Brown or a Temptations could play a single show before twelve thousand people at Madison Square Garden, the concept of thirty shows a week in a theater instantly became obsolete. (As a show of loyalty to the community and the owners of the Apollo, Brown was one of the few entertainers who continued appearing at the theater well into the '70s.)

Some critics treated the decline of the Chitlin' Circuit as a matter of the artists selling out by moving "downtown," but that argument never washed: In the heyday of the Chitlin' Circuit, even so-called superstars worked their asses off to eke out a living. Choosing more money for fewer shows in bigger venues over the lower pay, rigors, and risks of the old circuit was a no-brainer. Almost overnight, black music had hit the big time, and it would never look back.

4

I still didn't have a clue how I'd end up in show business, but I knew radio was a step in the right direction. Since WANT was headquarters for all the soul shows that passed through town, the radio station became my backstage pass, and I was determined to meet every artist, promoter, and road manager I could.

The most significant of these ventures, really a turning point in my life, was in July 1965. I can still picture myself arriving at the John Marshall Hotel in downtown Richmond around five o'clock in the afternoon, sweaty from lugging a not-so-portable tape recorder through the damp Virginia heat. The John Marshall was the city's most elegant hotel, the place where visiting dignitaries and celebrities usually stayed—the white ones, anyway. Recent law prohibited inn-keepers from turning away customers because of color, but Jim Crow habits didn't fade quickly—many of the black entertainers who came through town still stayed in the 'hood at places like Slaughter's or the Eggleston, two weary hotels across Broad Street. Not James Brown, however. Brown was all about going first-class. He prided himself on having the hippest wardrobe, the prettiest women, the biggest entourage, and the most luxurious hotel suite.

I mustered the courage to knock on the door and was greeted by a voluptuous, exotic-looking woman in a tight dress. She seemed surprised by my appearance, probably not expecting a radio guy in the person of a sweaty, skinny, red-haired, eighteen-year-old white kid.

A moment later, I was ushered into the master bedroom. And there he was, in bed, propped up on pillows against a backdrop of crisp white linen. I don't know what goes through the minds of other fans lucky enough to meet their idols, but my first thought on seeing James Brown was MY GOD, LOOK AT ALL THAT HAIR. His long processed "doo," not yet styled for that night's show, spread over the pillows like some great black halo. He greeted me enthusiastically, in a voice softer than I expected. Almost paralyzed by my excitement, I began to mumble anxiously.

"THANKS, MR. BROWN, FOR TAKING THE TIME TO TALK TO ME FOR MY SHOW. I'M REALLY JUST STARTING, AND I DON'T HAVE MUCH OF A TIME SLOT, I'M ONLY ON EVENINGS JUST BEFORE WE GO OFF THE AIR, BUT—"

"What are you talkin' about?" Brown interrupted, putting me somewhat at ease. "You got the prime time baby! It's summertime, people are off work by then and cruisin' the streets with the radio blastin'. Everybody's listening to YOU. So, I've GOT to talk to you."

And on he went, pumping me up with what I would later learn was his routine with DJs everywhere. He volunteered to tape station promos for me and assured me that, as a "hip young white boy," I was destined to become one of the biggest disc jockeys in America. I asked him about "Papa's Got a Brand New Bag," his new single, which was already crossing over to pop radio and shaping up to be a huge hit. He was right when he answered, "Son, you put that song on the jukebox with any other record you own, even any James Brown record, and it don't sound like none of 'em."

And we talked about race, the popularity of blue-eyed soul singers, and the relationships between artists and black companies like Berry Gordy's Motown. Looking back now, it's obvious that he was practicing with me. He was thrilled to finally be attracting the attention of pop radio but concerned about alienating his black base in the process. Despite me being white, in the months to come, he would be having our same conversation with important black radio programmers and promoters and, since I was a nobody in a small market, Brown felt safe to test the waters.

Of course, I had no sense of this at the time. Likewise, I had no idea that he was EVERY DJ's biggest fan. All I knew was that James Brown thought I was important, even seemed to like me. I left there fantasizing about working for him and I didn't even know that the Twisting Parkettes had recently become the James Brown Dancers!

Brown wasn't the only one courting my attention. It was easy to strike friendships with artists whose careers depended on the airplay we DJs offered their records. And access was never a problem; the backstage environment wasn't the formal, security-laden culture it is today. There were no TV news crews, gossip bloggers, or paparazzi anywhere in sight, so many a dressing room door stayed open. For example, when one of Irvin Feld's multi-artist tours stopped in Richmond for two shows at the Mosque, I found myself hanging out with headliner Joe Tex in his dressing room. Joe was a likeable, intriguing guy—perhaps the only soul-singing Texas cowboy to embrace the Nation of Islam—who had become a pal, more than just a guy hustling me for airplay. While we were casually chewing the fat, Motown producer Clarence Paul walked in with his ward, a teenage Stevie Wonder. The tour had been on the road for several weeks, and a noticeable camaraderie had developed among the performers. As Stevie sat down, Solomon Burke strolled in. Three major hit-makers, just kickin' it while waiting their turns on stage. Burke was on next and leaned over Tex to give the mirror a look, then turned in the blind youngster's direction and asked, "Do I look okay?"

Joe and Stevie cracked up and I tentatively joined the laughter, careful not to assume too much familiarity. Wonder finally snapped back, "Burke, you don't look any better than you did last night."

I was not only meeting the artists, but sometimes appearing on their stages as an emcee. Unlike Clayton and Ben, I took those jobs seriously. I would show up early, make a point to talk with all the acts and organize a schedule—letting each artist know their call times—something no one else in the clubs bothered to do.

Some artists, like Sam & Dave, Walter Jackson, and Jerry Butler began requesting my services when they passed through town, which did wonders for my self-confidence. In fact, I began to get a little cocky but that didn't last very long. One less-than-stellar night, I embarrassed myself in the star dressing room by barking out slangy obscenities within Gladys Knight's earshot. Her brother Bubba, one of the Pips, got in my face and rightly read me the riot act for having disrespected a lady. That humiliation brought me down to earth in a hurry. As a quiet means of apology, I gave their records a little more airplay after that.

Playing emcee was fun but Clayton, Ben, and I wanted a bigger piece of the pie. We wanted to promote our own shows but, first, we needed capital. In late August 1965, we rented a club and threw a back-to-school record hop. All the local promoters knew what we were up to and realized that we'd have an instant edge if we joined their ranks. Why wouldn't artists prefer to work for the very guys in the position to hype their records on the radio?

Still, the promoters were so accustomed to their status quo that they didn't really take us seriously. In fact, they laughed at the idea of people buying tickets just to see us spin records in a night club where the normal attraction was live entertainment. But we knew better. We knew from the radio station phone lines that we had an avid young fan base that loved the "trash" we talked and the music we played. I'll never forget the stunned looks on the faces of those promoters who dropped by our "back to school" show at the club called Rendezvous East. Young folks had lined up outside an hour before the doors opened and then packed the club to the rafters. The sound system was blasting, our sexy Tigerettes were workin' their stuff, and the dance floor was levitating to the sounds of Motown, Stax, and, of course, James Brown.

We scored big time and used the money to start booking real shows. First, we got Johnny Nash who had a sexy record on a new label he co-owned with a New York record man named Danny Sims—the same Danny Sims that would later move to Jamaica and manage Bob Marley. "Let's Move and Groove Together" wasn't a national hit, but it did very well in Richmond—particularly with the heavy rotation it received after Nash agreed to do a gig for barely more than expenses.

Later in the fall, we promoted a series of successful shows with artists like Sam & Dave, Walter Jackson, and The Manhattans. Even Otis Redding promised us his next Richmond date. But one show in particular stood out. We booked Jerry "The Iceman" Butler for a weekend.

Butler was a favorite of mine, a terrific performer and a regular guy. Like a lot of black performers who failed to crossover in large numbers, Butler was a much bigger star than history suggests. It so happened that Chuck Jackson was also in town, so late in the afternoon I drove the "Iceman" to where his pal Jackson was rehearsing. After Jerry introduced me to Chuck, the two singers spent a few minutes catching up. Before we left, Jackson asked Jerry, "Hey, what are you doing later?"

Jerry nodded toward me and said, "Ask him. I'm working for him tonight."

It hadn't occurred to me quite that way, but it was true. Jerry Butler working for me? I was on my way.

It only took four years. Four years of juggling radio, college journalism classes, a ton of daydreams, and chasing the James Brown tour bus all over the East Coast. I had become a familiar face backstage whenever the Brown tour was within reach. I hung out at shows in Washington, Pittsburgh, and all over Virginia, West Virginia, and Ohio, gradually developing what became life-long friendships with guys on the JB tour bus like tour manager Buddy Nolan, emcee/ valet Danny Ray, saxophonist St. Clair Pinckney, and Famous Flames Bobby Byrd and Bobby Bennett.

The backstage regiment at Brown's shows was stricter than most but, back in those days, the only backstage pass was an ability to talk your way in. Affiliation with a radio station usually did the trick but, once past security, I had to run the gauntlet of Brown's road crew who were well schooled in shielding their boss from intruders. It took a while but, eventually, I was familiar enough to be considered an insider.

My brother discovered how that worked when he accompanied me to a gig at Richmond's Mosque in April 1966. It was several hours before show time, and James was sitting at the organ while the band sound checked. I left a teenaged Eric in the wings while I went up front to visit with Tom Mitchell in the box office. Eric was in heaven, standing so close to the band he adored, when road manager Jimmy Smith appeared, prepared to chase him away. Brown himself waved Smith off and motioned for Eric to come closer as he whispered to his aide, "Don't mess with him. He's okay. He's with the DJ."

James seldom received visitors until after his shows—that is, after he dried off, sat in a robe under a hair dryer, and finally changed to street clothes. The wait could seem forever, but the conversations were usually worth it. A week after JB's tour of Vietnam, Eric and I sat spellbound into the wee hours listening to him describe being shot at in a helicopter and to his unique interpretation of the controversial war. A few months later, after "Say It Loud—I'm Black and I'm Proud" hit the market, he held court in a cold arena locker room, explaining the disc's significance, not just to blacks but to whites who needed to "recognize"—declaring that it was up to "liberated" whites ("like you, Alan") to spread the gospel in the white community because the race problem was "more about white ignorance than about hate."

Late in 1967, my busy little dream world came crashing down. First, WANT was sold and the new owners all but cleaned house. At the same time, I was re-classified "1-A" by the Selective Service, ripe to be drafted and shipped off to Vietnam. So, I decided to park my career and follow my family to Pittsburgh where I got into college and earned a student deferment. For the next year-and-a-half, I trudged from class to class, drifting towards a journalism degree until, one day, I got a call from Buddy Nolan, Brown's tour manager, asking if I'd be interested in fronting their upcoming concert at the Pittsburgh Civic Arena. You think?

For some reason, JB was at odds with the program director of WAMO, Pittsburgh's black radio station, and decided that he needed a reliable watchdog for the show's promotional campaign. I realized this was "the call." The door-opening opportunity that, performer or not, if you're bitten by the show biz bug, you dream about and wait for. If you're lucky, you actually get a "call." I was lucky. And I was determined not to waste it. That concert was going to succeed, even if I had to buy the damn tickets myself!

A year earlier, Brown had barely half filled that same venue but, thanks to my own relationships with some of the other WAMO disc jockeys and a lot of attention from the city's newspapers, my show sold out. James was astonished—particularly when I showed him the newspaper clippings with the kind of coverage black shows seldom received from big city dailies.

What Brown didn't realize was that the entertainment sections of middle-American city newspapers were often edited by drama critics who had little interest in, or knowledge about, popular music. But they had column inches to fill, so anyone willing to supply decently written releases about legitimate events was liable to benefit. It didn't hurt that the arts editor at the Pittsburgh Post-Gazette was an acquaintance of my father's. At any rate, my mission was accomplished. James asked me if I could get similar coverage in other markets and, if so, did I want a job. I had no idea if I could pull it off, but should I have said no? Not on your life. One school ended—another begun.

As I explained in a Brown obit for *Waxpoetics* in 2007, James knew I longed for a career in music. No, not just music, *Black* music. But I couldn't have picked a trickier time. In the immediate post-civil rights years, the Black music industry was about taking control of itself—overcoming decades of institutionalized exploitation by mostly white record companies, managers, agents, and promoters. And every move seemed to be under a microscope.

In that spirit, Brown understandably directed job opportunities in his expanding business empire towards the black community. But, fortunately for me, if someone fit his family, James wasn't about to disown them because of color. He once told me, "Of course we have to control our industry. And a lot of old-style cats got to go, both white and black. But, pretty soon, we'll have enough control to relax. And then the brothers will recognize we need white cats like you if we're ever going to get this music of ours out of the ghetto."

In November 1969, I set out for Cincinnati and a job with *that* James Brown, the same James Brown that I had nervously met just four years earlier. With or without the Twisting Parkettes, at least, metaphorically, I had earned my seat on the tour bus.

AT THE TIME I WENT TO WORK for James Brown, he had already racked up more hit records than any American entertainer other than Elvis Presley. He was hardly ever off the charts from 1960 into the mid-1970s, a one-of-a-kind consistency in the fickle, trendy music world. Today, his innovations and influence are all but taken for granted but, in 1969, that hadn't registered yet; he was viewed simply as a popular entertainer. In a sense, that's all he ever wanted. James aspired to be like Tony Bennett or Nat "King" Cole, a vocalist with high musical standards and an innate sense of how to work any audience. The fact that Brown became an innovator was almost accidental, a combination of innate genius, lucky timing, open-minded musical colleagues, and a career without artistic interference from managers or record companies. Maybe the impact of his street-level popularity just over-shadowed everything else but, for whatever reasons, critics hadn't begun to comprehend his artistic or cultural significance.

Some of us did—there was no one in black popular music or rhythm and blues as unique as James Brown. Over the years, his inno-vations grew more apparent—the way he put rhythm ahead of melody and de-Westernized what was considered popular music stretched beyond his own genre. The way some rock bands, punk bands, and jam bands construct some of their music today wouldn't be the same if it hadn't been for James Brown. A whole chapter of jazz icon Miles Davis' career wouldn't have happened the way it did if Miles hadn't been into James Brown. James simply changed the game.

But most of that was yet to come. From day one, Brown never felt his biggest obstacles or adversaries were musical. He viewed his career as an ongoing struggle with an industry that was stacked against him. By watching managers, agents, and record companies mismanage many of his contemporaries, he learned, early on, that his long-term prospects relied on retaining as much independence as possible. He was also savvy enough to recognize that the future hinged on his music and stage shows remaining unique. His business decisions frequently went against the grain of show business tradition, but usually to his advantage. Whenever he felt slighted, his strategy was to withhold his services. If he was unhappy with his record company, he would refuse to record. If he was unhappy with a promoter or a venue, he might refuse to perform. When other entertainers had tried that, they had typically proven replaceable, so James Brown's life mission was to be irreplaceable.

Whatever musical trends he adopted, Brown always added some-thing personal, enough to brand the styles his own. He packaged James Brown as a synonym for soul music. Anyone who wanted soul HAD to have James Brown.

Contrary to the many Horatio Alger stories that permeate pop music history, James Brown's career was full of ups and downs. His box office appeal was at its broadest in his later years, when his show regularly appeared at the most prestigious venues throughout the world. But that was long after his significance as a creative artist and record seller had diminished. During his peak years as a recording artist and a performer, the bulk of his gigs were off the mainstream radar screen, staged in arenas and aging theaters in front of audiences that were mostly African American.

Brown always welcomed white audiences, but never at the expense of his black fan base. Among the few concessions he made to mainstream show business involved appearances on national television programs whose budgets failed to provide for Brown's own musicians. On those occasions where he found himself performing with un-soulful studio musicians, he chose to sing standards such as "That's Life" or "If I Ruled the World"—arrangements the stiff but trained musicians could handle. "I always try to bring my band on TV, so I can present one hundred percent of what James Brown is about," Brown once explained. "But, when I don't have my band, I'd be crazy to do my own things. Their cats can't play my thing, so I'm better off getting in their bag."

With a music as personal as Brown's, it's no surprise that other musicians struggled with his rhythms and nuances. Even other soul artists seldom covered his songs. Legends like Aretha Franklin and Otis Redding tried with little success.

Brown's contemporaries both admired and envied his success and particularly his free agent status. In 1969, Ike Turner threw some digs in James' direction, while defending the pop influence in Turner's own music. "Go to James Brown and say, 'Hey, give me a pop tune.' He'll start singing some crap—that's what he thinks pop is. He doesn't know anything about music today." (I guess Ike somehow missed that Brown's "Mother Popcorn" started a dance craze and became that year's summertime anthem.)

In 1968, Joe Tex boldly painted "The New Soul Brother #1" on the sides of his band bus then called out Brown on Joey Bishop's late-night talk show. James agreed to take it to the stage, and they squared off in Atlanta's Municipal Auditorium. It was no contest. Tex rocked the house with his many hits but, five minutes into Brown's torrid set, the audience filled the aisles dancing with abandon until security all but stopped the show.

Despite his status, James could be surprisingly insecure, viewing every up-and-coming R&B singer as a threat. While headlining a star-studded tour in 1963, he supposedly told his band he'd fire them if they didn't "stop making that Marvin Gaye sound so damn good." Years later, when Gaye reflected on those early tours for his biographer, David Ritz, he referred to Brown as "a certified witch doctor."

Brown's paranoia should have been beneath him. His autonomy allowed him a distinct advantage over singers like Gaye and Tex, who lacked the resources or influence to completely control their music or their business. For instance, only after a decade of conflict with Motown guru Berry Gordy was Marvin Gaye able to successfully take his own reins and record his landmark *What's Going On*.

At the time of his tragic death, Otis Redding was probably Brown's biggest rival. As potential heir-apparent, Redding was on the threshold of mainstream pop music—something posthumously accomplished with the giant hit "(Sittin' On) The Dock of the Bay" and a filmed appearance alongside Jimi Hendrix, The Who, Jefferson Airplane, and Janis Joplin at the Monterey Pop Festival. But, in December 1967, Redding perished when his overloaded plane went down in a lake near Madison, Wisconsin. The funeral guest list read like a who's who in black music. Singers Joe Tex, Johnnie Taylor, Percy Sledge, Joe Simon, and Arthur Conley served as pallbearers. Brown wasn't formally invited, but he attended the services anyway—one of 6,500 people who jammed the Macon, Georgia, auditorium where both he and Otis had performed many times. An observer described the crowd to *Jet* magazine as, "acting like it was a rock and roll show.

When they spied James Brown outside, they surrounded him, tore off his coat and police had to wade in with night sticks to save him."

After the funeral, James went to the Redding family ranch to pay his respects, but was denied entry.

Jerry Butler was another singer whose career began around the same time as James Brown's. A member of The Impressions before going solo, in 1968, Butler told me of his first encounter with James years earlier: "We were all together on a show at the Uptown Theater in Philly, and James and his Flames were third or fourth on the bill. He'd just had 'Try Me,' a very big record, but they had country-looking hair styles and were dressed like a bunch of hicks. It was one of their first jobs up North and they weren't sure how to act, except when they were on that stage. They even talked funny—at least to us. Between shows, Curtis Mayfield and I would gather some of the other cats on the show, I think the Isleys were there too, and shoot some basketball. So, I decided to find James and ask if he wanted to play—kind of make him feel like he belonged. The first thing he asked me was how much money we were playing for! Then he challenged me to shoot free throws at fifty dollars a basket. That was a lot of money in those days, and WE were the headliners. I knew he didn't have that kind of money. I just told him that he was out of my league and walked away."

Almost apologetically, Jerry felt obligated to add more. "I feel helpless around Brown because I love his music and, when he plays Chicago, I'm right there in the audience with my kids, hollering and screaming like everyone else. And so much of what he says politically is right on target, but he's so competitive that he just doesn't know how to be down to earth. It's the old story of telling people to do as I say, not as I do. I want to embrace him as a brother, but I just avoid him because I know he's going to say something unnecessary that's going to make me mad."

Notwithstanding the boss' insecurities and competitive nature, James Brown Productions was an exciting place to be—in my case, a dream come true. In fact, his competitiveness turned every accomplishment into a victory of sorts, which, together with his activism in our inner cities, translated into being part of something special, something beyond just the music and my seat on the bus. By the time I entered his world, Brown had established a singular position in his industry. As Mal Watkins explained in an essay that appeared in *AMISTAD 2*, "James is not singing *about* black life…he *is* black life."

5

By 1969 standards, James Brown Productions was big business, the road show alone grossing in excess of $3 million. Most significantly, James was entirely his own boss, his manager Ben Bart having passed away a year earlier. Bart founded Universal Attractions in the late 1940s and built it into one of the industry's leading bookers of black talent—the only agency to have ever represented Brown. But, starting in 1967, James began booking the vast majority of his personal appearances in-house. It was called "four walling," whereby the artist's personal staff rented the venues, hired local promotion representatives in each city, bought the advertising, and kept all the profits. The unique and lucrative arrangement was a source of envy among peers like Otis Redding, Jerry Butler, or Wilson Pickett, whose appearances were booked and commissioned by agents and managers, usually to outside promoters for flat fees.

Ben Bart's son Jack ran Universal and never stopped trying to convince Brown that Universal's agents could better strategize and exploit his appearances. Jack insisted that he could position James in a more lucrative and prestigious variety of venues, at the same time saving the singer the cash outlay he was spending to front his own dates. But Brown held Universal at bay, limiting Bart's involvement to bookings outside the usual one-nighter circuit, such as international tours and mainstream night clubs. He wasn't about to sacrifice his hard-earned control, let alone allot Bart a percentage of everything.

Brown's first offices were in New York but, just before I came on board, they had moved to new digs inside the King Records complex in Cincinnati where the free rent was part of his renegotiated recording agreement. The tour dates were coordinated by Buddy Nolan and Bob Patton. Nolan had been part of JB's entourage for years, but Patton, an ex-disc jockey from Dayton, Ohio, had just taken the reins from two fellas who didn't make the move—Irwin Pate who opened his own promotion business in Buffalo, New York, and James Crawford who had variously served Brown's revue as a substitute Famous Flame, a solo artist, and a tour manager before becoming an agent at Universal.

Both Nolan and Patton became my mentors. Buddy knew every promoter and disc jockey in the R&B business. Patton was still learning the ropes but had a knack for cutting good deals and maneuvering Brown's show into better venues. They split their time between the Cincinnati office and the road where Brown's personal manager, Charles Bobbit, and road manager Freddie Holmes held things together.

King Records also housed Brown's recording enterprises—beside his many own recordings, he signed and produced a roster of artists including Hank Ballard and those who toured with the Brown revue, such as Leon Austin, Marva Whitney, and Vicki Anderson. Bud Hobgood was in charge of production and Eugene "Speedy" Brown (no relation) was the head of promotion. Hobgood worked out of the King plant but Speedy rated a desk in Brown's new office downstairs. The other new hire was Bobby Byrd, James' original alter ego who had returned as a staff writer and to generally assist Hobgood in the studio.

James Brown Productions was a windowless, somewhat claustrophobic suite of offices with its own entrance on Brewster Avenue. The drab décor made it seem even cozier than it was. Underneath the wood paneling were cold stone walls that originally housed part of the King Records warehouse. To the right of the reception area was a stubby hallway leading into a room crammed with desks, each hosting a bank of telephones. Descending from a false ceiling at the opposite end of the suite was a tightly coiled spiral staircase that led up to a Brown's own executive office, off limits save the few days a month that the boss was in residence. Set amidst garish black leather furniture was the floor piece, an enormous marble-top desk that once belonged to King founder Sydney Nathan.

Brown was on the road the first week I was there, but then he unexpectedly decided to spend three off-days in Cincinnati. That morning, the office burst with newfound energy. Bob, Buddy, and Speedy hurriedly sifted through papers strewn about the desks, putting away anything that might arouse their boss' curiosity. I didn't understand what bordered on paranoia. I would later.

An hour later, Brown stalked into what had turned into the most orderly office in show business. The only thing the neat façade failed to disguise was the tension that tied desk to desk, employee to employee. Everyone held their breath, trying to read the mood of their volatile boss—prepared to greet him but not until spoken to.

James strolled through without anything resembling an acknowledgement, turned toward Nolan and Patton and began questioning the advance ticket sales for upcoming concert dates. They were obviously accustomed to having such information on the tips of their tongues. Mid-sentence, Brown bolted towards office manager Christine Tate and asked for a copy of his latest record. Patton jumped up to turn on a stereo, but Brown waved him away.

"I don't wanna hear it. Don't you think I know what it sounds like? I wanna look at that mutha!" he all but shouted.

Turning back to Miss Tate, he growled, "Get Mr. Hobgood down here."

As an afterthought, his voice took on a sugary drawl and he flirtingly added, "pleeeeze."

Moments later, Hobgood, a gangly white Kentuckian with a high forehead and a bulbous W. C. Fields nose, whizzed into the office like Road Runner. James lashed right into him.

"Bud, all these damn records are pressed crooked, they're off center. Everywhere I go, the disc jockeys complain. What the hell's the matter up there? I put you upstairs to watch over those guys and you can't even get them to make a round hole for the records!"

The records *were* slightly defective, and someone in the King Records pressing plant next door should have noticed, but quality control wasn't really Hobgood's jurisdiction. Still, he fumbled for an excuse. Brown knew Bud wouldn't rest until the problem was corrected.

Meanwhile, I was just taking all this in. The warm, friendly James Brown I knew as a sponsor and friend was nowhere in sight. This James Brown hadn't even yet greeted me. When he finally did, I offered a meek response, but he cut me right off, "Have Mr. Patton give you all the information on next month's dates. I want you to get those stories you write in all the newspapers everywhere."

MR. Patton. MR. Leeds. And, of course, MR. Brown. Addressing each other by surname was the rule of thumb. In fact, from the day I met him, it always seemed awkward calling him James. One of the initiations into the inner circle was exchanging James for Mister. It was reciprocal. I went from Alan to Mr. Leeds.

I remember asking him about the "mister" thing. "Alan," he said, "until I was twenty years old, all I was ever called was Jimmy. My name was never Jimmy. It was James. But nobody saw no James. They saw Jimmy. Now, if they didn't see no James, you KNOW they didn't see no mister. I knew, if taking over my own business was going to work, I had to get the respect of someone running a business. If that's all they hear us call each other, they won't know nothing else to call us but mister. They might still wanna call me Jimmy, but, if they want to book the James Brown Show, they gonna have to do business with Mr. Brown."

We were also required to wear dark suits and ties. Even the band was glued to a strict dress code. They could be living on the bus for days on end but, when they got off that bus, they'd better be looking fresh. In the pre-Afro days, a doo rag in public was never an option. It really was a respect thing. Imagine the effect it had in hotels or restaurants when a busload of musicians descended looking like they just stepped out of G.Q. Support acts, stage hands, and even promoters were often intimidated by the band strutting to their dressing room, as sharp in their street clothes as they were in their stage uniforms. You could say it was elitist, even cult-like, but it represented family. The James Brown family, and James Brown cared about the impression that family left behind.

Back at 1540 Brewster Avenue, Brown was off to the King studio around the corner. We didn't see him again for two days. Meanwhile, I tackled my mandate, phoning the entertainment editors of countless newspapers across the country and planting stories about my new boss, Soul Brother #1.

Later that week, Brown caught up with the show bus for a series of dates in California, which led up to an important three-week booking at the brand-new International Hotel in Las Vegas.

With the boss away, the office exhaled. I fit in well with Nolan and Patton, but I was a curiosity to the others. Speedy Brown embraced me just a little too much—as if he wanted to be in my good graces, at least, until he figured out my relationship with the boss. Miss Tate was accommodating but distant and soberly professional. On the other hand, Bud Hobgood barely acknowledged me. He was the liaison between Brown's business and King Records but had nothing at all to do with the tour operation. Since they all had the boss' ear, Hobgood was guardedly territorial with Bob and Buddy.

It didn't take long to recognize that everyone's priority at James Brown Productions was keeping the boss happy. Wherever he was on the planet, he called into the office several times a day expecting up-to-the-minute ticket counts for his upcoming appearances and sales figures of his current records. Anyone who answered his call was subject to the oral exam. Flunking the test risked a place in the JB doghouse or worse. As a result, most JB employees were always accumulating fodder for the phone calls. Hobgood and Speedy, even my pal Buddy, concealed anything that might upset JB. Whenever possible, that included dodging accountability if a tour date or record promotion was less than satisfactory. Truth didn't seem to matter if meant keeping their butts off the firing line.

Only Bob Patton seemed to value reality beyond just pleasing the boss. That honesty sometimes trapped him in compromising positions, but Bob was a master juggler and managed to keep the boss satisfied most of the time. Patton wanted to win. When things went wrong, he took it as seriously as JB did. For whatever reason, he saw me as a like mind and quickly became my rabbi, schooling me on how to stay a step ahead of our nosy boss without compromising the integrity of our work. In a perfect world, Buddy would have been like Bob too but, by the time I came along, he had lost his fight. While he almost relished confrontations with anyone else, he did everything he could to avoid bumping heads with the boss. In their own ways, both Patton and Nolan guided me through the maze of double-talking promoters and agents that were attached to our lifeblood, The James Brown Show.

It took a while to get the hang of things. Brown seldom asked for me when he called in; Patton and Hobgood usually had the information he wanted most. Then, one morning, Bob motioned to me while JB was on the phone. The boss wanted me. "Mr. Leeds, how you liking Cincinnati? What's happenin' today?"

I quickly responded, "Oh, Mr. Brown, everything is terrific. Nothing happening today. Everything's cool."

WRONG! To say "nothing's happening" meant to Brown that you hadn't done anything worth talking about. You weren't earning your keep. From that day on, I kept a cheat sheet of notes by my side 24/7. Whenever I got his call, in the office, at home, or on the road, I had something ready to tell him. He'd never again think I wasn't busy.

But the fact was that, after a couple weeks in Cincinnati, I wasn't very busy. I had contacted and serviced every newspaper in the cities the show was appearing. Meanwhile, Patton began assigning me tasks that were directly tied to the tour's promotion—beyond the parameters of publicity. I was grateful for each learning experience and equally grateful that pay day was coming. My temporary home was a couch in the Patton living room, an arrangement close to wearing away its welcome. I had an apartment on hold and was eager for a pay check.

Each Sunday, Freddie Holmes or Charles Bobbit wired the office payroll out of the show's road receipts, after which Hobgood would make up individual pay envelopes for the employees. But there was none for me. An understandable oversight? Perhaps. Bob thought so. It made me feel better to simply agree. But, a week later, the same thing. Hobgood claimed he didn't know why. No one else did either.

Now I had a problem, a new job without a pay check is no job at all. My pockets were frighteningly close to empty and I didn't know where to turn for help. I tried getting JB on the phone but couldn't get through the hotel switchboards he had trained to block calls. Buddy was on the West Coast with Brown, and Patton was getting ready to join them. Bob asked me not to panic, promising to straighten things out.

What none of us knew was that James had asked King president Hal Neely to put me on the label payroll. But Neely had no idea who I was or why I was there, beyond James telling him I would get great press. After another week went by, a disinterested Hobgood admitted that Neely had refused. I had become a political football between artist and label and Hobgood, who had no horse in that race, wasn't about to get involved. He simply shrugged and told me to "do whatever you gotta do."

Doing what I "had to do" turned into packing my car in the middle of the night and dejectedly hitting the road heading east. I couldn't face returning to Pittsburgh and my friends who had thrown me a going away party just weeks earlier. So, I kept going, all the way to New York and a hastily scrounged up entry-level job with Gene Redd, Jr., record producer and manager of the fledgling Kool & the Gang. Irony: Gene's dad had been a long time King Records producer who worked with James Brown in his early days.

My connection to Kool & the Gang was an old school road rat from Chicago. Herferth "Tiny" Blue was a veteran of tours with B. B. King, whom I had befriended when he was road manager for singer Walter Jackson. He was a wheeler dealer with a rich sense of humor that I would have liked just because I had never met a Herferth (and still haven't met another). Blue had ended up in New York where he was building a career as an independent record promoter, when he attached himself to Gene Redd, Jr. Kool & the Gang was a young band from Ohio that had settled in Jersey City—close enough to New York. Their self-titled debut single was enough of a hit to get them started. Enter Alan Leeds, the guy Tiny Blue hyped as having learned the ropes working for James Brown.

Redd offered me 10 percent of any gig I booked for the band and agreed to cover the cost of a room at the Howard Johnson Motor Inn on 8th Avenue, just a few blocks from his 57th Street office. As soon as I got settled, I began cold-calling R&B disc jockeys up and down the east coast soliciting gigs. I knew the band wasn't popular enough yet to warrant any serious attention from promoters, but many disc jockeys had venues with built-in audiences and were willing to book an unproven attraction whose record they could blow up on the air.

Soon, I had enough gigs booked to rent a station wagon and put Blue and the band on the road. Unfortunately, it was a lot easier getting gigs from disc jockeys than getting paid. Young artists relied on the exposure the DJs provided, which became leverage when it came time to settle in the box office. Each gig was a crapshoot—some nights they got paid, other nights, they didn't. Then I got a threatening call from a Days Inn somewhere in Virginia or Maryland, claiming the guys had made off with every pillow and blanket they got their hands on. It was a struggle, but the guys were committed, and as long as they had enough money to eat and put gas in the wagon, they kept rolling. Now they even had blankets to stay warm!

Musically, the band was on fire; these kids could really play, so all the gigs were well received. But, after the costs of gas, food, and hotels, there wasn't much left, for Leeds or anyone else. 10 percent of nothing is nothing.

Around the time the band got home, the Howard Johnson let me know that payment was overdue on my room by locking me out. There is no more dehumanizing of a feeling than to put your key into a hotel lock that won't work. And I'm convinced there is a certain kind of hotel clerk who relishes having a guest approach the front desk crying for access to a locked room. They had me over a barrel, my belongings on the other side of that locked door. I promised the snide clerk that I'd return shortly with the payment, and raced back to the office.

Problem was, no one had seen Gene in a few days. His sudden absence seemed strange, but Blue was there and so was one of Redd's cronies, a somewhat mysterious guy that Tiny simply referred to as Gene's money man. So, I asked Mr. Money Man to please pay my hotel bill. That's when Blue and money man sat me down and explained that, a few months prior, Gene had borrowed some street money to keep his company afloat but had fallen behind in his payments. The *vig* (interest) had gotten out of control, so now he owed way more than he had borrowed. Naturally, his street bankers were unhappy and anxious to find him. In short, the company had no money and Redd was on the lam, hiding from unfriendly loan sharks.

Blue offered me his living room couch, but the girl Tiny lived with was a part-time hooker and I didn't want to be around that madness. Instead, I bought some toiletries to hold me until I could sort things out with the hotel. Then I cleared off my desk and spread out a pillow and a blanket I spotted in the corner. Not surprisingly, they had Days Inn logos on them.

While I spent the next few nights on the desk, we all waited for Gene to surface, hopefully with some money. It didn't seem too much to ask, since the money we needed in the office was small potatoes compared to what Redd owed "the boys." Finally, he called in from a pay phone and announced he had collected some cash from one of his label's distributors. The only problem was arranging a discreet meeting place. What we agreed on was like a bad movie, a 3:00 a.m. meeting in an obscure stairwell deep inside the Port Authority bus station. Thankfully, these were the days before there were security cameras everywhere, or I'm convinced we both would have had some explaining to do at the nearest police precinct.

Fresh cash in hand, I went straight up 8th avenue to the HoJo to reclaim my room. The night clerk explained that, to avoid any further issues, the bill should be settled every Friday because while the hotel registration had billing set up to Gene's company, there was no credit card on file to guarantee the charges, so I remained on the hook for future charges. Tired of desks and other people's couches, I prepaid a week. After that, I somehow fell between the cracks, and they let me ride for a second week. By the time they next hunted me down, I was gone.

All the time I was in New York, Bob Patton, God bless him, was missing his protégé and the help I had briefly offered in Cincinnati. We spoke several times a week, me hoping against hope to collect the back pay owed me. Then Buddy Nolan got fired in California, leaving Patton alone to run the tour. He was suddenly swamped and in serious need of real help. Bob begged James to re-hire me. It turned out that Bud Hobgood had co-signed my termination, suggesting to JB that I didn't do enough to justify being there. So, Bob had to convince the boss that Bud didn't know what he was talking about, that he felt he could train me to replace Nolan. Brown relented, so Patton begged me to swallow my pride and consider coming back. I was unsure, still angry that Brown hadn't taken the interest to figure out what had gone down in Cincinnati. How could I trust him? On the other hand, dodging hotel clerks and sleeping on office desks wasn't my idea of fun. Brown had a one-nighter in Rochester, New York. He told Patton that if I was in Rochester that night before the show ended, I'd have a job. I threw my things together and scrambled onto a Greyhound bus that reached Rochester about 10:00 p.m. A quick taxi ride to the War

Memorial Auditorium, and I slipped backstage just as the show was coming down. An hour later, I was flying to Cincinnati with Brown in his private Learjet. I had about ten dollars in my pocket, but I'd gone from Greyhound to Learjet and from Days Inn blankets to a suite in a Hilton in less than twenty-four hours. AND, I actually had a job, a real job with a real salary. 100 percent of something is 100 percent.

THE JAMES BROWN I WENT TO WORK FOR in 1969 was not the caricature he became in the latter years of his career—the iconic James Brown that people under forty years of age today are familiar with. Rather, the James Brown I worked for was an enterprising businessman, a snappy minded, uncompromising perfectionist who also happened to be a world class entertainer. The payroll I finally landed on included over thirty performers and a sizeable staff that ran the gamut from tour managers to valets. Nevertheless, James stubbornly insisted on making most business decisions himself. He produced nearly all his own recordings, usually with his own bands and vocalists. His unusual working agreements with King Records, and later Polydor Records, allowed him to schedule recording sessions on a whim. He decided which recordings were issued and when, all carefully promoted by his own staff but subsidized by King.

Dick Kline, then a Polydor Records vice president, told *Downbeat* in 1980, "Working with James has always been a trip…he's always had his own methods, his own thoughts, and his own direction. James Brown is the greatest promoter of James Brown there ever was."

James had a rare aura. He was one of those guys whose presence you felt like a breeze through the room. Both his brazen smile, or the cold glare of his boxing-scarred eyes, could instill caution. His theatrical way of speaking, his voice harsh and raspy when excited or annoyed and disarmingly breathy otherwise, always enhanced his words. His every mannerism seemed intended to place anyone around him on defense, as Doon Arbus discovered when interviewing him for the *New York Herald Tribune* in 1966. "He used my first name from the start," remembered Arbus. "It put him in control, implying intimacy while remaining aloof."

Vicki Anderson, a songstress who spent several years with Brown's show, firmly believed that he had secretly mastered a subtle form of hypnotism. Many who worked for him felt he was clairvoyant. He really could make the most ridiculous things sound plausible. Once, after a European tour, he nearly had me believing there were *satyrs* in the German Black Forest. He was so adamant that it was pointless to argue.

I soon discovered that my initial coming and going was business as usual in the whirlwind that was James Brown Productions—an initiation, so to speak. James thrived on wielding his authority about his little empire, and no one escaped the arm of his law forever. He impulsively hired, fired, and rehired. Faithful employees accepted that side of him as the price of doing business. The less loyal quickly disappeared.

Sitting in the penalty box might last six months, six weeks, six days, six hours, or even six minutes, depending on the circumstances and the employee's reaction. Once, Buddy Nolan was in the process of getting fired when a phone call interrupted the boss' tirade. After a few minutes, James turned back to Buddy and gave him instructions for the coming work week, as if nothing had happened.

Another time, Buddy wasn't so lucky. The local promoter of a less-than-successful one-nighter had thrown the blame on Nolan, claiming that Buddy had come to advance the date but never left his hotel room. Soon thereafter, Brown called a staff meeting to which Nolan arrived by way of Baton Rouge where he'd spent a few days advancing another date.

James opened the agenda by asking Buddy where he'd been earlier in the week. The bewildered Nolan reminded him of his Baton Rouge assignment. "I was down there for three days, just like you asked me to. And I stayed where we always stay in Baton Rouge, Mr. Brown,

The White House Inn," he responded. "I even tried calling you the other night and, when Mrs. Brown answered, I gave her the number where I was."

James glared for a moment and then was off to the races. "I know what you told her but, when I called you back, you weren't there. That hotel had no Mr. Nolan registered. You ain't doin' nothin'. You're bullshittin' out there, Buddy, and I can't have that no more. You ain't doing nothin'. I gotta let you go." Nolan's jaw dropped. Then he reached into his briefcase, withdrew a hotel bill, and tossed it in front of James. The boss picked it up, glanced at it, and dropped it back on the table.

"This don't mean nothin'. Nothin' at all," said James. "I called you and you weren't there. I can't call a piece of paper—I gotta call a man. They said they didn't have a Buddy Nolan. You were hidin' out and you got caught."

After Buddy sulked away and the meeting wound down, I picked up the hotel bill off the table. It itemized a fully paid three days at the White House Inn, registered to James Brown Productions! In registering in the company name, often the only type receipts Brown would readily reimburse, Buddy's own name was missing from the form, a copy of which was usually sent to hotel switchboard operators in the pre-digital days. The only way a caller could have reached Nolan's room was to ask for James Brown or James Brown Productions!

Road manager Freddie Holmes was once fired while flying in the singer's private Learjet. James simply concluded a tongue lashing by telling Holmes, "As long as this plane is in the air, you've got a job."

The thing that kept us around was that, no matter how crazy things got, James felt more like a patriarch than a boss. No matter how angry he got or how often you got fired, you always had the feeling you could still "go home" if you were willing to kiss the ring and take a little heat. It didn't take a genius to figure out that the loyalty and attentiveness that Brown required knew no boundaries. Sour grapes and inside jokes understandably flowed behind his back but, in his presence, many employees competed like juveniles for his attention and approval. Bob Patton once grumbled, "This company could run so much smoother if everyone just did their job instead of trying to score points with James. Certain things that happen day to day go better untold with an emotional man like him, but you can bet any little thing finds its way back to him."

Brown relished and instigated competition among his staff, viewing any overt fraternal camaraderie as a threat to his authority and control. Interestingly, the Brown philosophy wasn't immune to blatant stereotypes. Once he tried explaining to Buddy Nolan that his effectiveness had its limits because "white cats like Mr. Leeds here will outwork you every time. He got that schooling you don't have, Mr. Nolan. Discipline."

A split second later, before I could gather any false sense of security, he turned to me and said, "Mr. Leeds, you could never know as much as Mr. Nolan about certain things out here because you ain't been where he's been. They don't teach that in your schools."

Of course, given our respective backgrounds, this actually made sense. Then he added, "In fact, some of the places Mr. Nolan been you *can't* go. You don't need to go."

Stereotypes aside, James Brown Productions was an equal opportunity employer and I never seriously felt either advantaged or disadvantaged by color. In fact, Brown got a charge out of how Bob Patton and I fit in. Enough so that, one night after a show and a couple of cocktails, James looked at us and laughed, "Look at you and Mr. Patton," he said affectionately. "I thought I hired me a couple white boys and I got me two more niggas." Many decades before the hip hop generation authorized young white kids to refer to each other that way, we took Brown's observation as a compliment.

Of course, the ceaseless gamesmanship made for frequent stress. Most employees developed their own individual strategies for placating the boss without sacrificing their peace of mind or dignity. It was a delicate balance, and those closest to Brown either learned to cope or risked self-destruction.

Danny Ray, for example, was adept at remaining agreeable with James while biting his tongue. Doubling as the show's emcee and Brown's valet, Ray spent more time in the boss' presence than most and usually hid his tired, weed-reddened eyes behind dark glasses. On one occasion, Brown studied Danny preparing the singer's wardrobe, chuckled and started in on him. "You know, Mr. Ray. You're crazy… really crazy. Look at you with those glasses—and it's as dark backstage as it is outside."

Danny never looked up. Not to be intimidated, he started mumbling under his breath. "You're right, Mr. Brown, definitely right about that. Crazy is the word and it sure is dark. I like it dark. Yeah, I'm certainly crazy alright. Uh-huh, no doubt about it. If there ever was a word to put with my name, it's got to be crazy. Yassir. In the dark and crazy."

Brown had walked out of the dressing room. I'm not even sure Danny noticed.

THE FEW MONTHS I'D BEEN AWAY had been turbulent in James Brown's world. First, his girlfriend-protégé singer Marva Whitney had quit and given *Soul* magazine an angry interview claiming she suffered from all sorts of exploitation on "plantation Brown." Meanwhile, the heralded James Brown Band's morale was sinking, marked by disputes over off-day rehearsals, salaries, composer credits, and road expenses. In March, frustrations boiled over and the fellas issued an ultimatum—either acknowledge some of their grievances or they'd refuse to play the next gig. The boss answered by secretly flying in a replacement band—a group of youngsters from Cincinnati whose bright spots were teenage bassist William "Bootsy" Collins and his guitarist brother Phelps "Catfish" Collins.

On an otherwise normal Monday night on the road, the veteran band gathered around the stage in Columbus, Georgia, awaiting their boss. As show time approached, they realized Brown was calling their bluff. Suddenly, James burst from his dressing room jogging towards the stage, followed by the six scruffy youngsters and drummer John "Jabo" Starks, the lone loyalist of the old band. Minutes later, the house lights dimmed, and Soul Brother #1 began what must have been his most ragged performance since the 1950s, the nubile band laboring their way through whatever Brown tunes they knew.

Meanwhile, Maceo Parker, Jimmy Nolen, and all the others who had been part of a musical legacy, slowly gathered their personal belongings and solemnly drifted through the backstage shadows into the cool Georgia night.

Nobody really thought that James would let the band go. They were the elite unit on the circuit and the envy of every other soul singer. But the boss felt control was the primary issue and caving in would be fatal. I suppose, at some point, he reminded himself that HE sold the tickets. It was HIS name on the records. James took it as a challenge, and he loved having something to prove.

Thankfully, there were three off days before the next gig in Fort Wayne, Indiana, during which James hoped to whip the youngsters into something worthy of the King of Soul. But he needed a band leader. As always, old pal Bobby Byrd came to the rescue. But, in the wake of Marva Whitney's quitting and now the band, the soul grapevine was abuzz. Most of my first week back was about putting out those fires.

Meanwhile, now convinced that I "really wanted to be part of the organization," James suggested I ride the band bus for a week of one-nighters, after which we could sit and brainstorm when the show settled into an extended engagement at the Latin Casino outside Philadelphia.

Brown couldn't have known the significance of his suggestion. Splitting my time between the office and the road didn't justify a full-time seat but, after six years, I had made it—ON THE BUS!

6

My first ride on the James Brown tour bus couldn't possibly have lived up to my romanticized vision, but it was quite an experience just the same. Gertrude Sanders, Brown's long-time wardrobe mistress, was his eyes and ears on the bus and she ruled her domain with every ounce of her solid frame. She quickly squelched any behavior that infringed on what little privacy existed aboard the JB express. Everyone respected her unique access to the boss, so her authority was seldom challenged.

This was no luxury custom coach—it was a standard, late model long distance tour bus leased from Trailways. The seats reclined, and some had been removed to provide extra leg room but that was it. As the bus raced through darkness, I was too excited to sleep. Mindful of my rookie status, I looked around to see how the pros coped.

The entourage was a mix of veterans with rookies who had little more road experience than me. Holly, the driver (his last name forgotten to the ages), an ex-trucker from New Jersey, happened to be white and most of the passengers happened to be black but there was no color line, just a pack of road rats—the real James Brown family. Seniority dictated choice of seats and most everyone had two seats to themselves. The old hands like Jabo Starks and roadie Kenny Hull sat near the front, lulling themselves to sleep with a bottle of gin. Gertrude sat behind Holly where she waged a running battle over road directions designed to make sure he stayed awake. I never did figure out when Gertrude slept—seemed like she was always running her mouth about something or other.

Comedian Clay Tyson and Danny Ray were self-appointed commentators, cracking wise about every billboard, dilapidated building, winter-weary farm animal, and downtrodden hitchhiker that we passed. Nobody seemed to pay their non-stop babble any attention. I don't think they even listened to each other, but it's too bad we didn't have today's portable technology to record them because they were drop-dead hysterical.

Bootsy Collins, his brother Catfish, and the other youngsters in the band, only three weeks on the road, secluded themselves in the back, sharing reefer (or acid) inspired giggles and picking out Jimi Hendrix riffs on their guitars. There was a glaring generation gap on the bus. Weed versus gin, Hendrix versus Basie, and I fit somewhere in the middle. I was just a few years older than the other rookies and certainly shared their preference of weed over alcohol, but I had other things in common with the veterans, many of whom I'd known for several years. None of that really mattered because my management status dictated that Gertrude seat me near the front, which discouraged any thoughts I had of hanging with the band. The last thing I needed was for the boss to think his "new executive" was already letting his hair down with the boys. And, believe me, he would have found out—Gertrude wasn't the only one aboard with loose lips.

The biggest benefit of being on the bus was getting to know road manager Freddie Holmes, who schooled me on what Brown did and did not want to hear in the nightly box office reports. But nobody wanted to talk business very long after a long show day. The idea was to get some sleep. Unfortunately, despite my experience on Gene Redd's desktops, my body didn't easily adjust to awkwardly sprawling across the bus seats. Once the novelty of being on board wore off, I was left with the reality that any bus trip over a couple hundred miles was a grind—hardly the equal of a night in a hotel. The thought that some of these guys had spent the better part of their adult lives on buses like this was mind-boggling.

Being on the road did give me the opportunity to be a fan again. Periodically, I'd wander off to catch part of the new show, which was improving quickly but still didn't compare to the productions Brown was known for. The good news was that, unlike their predecessors, some of whom were dedicated to jazz and viewed the Brown band as a pay check and stepping stone towards more challenging gigs elsewhere, Bootsy and his gang grew up on James Brown music and loved playing it. The bad news was that, other than the Collins brothers, the little eight-piece band didn't have enough chops to give James much to work with. The weakest musicians in the group were the horn players, so JB had cleverly shifted emphasis to the rhythm section, where Bootsy, Phelps (and Jabo) could shine—and, in fact, eventually reinvent Brown's trademark funk. But that was still to come. The band was still struggling when they arrived at the Latin Casino, so James opted to augment them with a group of local union musicians.

The week at the Latin Casino, a supper club in Cherry Hill, New Jersey near Philadelphia, marked the new band's first appearance in a major market. James rehearsed the anxious but soon exhausted musicians to death, hammering out a precision that belied their limitations. The gig was a revelation for me. I had seen James perform in countless theaters and arenas, but this was my first time seeing him perform in a night club. As the week went on, the show seemed to benefit from the repetition of two shows a night without the grind and distraction of travel.

It was also my first experience watching James operate in the company of other celebrities and well-wishers, including Muhammad Ali. The usually boisterous champ was surprisingly deferential to Soul Brother #1. First, the boxer listened quietly as Brown offered his two cents about Ali losing his heavyweight title to an Army draft board. Then James rambled on and on about blackness, politics, and a role model's responsibilities, boldly contradicting some of the Nation of Islam's teachings that Ali subscribed to. In Brown's presence, Ali seemed just another plebe; humble, and attentive.

(It wasn't quite the same ten years later, when Ali accompanied James to NBC-TV's *Tom Snyder Show* and an odd panel discussion that was supposed to be about unrest among youth in the African-American community. Brown stayed on subject, offering himself and Ali as role models for young blacks and claiming the media distorted what went on in the black community. Ali, however, ignored the unrehearsed show of unity and stunned host Snyder by sheepishly admitting that he didn't really know why he was there except that his 'good friend' James had requested his presence and NBC had offered to pick up the tab. Visibly disappointed, Brown's already-somber tone turned maudlin as Muhammad smiled and added, 'It's always nice to get a free trip to New York.'")

The Latin Casino housed us at the adjoining Rickshaw Inn, which meant a week in suburban Cherry Hill, where there wasn't much to do but strategize upcoming tour dates with the boss or sneak off to the nearby shopping mall. When I think about it, we didn't use the word tour very often back then, since the Brown show stayed on the road as much as fifty-one weeks of the year. That meant carefully routing itineraries that avoided over-exposure in any one region. There were only so many places to play, and James seemed to know them all. He had an encyclopedic knowledge of cities and their venues and an atlas-like sense of distances, the result of his early years trudging around the country in a station wagon. Thanks to his uncanny photographic memory for names, places, and statistics, Brown had a skillset the envy of any booking agent.

Early on, manager Ben Bart recognized that James Brown wasn't just any artist. Most of the singers and bands signed to his Universal Attractions took whatever gigs the agency offered without question but, from the beginning, James insisting on learning the reasons behind every decision made on his behalf.

When Brown's marquee value grew in the early 1960s, Bart curtailed selling dates to outside promoters and backed many shows himself. I suppose Ben justified his additional promoter income by putting up the front money and shielding his artist from the notorious "bad pay" promoters that haunted the Chitlin' Circuit. But it didn't take James long to catch on to the potential conflict of interest and demand a partnership in the promotion, adding to the flat fee Bart had been paying (and assumedly commissioning). From that point on, the hardest-working man in show business was as much a promoter as he was a performer or, as he preferred to explain, "seventy-five percent business and twenty-five percent artist." Inevitably, Brown took over the reins and, by the time Bart died in 1968, he had been reduced to a semi-retired, albeit beloved, consultant.

And so, in early April 1970, I sat with James in his hotel suite and mapped out a wish list of bookings for May and June—the first of many such sessions we'd have over the next few years. First, he selected the more lucrative large cities, allotting one per week and then filling in around them. After a while, I acquired Bob Patton's and Buddy Nolan's familiarity with the circuit, but it wasn't unusual for Brown to throw us a curve when we were stumped. Whenever we were troubled to find somewhere to fill in a date, he was likely to come up with some small town that fit the radius. "There's an old theater there on the main street that holds about three thousand people. Look it up," he'd say. He was always right.

Juggling the available dates in buildings that also housed stage plays, circuses, ice shows, sporting events, and concerts of all kinds was a complicated task but, somehow, we usually managed to stick close to James' outlines. Once a month's worth of shows was locked in, Brown would divvy the responsibilities of the various shows between us based on our individual strengths. For example, if only because James still associated me with Richmond, I got all the shows in the southeast. Patton and Nolen were held accountable for most of the "A" markets, except for New York, which Brown ceremoniously put in my column—although, in practice, we approached the Big Apple and other media centers as a team.

After leasing a venue, our next step was to select a local promoter, usually someone James knew and had history with. Sometimes they were experienced, professional promoters but, more often, it was someone associated with a black radio station—a station manager or a popular on-air personality. We would scale the house and order tickets ourselves to head off any counterfeiting—control was everything. Posters and handbills were printed and shipped to the local rep for distribution. Then we put our Mad Men hats on, researched what radio stations and newspapers would best reach our audience, and bought the advertising.

Posters and newspaper ads were always part of the plan, but black radio was the undeniable foundation of our promotions. Most radio personalities maintained a high profile in their communities and could do a lot to make or break a concert. Brown had courted their loyalty throughout his career and we'd often invite them to make paid appearances on stage as guest emcees—a thinly disguised encouragement to keep playing our records. It was no accident that Brown's music received steady airplay throughout what's become known as the urban (read: *Black*) radio world.

Once promotions were underway, we had to keep tabs on each campaign, including a keen eye on daily ticket sales. In those days, with the Brown show playing most markets twice each year, sellouts weren't guaranteed and "walk up" or day-of-show ticket sales were a significant portion of our business. That meant keeping abreast of variables like local economies and weather forecasts. Whenever ticket sales lagged, we would hit the road and troubleshoot—spending as many days as necessary in the problem areas, adjusting advertisement and scheming up any promotional gimmick that might turn things around.

One such situation inadvertently illustrated what James had explained to me about the "mister thing." It also demonstrated that I still had a lot to learn about the deep South. I didn't fully understand how much many Southern men had in common, regardless of color. Despite their jaded history, white and black Southerners shared the same drawl, worked the same land, ate the same kinds of food, drank the same moonshine, and worshipped the same God. I was reminded of all this thanks to a visit to Mobile, Alabama.

The first thing I noticed when I got off the plane in Mobile was that all the locals were either wearing overalls or drab, generic business suits. My trendy leisure suit was a neon sign blaring "Yankee." I caught a cab to the Municipal Auditorium for a meeting with Buddy Clewis, the venue director. A dyed-in-the-wool good ol' boy who was somewhat of a legend in the arena business, Buddy could have played a bartender in a Western movie. He had a little round, reddish nose and wore a thin bolo tie on a white shirt with a rumpled collar. All he lacked were garters for his sleeves. Most noticeably, a huge Confederate flag hung on the wall behind his desk alongside a framed photo of him hugging Gov. George Wallace, the renowned segregationist. Before I said a word, thoughts rushed through my head of all the civil rights workers who were beaten or worse in the swamps and bayous of Alabama, Louisiana, and Mississippi. Clewis stood and extended his hand.

"Well, well, I do declare. Who'd ever thought ol' Mr. Brown woulda sent a Yankee white boy down here to see ol' Buddy," he drawled.

There was that mister thing. "Mr. Leeds, let's you and me see how we can make some money with ol' Mr. Brown," he continued. "Mr. Brown's been awful good to Mobile and ol' Buddy. Maybe he'll be good to you too."

I was momentarily speechless. But, before I exhaled, I remembered that one of Mr. Brown's policies was to reward venue managers with a generous tip on successful dates. Long before their corporatization under the Live Nations and AEGs of the world, venue managers were usually modestly paid city employees who had the authority to book their venues as they saw fit. Having them in our pocket gave the

James Brown Show first crack at the most lucrative dates and a host of assorted promotional favors. Business was business, and Buddy Clewis was delighted to be in business with Mr. Brown.

Unfortunately, every relationship wasn't that easy. With too much on his plate, Bob Patton had been relying more than usual on local promoters. The local guys always stood to benefit from a successful show, but their jobs didn't depend on it like ours did. Some were very competent and responsible, but others were just watch dogs and failed to share our sense of urgency when things got dodgy. These guys might just be hustlers who enjoyed showboating their relationship with Soul Brother #1 or took the gig for whatever local prestige it mustered. Either way, they might spend more time promoting themselves than our show. Worse yet were the few that envied or even wanted our jobs and weren't above throwing us under the bus to make themselves look good.

The danger was that, when things went badly, James could be very impressionable. Inevitably, he'd confront the local rep who'd predictably pass the buck in our direction, perhaps claiming we ignored his advice on matters like ticket prices and advertising strategies. It didn't help that we weren't always on the road to defend ourselves. That usually meant an angry middle-of-the-night phone call from the boss.

On the other hand, James could be quick to stick up for us. Once, after a sparsely attended show in Raleigh, North Carolina, Brown took out his frustration on Buddy Nolan in front of the local promoter who shared at least some of the responsibility. As they were leaving James' dressing room, the local guy started taunting Buddy, calling him "James Brown's flunky." Nolan shoved him but was knocked back by a sucker punch. Brown heard the commotion and suddenly appeared in the doorway. Wearing a robe and slippers, his hair in curlers, he held a pistol in his hand—leveled at the local guy.

"Mr. Nolan works for me," he barked. "I can tell him anything I want to, and he can either listen or quit. But you better not say another word to him as long as you live!"

7

The first date I was responsible for was in Petersburg, Virgina, a campus concert at Virginia State College. The show was a quick sell-out, and the box office settlement went smoothly so I had time to catch some of the show. Just as I neared the stage, James tore into a new arrangement of "Give It Up or Turnit a Loose" that I hadn't heard before. The song had been a show-stopper ever since it was released in 1968, and the new version was funkier than ever, built on an infectious Phelps Collins guitar line. After the show, I asked JB about it.

"Oh, that's gonna be my new tune," he answered with an impish grin. I didn't understand how an old record could also be his "new" tune, but all he said was, "Wait until we get to Nashville tomorrow. You'll see."

Then he turned to Charles Bobbit and reminded him to get King engineer Ron Lenhoff to Nashville, where James had scheduled a late-night recording session after the next show. Brown would be flying to Nashville in his Learjet, but the band and crew faced a grueling drive. There was a lot of highway between Petersburg and Nashville, and none of us looked forward to the ride. Evidently, neither did the bus.

Once or twice a year, the bus breaks down and strands the show somewhere. Sometimes, the bus is polite enough to select an off day, but not this time. Not at 2:00 a.m. in Petersburg, and the next show eighteen hours and 500 miles away. Holly was convinced the breakdown was serious enough that the bus couldn't be repaired in time to make it, so we flipped into emergency mode. That meant finding local transportation to get everyone to the closest airport, Richmond's Byrd Field, and then figuring out flights to Nashville.

It took a couple hours to find enough vans to make the move. The band gradually drifted into the terminal, only to learn that they had a five-hour wait and the restaurant wasn't open yet. Then I spotted Kenny Hull, who should have been riding shotgun in the equipment truck, which I had assumed was well on its way to Nashville. But it turned out that the truck was necessary to get all of the band's luggage from the bus to the airport. I didn't waste any further time pointing out that they could have just taken the luggage on to Tennessee. Kenny tried convincing me that the truck would make it in time for load-in, but Freddie Holmes and I weren't convinced. As a safeguard, we decided to fly at least one set of drums and guitar amps with the group. That meant digging into the truck and, before long, the main rotunda of cozy Byrd Field was littered with audio equipment, amplifiers, guitar, light racks, and drum cases.

Once sorted, we shoved the gear towards the ticket counter. But Piedmont Airlines balked at the extra weight on their small commuter jets. Worse yet, they were two seats short of accommodating our entourage.

Fast forward a couple hours, and there were Freddie and me pacing around our gear, now strewn about the lobby of a private executive terminal. We were waiting for a pilot we had awakened and bribed into flying our gear to Nashville, along with any of us who could squeeze into his small cargo plane. Once we finished loading everything, Kenny and audio engineer Jerry Shearin climbed aboard. There were no seats; they'd have to lay prone and hug the road cases all the way to Tennessee. As I watched the over-loaded Piper struggle into the air, I seriously wondered if I'd ever see any of them again.

Luck was on our side. Everyone reached Nashville in time. The show went on without a hitch, although James had a fit when he learned what it cost us to get there. After the gig, a charter bus idled outside Municipal Auditorium, waiting to carry everyone to Starday Studios on Dickerson Road in suburban Madison, Tennessee.

Starday was an old-school country and western label that had merged with King Records in 1969. Starday-King president Hal Neely was thrilled that James had agreed to try Starday's freshly refurbished studio. Brown really had no preference in studios, and the facility's country music pedigree was of no concern. After all, he had cut his breakthrough hit, "Papa's Got a Brand New Bag" at country guitarist Arthur Smith's Charlotte, North Carolina studios in 1965.

The Starday staff was eager to host the label's primary money-maker and his first session with the new band. When the guys arrived just after midnight, they were met by a studio full of hospitable if curious employees. It was safe to bet they didn't record too many funk groups out on Dickerson Road.

About 1:00 a.m., James and Bobby Byrd walked in carrying a jumbo show poster on the back of which were some hastily scribbled lyrics. JB went right to work, counting off the new arrangement of "Give It Up or Turnit a Loose." After a few minutes spent tinkering with the rhythm parts, James began practicing his new lyrics. But not for long. Suddenly, he cut the band off and said, "Fellas, that's real good but, if we get it too perfect, we're gonna blow it."

He meant blow the *feeling*, always the most important element to Brown—even at the expense of precision. After quickly reminding "Jabo" Starks to emphasize the "one" on the bass drum, Brown kicked things off.

"Fellas! I wanna get up and do MY thing. You know…like a sex machine!"

James put the emphasis on "my." That amused me. In a day when everyone was encouraged to do THEIR thing, Brown was insisting that HIS thing was still definitive.

After an abbreviated false start, "Sex Machine," officially titled "Get Up I Feel Like Being Like a Sex Machine" was on tape.

Brown instantly knew what he had. He told his inexperienced band, "That's all right! We got all we need," before turning in the direction of engineer Ron Lenhoff and continuing, "That is, if we've got a good balance."

Lenhoff shook his head no, a responsibly cautious excuse to request a second take. Interestingly, the second run through was less cohesive, Brown's partially ad-libbed lyrics sometimes struggling to fit the funky vamp. Still, at the end, the entire studio, the giddy band, and the Starday staff alike, erupted into cheering and applause. Although James sarcastically declared, "I'm scared to listen to that one," folks crowded around the playback speakers. Thirty seconds into the song, everyone was smiling, laughing, dancing in place and slapping high fives. The first take was definitely the keeper. During the next few days, James would have Lenhoff electronically up the tempo a smidgen and add some echo. Four weeks after the session, the single was on the streets.

A group exhale had been building since the young band's surprise call to join Soul Brother #1. They left all the tension of their first month behind at Starday Studios, the tense, grueling rehearsals, the interminable bus rides, the hectic week at the Latin Casino and the fiasco the night before in Petersburg.

Brown was pleased. "Sex Machine" rejuvenated his music— Bootsy Collins' "in your face" bass, Bobby Byrd's catchy co-vocals, and JB's own piano interlude all broke formula. James panned the room, studying facial expressions and body language. Finally, he hushed everyone and announced that, three nights later, he would introduce the band to the nation on *The Tonight Show starring Johnny Carson*. Believe it or not, everyone cheered—again. Actually, yelled and screamed. Well, maybe not everyone, but even old Bobby Byrd and Jabo Starks wore silent smiles of approval. And I was too busy jotting down the instructions that James began throwing my way. He had questions about four Carolina dates that we had scheduled after the Carson show.

Upcoming shows in Charlotte, Greenville, Fayetteville, and Raleigh were all within a region dominated by two veteran white promoters, Joe Murnick of Norfolk and Jim Crockett of Charlotte. The foundation of their loose partnership was an eternally profitable professional wrestling circuit and their control of several key venues. Recognizing their strengths, JB chose to co-promote his Carolina appearances with them. The deal was 60/40, 60 percent of the gross for Brown and 40 percent for the promoters, out of which they would be responsible for all venue and advertising expenses. Bob Patton and I loved the deal, since the promoters put up the front money and did the bulk of the work. But I quickly realized there was a downside.

With the first date less than a week away, ticket sales were lagging, so James agreed to do phoners, on-the-air interviews with radio stations in each town. When a Raleigh radio personality casually referred to Crockett-Murnick's advertising campaign as modest, JB hit the ceiling. Theoretically, we couldn't spend the promoter's money for them but, if it had been our own promotion, we would have quickly increased the radio time buys. The terms of our agreement with Crockett and Murnick were just a technicality to James; he instructed the station to triple the advertising and bill it to the promoters. When the radio station called Crockett for approval, it was his turn to snap out. After an angry, confrontational conference call, he agreed to increase the advertising on the condition there would be no further tampering from our camp. Bob Patton later explained to me that this kind of friction was typical. Brown appreciated the benefits of the 60/40 deals in theory, but he hated feeling beholden to outside promoters. That wasn't a recipe for a smooth relationship.

Later that week, I met the show in Greenville and ended up spending the weekend rolling with the boss and his Learjet. To say it was a huge difference from riding the band bus is an understatement. An hour flight on the speedy jet was as ordinary to James as a drive to the grocery store for anyone else. Considering that he had people to pack and drag around his considerable luggage, had his plane warming up on the runway after a show, and two rental cars waiting when he landed, travel in JB's world was a breeze. The first rental car was a sedan that James usually drove himself. The second vehicle, a station wagon, stayed behind for the bags. Over the years, James learned his way around most cities. I was amazed at how he'd effortlessly wind his way from airports to venues to hotels.

One of the advantages of the plane was the flexibility to spend the nights in pet cities and hotels rather than the tank towns we sometimes played in. For example, less than two hours after the Greenville show, we landed in nearby Atlanta and were heading towards the sparkling Hyatt Regency, which was known for its then-innovative atrium design and glass elevators. When we pulled into the hotel driveway, James spotted Pearl Bailey coming out of the main entrance. He leaped from the car and grabbed her in a playful hug, oblivious to the throng of youngsters following her with autograph books. We had driven from the airport alone, no security, so I jumped to his side as the approaching fans began recognizing him. I tried guiding Brown into the lobby, but he'd have none of it. James stayed on the steps with Pearl signing autographs for almost fifteen minutes. It was a gallant gesture because, if he had turned towards the lobby, fans might have followed us inside, leaving Ms. Bailey behind. I was pleased with his sensitivity.

Fayetteville came and went. As we were taking off for Charlotte, it began raining. JB hated rain—it was bad news for ticket sales, discouraged walk-ups. I hoped for sunshine in Charlotte but had a hunch we were in for a long night.

Sure enough, it was pouring when we landed, and Brown's mood changed from bad to worse. James frantically surfed the car radio for any station advertising the gig as we raced down the highway—and raced right past the Coliseum exit. He jerked onto the culvert, backed up about fifty yards, and screeched down the ramp towards the venue.

Frustrated by his inability to find an ad for the show, James turned cynical. "Those stations never air the last spots before a show because they figure the promoters are too busy to listen for them."

As we pulled into the secured driveway behind the Coliseum, James' dire expression suddenly exploded into a cheesy grin as he lowered the window to address a guard. "Hi," he drooled. "I'm James Brown. Hey! I remember you from last time we were here. Yeaahhh, my man!"

Brown extended his palm out the window expecting a slap of five. The officer missed the point, instead grabbing his hand and shaking it vehemently as he directed us into the backstage area. Before we parked, James turned to me and said matter-of-factly, "Go right up front and get the latest ticket count. Then call each radio station and get their schedule of advertisements for today. Mr. Crockett needs to know we watchin' him."

The car lurched on its axles as James slammed on the brakes and opened the door in one motion. Suddenly, we were surrounded by activity. Valet Henry Stallings rose from the station wagon tailing us and dove for the trunk, as Gertrude Sanders and Danny Ray appeared out of nowhere to help unload. James strutted towards the stage and a waiting sound check as manager/confidante Charles Bobbit dutifully swooped to his side. Bobbit wanted to warn James that there were a bunch of folks wandering around looking for autographs, but Brown ran to the stage before Charles could hold his attention.

Bobbit didn't know the back story. As part of the promotion, James had persuaded Jim Crockett to donate gift food certificates to ten needy families. The two black radio stations in Charlotte had each submitted five such families and, in their enthusiasm, had invited them all to the show. It was this collection of fathers, mothers, sons, daughters, nieces, nephews, uncles, and aunts that ambushed James between the stage and his dressing room after sound check.

But James didn't connect these people with the food certificates, he just assumed they were fans who had somehow eluded security.

Finally, one of the local disc jockeys rushed forward explaining things and asking JB to pose for pictures and sign some autographs.

The boss was caught in his tracks. He hesitantly explained that he needed to prepare for the show and suggested that the DJ escort them backstage again afterwards when he would have time to visit. Not everyone understood. As the group was escorted towards the front of the Coliseum, a couple of women with small children muttered about Brown's lack of hospitality. I had been in the box office during the whole scenario, so I had no idea what the disc jockey was talking about when he came in demanding a bunch of tickets. His story sounded legit, but I needed to run and get the boss' approval before I could cut loose fifty some comp tickets.

"How many are there?" he asked. I told him more than fifty.

"Oh man, sounds like family reunions out there. Tell Mr. Crockett he's got to pay for the extra tickets, I never told him to have all those folks back here."

Before I could tell James that Crockett had already refused, he had a change of heart. "Actually, Crockett would never have told those radio fellas to bring all those folks; he's not that crazy. But we need that radio station on our side and so does Crockett. So tell him we'll split the cost. And be sure to tell those disc jockeys we bailed them out. Make them understand that!"

Despite the rain, a decent walk-up salvaged the date, after which we flew to Cincinnati for the night. On the flight, James talked about how he wanted to approach the Carolina markets next time around. He was unhappy with Crockett and suspected that the local black media resented his using white promoters. "That sixty-forty made a lot of sense, we didn't need to front the bills. But pretty soon 'Sex Machine' is gonna have us red hot again. Then we can bankroll things ourselves and make a killing. And, if Mr. Crockett tries to block us, we'll use the radio stations to get the dates. Those buildings don't want black radio stirring things up in their communities. 'Sex Machine' is gonna turn things around. That record is a mutha!"

I reminded him that we still had one more show with Crockett. "Tomorrow? I'm not sure about tomorrow," Brown replied. "Folks in Raleigh don't like that old Dorton Arena. We really should be playing in that other building there, but I think Mr. Crockett went to Dorton because it's cheaper. You know we're doing a TV show there in the afternoon. Maybe that'll help get us through."

Like Atlanta, Cincinnati was one of JB's nocturnal haunts—understandable, what with the office and record company there. But it was a weekend and James really went to Cincinnati because he had a favorite late-night barbecue joint, and there were all-night movies on local television—remember, this was before cable or hotel pay-per-views. The fact that Cincinnati TV's late-night host, a middle-aged bartender named Bob Shrieve, was a Brown admirer and had a polka album on King Records added to the attraction.

After stopping to pick up barbecue we got to the hotel about 3 a.m., I was beat—I turned on the TV and jumped in the bed. And there was good old Bob Shrieve. The first thing I heard him say was, "We'd like to say hello to that great soul singer, my good buddy James Brown, who's with us tonight for all-night movies."

Then the phone rang. Guess who?

"Hey, Mr. Leeds. Did you hear him talkin' about us on TV? Ha, ha, ha. Sure is nice…nice to be where you feel at home. Don't you worry about these dates, son. Things gonna get better real soon. You know we're leaving early tomorrow…gotta do that TV show." Click.

No goodnight. No nothing. In fact, I didn't breathe a word after "Hello." I turned everything off and for a minute I imagined I was on a quiet beach—some place where they didn't have telephones, televisions, and hadn't heard of James Brown. At least for one night. I had only been on the job for a month, and jockeying back and forth between the regiment of the office and the erratic pace of the road confused the hell out of my system. I was learning something new every day, but everything was happening so fast I couldn't get a rhythm.

Eight hours later, I rubbed my eyes and realized that the sun was already high. It was noon. I dressed and packed quickly then ran into Bobby Byrd at the front desk when I went to check out. Byrd was waiting with a bellman to get James' luggage. Turns out James had just gotten up.

"I just called him again to make sure he's up," Byrd told me. "That girl he's got up there wouldn't wake him."

Girl? Damn. Who was she and where did she come from?

Bobby seemed surprised at my naivete. "You should know by now," he said. "That man never sleeps alone. He got girls everywhere."

In fact, Brown once boasted to writer Phillip Norman, "When I'm on the road, I behave like a teenager—bang, bang, bang. That racehorse don't run if he ain't got no lust."

It turned out that JB had a revolving door of companions that would fly in and out of damn near any town we slept in—sometimes different women stashed in different rooms of the same hotel.

About twenty minutes later, James strolled across the lobby—alone. Evidently that horse doesn't linger in the stable.

It was clouding up when we took off for Raleigh. Down there, it was already raining. After we landed, James got behind the wheel of our rented Buick Riviera, and off we went to a telethon being broadcast from a school auditorium.

The immediate area around the school was blocked to traffic and there wasn't a guard anywhere in sight, so we parked as close as we could. The auditorium floor was covered with makeshift sets—giant props, false walls, and gaudy artwork. Technicians, cameras, and cables were everywhere.

We had a tape to which James could lip-sync, so they scheduled him to do a song and a quick interview. Distracted by the maze of cables and gear, we failed to notice that the bleachers along two long walls of the auditorium were filled with kids. As soon as they spotted Brown, the bleachers began emptying—a wave of teenagers moving onto the floor, taking up every inch of space surrounding the set.

As JB finished his performance, the kids started screaming, all but drowning out the brief interview.

Bobby and I realized we were in big trouble. Without any security, how in the hell were we going to get to the car in one piece? We felt the kids surging forward ever so slowly, anxious for the segment to end, so they could pounce on their hero. As soon as the TV host broke for a commercial, Bobby and I reached out and pulled James in between us and jetted towards the door.

It took the fans a few seconds to react, so we actually beat them to the door and out into the rain, but they weren't about to give up. Five or six kids caught up with us before James could start the car. As he turned on the ignition, he lowered his window to sign autographs for the few who were prepared with pen and paper. He gradually lifted his foot from the brake and we slowly pulled away, JB's fist held high through the open window, clenched in the black power salute.

Despite the avid fans at the school, the Raleigh show was a loser. As the date went quietly into defeat, I bid James *adieu* and headed for a hotel. James was flying home to Augusta, but I had a Monday morning flight to join Bob Patton in Nashville and try to make heads or tails of our new makeshift office. Nashville?

8

Nashville? The story was fit for Ripley's Believe It or Not. Multi-millionaire entertainer closes his office rather than pay the phone bill! Indeed, Ma Bell had suspended our phone service in Cincinnati. The outstanding bill was several months in arrears, and the issue was what James claimed were unauthorized toll calls made by former employees. True or not, I couldn't see how James could blame the phone company. James couldn't have cared less—he just wasn't in the mood to pay the substantial bill.

The first few days without service were a pain in the butt, dashing up and down the stairs to King where we commandeered a couple of phones from which to conduct our business. Remember, this was before answering machines, let alone cell phones, so any callers we had been doing business with—venues, promoters, radio stations—reached a suddenly disconnected line with no further instructions. Not a good look. Meanwhile, the King switchboard operator was going crazy trying to keep up with us. As soon as she thought she had us pinned down at one extension, we'd disappear back down-stairs. The walk was a long one, the length of the building and down through the warehouse and shipping dock. Soon, everyone at King was monitoring our movements, paging us and forwarding calls from one part of the plant to another. It was disruptive and, finally, Hal Neely had enough and confronted James.

Brown still didn't want to know about the phone company. I suspect he was hoping that Neely would offer to settle our bill. Instead, Hal offered to temporarily house us in Nashville where they could better accommodate us. We had no way of knowing how long we'd be there, so Patton and I packed a bunch of files, dumped them in Bob's car, and drove south.

Starting the next day, callers now expecting to find us at King's Cincinnati number were referred to Starday in Nashville. The staff there, some of whom we remembered from the "Sex Machine" session, laid out the red carpet. Nevertheless, it was awkward and inefficient having to ask for help every time we needed something. And Nashville wasn't exactly my favorite town. I couldn't wait for the weekend and an excuse to meet the show somewhere. Anywhere! So, guess where. The show was playing dates in Ohio, and James, naturally, based himself right back in Cincinnati.

Speaking of "Sex Machine," the single was racing up the charts— the R&B charts, that is. Pop radio was resistant, many stations claiming the lyric was too risqué. Imagine an era where just a title like "Sex Machine" could be controversial. Worse yet, the disc's popularity hadn't yet translated to ticket sales. Attendance in Ohio was as lackluster as it had been in the Carolinas. Bob and I began advancing summer dates, and the promoter feedback was hesitant. Word was out, the James Brown Show was ice cold.

Of course, Brown remained predictably optimistic. "By the time we get to California, we'll be hot as cayenne pepper," he claimed. But Bob and I were facing another problem, venue rent deposits and advertising costs for future dates were coming due, and cash flow on the road was thin. We badgered Charles Bobbit and Freddie Holmes on the road, hoping they could scrape together some cash to keep things afloat, but the boss insisted on personally authorizing every dime spent and, sometimes, he just didn't want to deal with it.

After another week in Nashville, I caught up with the show again at Bushnell Hall in Hartford. Ticket sales were reasonably successful, but I avoided James most of the night. I was worried about my date in Pittsburgh two nights away, and I knew he'd be asking about it. Ticket sales for this hasty return booking simply weren't on par with the sell-out that started my adventure a mere six months earlier. After the show, James asked me to ride the show bus to Dover where I could "keep an eye on things" the next night.

What he meant was keep an eye on my old Richmond crony, promoter Allen Knight. Somehow, Knight had secured a modestly sized auditorium on the campus of Delaware State University and convinced JB to try a show there. Their history was full of confusion and dispute, so James always kept a keen eye on every aspect of Knight's promotions. Since Brown knew I was hip to most of Knight's shenanigans, I was a natural point man.

No matter how exciting a performance was, no matter how enthusiastic an audience was, nothing ever stood between Mr. Dynamite and his first question as he walked off stage, "How did we do?" He never lost sight of the fact that everything that happened on that stage was designed to please the people who had bought the tickets, and that those ticket sales were the ultimate barometer of a show's success.

Settling the box office began as soon as the ticket windows closed, usually about an hour after show time. By then, the advance sales had been verified, as had the vast majority of the show costs, all except any venue labor that might be affected by the show going into overtime. Our primary representative in any box office settlement was road manager Freddie Holmes, accompanied by Brown's manager Charles Bobbit, Bob Patton, or me, when we happened to be on the road. But Holmes kept the books. Most venues supplied detailed, multi-page settlements along with copies of all the receipts, but Brown seldom asked to see these. Instead, every night Holmes showed him the same one-sheet template that he was familiar with—one on which he could quickly scan our profit or loss, how much we spent on advertising, and how many comp tickets had been issued. It usually took Freddie fifteen or twenty minutes to transfer the key data from the actual settlements into our "book." By then, the show was usually either close to finished or already down. If Brown didn't see Freddie soon thereafter, he'd get impatient and send an aide to determine what was taking so long.

James' post-show ritual seldom varied. A towel around his neck and soaked with sweat, he'd trot to the dressing room accompanied by Gertrude Sanders, a security guy, maybe James Pearson or Leon Austin, and a valet, usually Henry Stallings or Danny Ray. Visitors, even V.I.P.s or those of us on payroll, had to wait outside until he decompressed. Inside the dressing room, he'd open a cold drink, usually a soda, and gradually dry off in a terry cloth robe. Once he caught his breath, whoever was doing his hair—in the 1960s, Frank McRae or Famous Flame Bobby Bennett, but now either Stallings or Austin—did their thing and put him under a dome-shaped, beauty-salon type hair dryer. In the old days, they'd first wrap his hair in curlers but, since he began sporting an Afro, the procedure was a little simpler. Once he was seated under the dryer, he was ready to look at the "book." That meant Freddie and whoever else was on duty would sanctimoniously walk in and silently surround Brown as he studied the night's report.

It was like facing a teacher at the end of class; you never knew if you were going to be commended and given a star or if you would be called out and embarrassed, and made to stay after school. Sometimes he would fool you. If the date had been a sell-out, rather than celebrate, he might quibble over something inconsequential like the number of comps given away by radio station promotions. On the other hand, when you had your seatbelt fastened because of a poor date, he might shrug it off with a pep talk designed to salvage morale. His reactions unpredictable, I always believed his whole point was to keep us on our toes.

Most established venues we played had bonded box office personnel, so we seldom touched any money until the end of the night, but Delaware State was a mom-and-pop gig with a potential for the very kind of orchestrated chaos that Allen and his crew thrived on. That meant tediously counting all the ticket stubs by hand to balance against the cash receipts. The show had sold out and, to my relief, the settlement balanced. Still, James hit the ceiling when Freddie and I showed him the final numbers in his dressing room. Knight had overestimated the hall's capacity—the place had been packed to the rafters, but what he had claimed would be 3,000 turned out to be just a little over 2,000. JB rightfully pointed out the revenue we lost by having to turn away several hundred folks. Finally, he threw the ledger across the floor and barked, "That's it. No more dates for Knight! We could have sold another thousand tickets. Cancel all his future dates and tell him I said so!"

Knight was holding a few "B" market dates in the coming months but, when I gave him Brown's edict, he just shrugged and replied, "I don't care. We all made some money tonight—better than he did with Jim Crockett last month. Your boss is the only guy I know who's harder to deal with on sellouts than flops."

Later in the year, Knight would eat those words, and we'd eat some too, but I'm getting ahead of myself.

The bus left Dover about midnight heading for a tavern owned by a friend of Gertrude's. The joint was out of our way, in some remote township near the Chesapeake Bay, but worth the drive. Bus rule #1: never turn down a free meal. The owner and her attractive daughter were great hostesses and made sure there were plenty of local girls for atmosphere. We served ourselves cafeteria style. There was chicken, pork chops, baked beans, potato salad, beer, wine, and even a little weed if you were lucky enough to meet the right young ladies. All in all, it was a delightful change of pace from the usual night on the bus. But, just as a few of the guys were making headway with the girls, we had to hit the road.

Between a foggy drizzle and the poorly marked back roads, Holly had trouble finding the turnpike. He must have driven about fifty miles in the wrong direction before Gertrude threw a fit and convinced him to turn around. With the exception of Gertie's grumbling, the bus was unusually tranquil. Kenny Hull tried luring someone, anyone, into a poker game but everyone fell quickly asleep. Except me. Worrying about Pittsburgh ticket sales, as we approached the foothills of the Alleghenies, I found myself hypnotized by the beads of rain tumbling down my window.

Suddenly, the solitude was violated. A few rows behind me, Vicki Anderson had gotten up to grab a pillow from the overhead rack and stumbled over dancer Ann Norman who was wrapped in a blanket, cuddled across two seats, with her rather noteworthy legs stretched into the aisle. Some of us wouldn't have minded getting tangled in Ann's legs, but Ms. Norman was off limits—she belonged to Mr. Brown and didn't mind letting you know it. Vicki had mumbled something under her breath that woke Ann for a hazy moment, just long enough to snap, "You only wish they were *your* legs." Then she dramatically hoisted her butt and reeled those legs out of the way.

Vicki, a.k.a. Mrs. Bobby Byrd but "Mommy-o" to all of us, wasn't one to back down. But Gertrude shouted for them to both "keep quiet so people can sleep," in so doing, waking everyone else up. But not for long. Even I finally fell asleep. Next thing I knew, we were just a few miles shy of the Steel City. The rain had cleared, and it was a gorgeous spring morning. I hoped the weather was a good sign, I knew James expected me to salvage the date, despite the disappointing advance sales.

We still didn't have a dependable local man in the 'burgh. James had elected to give the date to Al Brisbane, a disc jockey he had known in Buffalo prior to his joining WAMO in Pittsburgh. Brisbane was both inexperienced as a promoter and unfamiliar with his new city, so I had to pretty much walk him through the entire promotion, a task complicated by my long friendship with "Brother Matt" Ledbetter, another WAMO DJ who wanted to get into fronting shows. I had visited Pittsburgh twice during the course of the campaign, leading Brisbane all over town, from the legendary Crawford Grill in the Hill District to newer clubs in trendy Market Square. Al was a nice enough guy, but he enjoyed telling folks about hanging out with "James Brown's man" just a little too much. That's how he was introducing me in what had been *my* hometown!

Brisbane did everything we asked him to do, but when I needed a real pulse, the street buzz, I had to call Matt. It was delicate explaining all this to the boss. I wanted to position Matt for the future, but all I could do was plant the seed; I couldn't throw Brisbane under the bus because he had been Brown's own choice. But, every time we discussed the gig, I maneuvered Matt's name into the conversation.

The show turned out to be the disappointment I had feared, but we were spared a total disaster by a reasonably decent door sale. On a positive note, it was the first audience to knowingly react to "Sex Machine." Maybe the record accounted for the last-minute walk-up, and the general feeling after the show was that we were headed for better days.

Overall, I was relieved. Pittsburgh meant a lot to me, for obvious reasons. It meant a lot to James too. He was on a first-name basis with several local politicians and had also taken an interest in a group of youngsters from Homewood, a section of the "hood" in the eastern part of the city.

The previous November, a group of young fellas, clad in black from berets to combat boots, had surfaced outside James' dressing room, where they waited quietly for an audience with Soul Brother #1. Nobody in Brown's camp knew who they were or why they were there, so they were kept waiting well over an hour, while JB visited with disc jockeys and other friends. The group waited patiently, mannerly but determined to see James. Somewhat apprehensively, JB agreed to meet with their spokesman.

The youngster explained that they were a volunteer, non-violent security force—a precursor to the Guardian Angels, so to speak. They had formed during a 1968 racial disturbance, cruising the city to protect residents and merchants from both looter violence and over-anxious, trigger-happy police. Intrigued, James asked to hear more and learned that, following the riot, the group remained intact, donating their services to any and every event that assembled African Americans, from playground sporting events to street fairs and concerts in the parks.

They had a proposal for Brown. Pointing out that relations between the black community and the Pittsburgh police were at an all-time low, they believed that the kind of audience disruptions that too often marred shows like ours were almost always a result of an overbearing police presence insisted upon by venue managers or promoters. They, the Black Guerillas, would offer their services as concert security, replacing uniformed police at events where a rapport with young blacks would be beneficial. Impressed, JB promised to employ them at his next Pittsburgh appearance.

Sure enough, as soon as this gig was announced, the Guerillas contacted me. I was all for giving them a shot, but there was a roadblock. The Civic Arena was a city-owned building, so the hiring of any private security would be subject to a drawn-out, bureaucratic bidding process. What's more, the chief of police had the authority to assign—in essence, force upon us—however many officers he felt necessary, whether we used them or not. Furthermore, the venue director told me that the chief was hesitant to lend credibility to a group that he viewed as unprofessional renegades. With that news, I spoke to James and we decided to pay the Guerillas ourselves. They would work for us and augment, rather than replace, city police.

As it turned out, many of the city cops assigned to the show were only too happy to relinquish their posts as long as they still got paid. So, with the cautious support of leery arena management, we positioned the Guerillas in front of the stage and at key points throughout the building, impressing upon them that their success depended on their willingness to work *with* the building and the police. The show went down without incident and everyone went home happy. Most of the city cops spent the evening getting paid to sit backstage playing cards.

Later that summer, we donated five hundred James Brown albums for the Guerillas to sell as fund raisers from their display booth at Pittsburgh's annual Black Solidarity Fair. By 1972, the Civic Arena was recommending them to the promoters of other black events, and the size of the expensive police details gradually diminished. I was proud to have played a role.

9

I spent the next week in Nashville setting up dates for fall, while Patton tried to make heads or tails of the upcoming West Coast shows. The lack of adequate front money was becoming critical. In that sense, our transient telephone situation sometimes served us well, an excuse for dodging calls from California arena managers seeking overdue rent deposits. James finally felt our panic, or maybe he was just tired of us bugging him for money. Whatever the reason, he called a staff meeting in Dallas.

Charles Bobbit had phone lines installed in a hotel conference room for what we all assumed would be a day-long head banger. But we never left Brown's suite—beginning the meeting unbeknownst to Bobbit who waited nervously in the conference room. James raised a few off-the-wall questions and then stunningly announced that he wanted to cancel every date scheduled for the next three weeks, the entire West Coast swing.

"Everything is too far behind," Brown said. "We need the time to re-group." The boss was right. I wanted to feel relieved, but I worried about where and how the blame would fall. It wasn't our effort that was lacking, it was operating capital, money JB could have easily come up with. More disappointed than angry, JB even hinted at retirement. "This business is changing, but so is the economy—worst it's ever been for blacks," he claimed. "Poor people can't afford to buy records or tickets to shows. If things don't change soon, we'll all have to give this up."

Just my luck, I mused. Work all these years to get into the business and, as soon as I make it, Brown hits a cold streak and throws in the towel. But I knew better; he was just convincing himself the cancellations were the right thing to do. And they were. The shows were under-promoted at a time when they needed all the help they could get. The good news was that "Sex Machine" had grown into a bona fide smash hit. And we could reclaim our office, since James got tired of paying our considerable hotel bills in Nashville and finally coughed up the money to pay off Cincinnati Bell.

Patton and I made good use of the hiatus, getting ahead of our next cycle of dates. Our first show back was June 24th in New Orleans and, lo and behold, the Municipal Auditorium was sold out. After equally successful dates in Little Rock, Oklahoma City, and Denver, James recorded his next single, "Super Bad."

A ferocious slice of hard funk, "Super Bad" was over nine minutes long, with enough hook to suggest another monster hit. It didn't have the crossover potential we had thought was in "Sex Machine" but nobody cared. A pop hit would have been welcome but, by this point, James viewed pop acceptance as an occasional bonus. He was more concerned with continuing to satisfy his base audience, and that meant staying true to his musical roots.

King advertised "Super Bad" as the first "three-part single"—compressing Parts 1 and 2 onto the first side, with Part 3 on the flip side. I suppose that's a disappointingly mundane explanation of what they exaggerated as a "revolutionary" concept, but what did people expect, a third part on the edge of the disc? At least the center holes were perfectly round, which brings us back to Bud Hobgood, who had taken seriously ill. In fact, he never recovered from an unexplained ailment, probably some form of cancer that Brown chose to blame on Bud's bad teeth. "Mr. Hobgood, your face is collapsing," James insensitively told poor Bud in the hospital the week before he died. "That's the sickness in your mouth and the poison is spreading. You should tell your doctor to call in a dentist."

JB often professed that, "A man with good teeth and hair has everything. Without that, he's in trouble." He acted as if any other ailment could be willed away.

THANKS TO "SEX MACHINE" AND OUR TIME OFF, we turned a corner. Well-attended shows continued into July, the bus stopping in Atlanta, Virginia Beach, Baltimore, Albany, and Montreal, before heading to Cincinnati and a hastily arranged recording session.

The idea was to complete a *Sex Machine* album that would be marketed as a two-record live set. James had recorded a 1969 gig with the old band in Augusta, Georgia, which he originally planned to release as *Live at Home With His Bad Self.* But the project was cancelled after the band mutiny in March. The new plan was to compile an abbreviated set from the Augusta show for the new album's first disc and couple it with a simulated concert set of new material including "Sex Machine." James planned to record the second disc at King studios, then over-dub audience reaction to duplicate the ambiance of the live record.

I knew from the road show performances that the new version of "Sex Machine" would be killer. On the other hand, it was impossible to disguise the fact that the two discs were recorded with entirely different bands except for the drummers, "Jabo" Starks and the recently returned Clyde Stubblefield. The newer recordings also introduced conga drums to Brown's music in the name of percussionist Johnny Griggs, the newest member of the recently dubbed "J.B.'s Band."

As exciting as the performances proved to be, the session was a technical nightmare. Engineer Ron Lenhoff, whose personal compatibility with James was as crucial as his skills, was on vacation. King President Hal Neely had no choice but to press an intern into duty, a petrified young man who had never run a session.

As the novice engineer frantically attempted to test and balance microphone levels, a typically impatient Brown counted off "Sex Machine." Halfway through a solid take, Neely and the apprentice realized that two of the microphones were not on and waved things off. Pissed at the interruption, James began a second take stalking around the studio, sarcastically calling out each band member to test their mics, a comical ad-lib that was later edited from the final master.

"I'm ready to get up and do my thing," Brown bellowed as he began his stroll. "Hey, Bootsy, are you ready to do your thing? Let me hear some of that bass. Alright, now horns, are you ready? Let me hear some of that sax there, brother."

And so it went, as Neely realized that JB was satisfying himself that everything was in working order. That take became a classic, as did "Give It Up or Turnit a Loose," recorded a few minutes later, but the tone and equalization on some of the instruments were so distorted that the overdubbed audience reaction served a greater purpose, obscuring the session's inferior sonic quality.

The next stop was Cleveland, and I tagged along with JB on his jet. In fact, James suggested we take our girlfriends along. His live-in mate at the time was fiancé Deidre Jenkins. Meanwhile, against her will, I convinced Deborah, my girlfriend from Pittsburgh, to start packing. Neither of us were thrilled at the idea of spending a Sunday in Cleveland with the boss, but duty called.

Deidre, or Dee Dee as we knew her, was a sweetheart, friendly, and genuine whenever James wasn't around. But, in his presence, she was relegated to play the ever-loyal silent partner, hardly a recipe for a fun excursion. James already seemed edgy when we took off. Once airborne, he decided to make an issue of Deb's lip gloss. Her tasteful and otherwise modest make-up was stylish—apparently too stylish for the parochial side of Soul Brother #1. Despite our single status, he referred to Deb as "Mrs. Leeds," just as Dee Dee was prematurely "Mrs. Brown." "Mrs. Leeds, you know down south we don't have that," he said, too condescendingly to be accepted as sensitive advice.

"No one wears that gloss but loose women. Don't you know that? You need to be glad we're up north."

Now I was edgy. Deb wore her pride on her sleeve, and I was afraid she'd walk into his trap and fight back but, thankfully, she played him off. Never one to leave things alone, James turned to Dee Dee and started reminiscing about how he and Bobby Byrd used to wear lip gloss on stage in their early days, "That's what that stuff is for," he insisted. "Show people and street walkers."

Once we landed, Dee Dee pulled Deb aside to console her, but she was already laughing it off. I was never so happy to see Cleveland. Two shows later, well after midnight, JB unexpectedly decided to spend the night there. I found him a suite at an upscale hotel, but it was otherwise sold out, so Deb and I rode the bus to where the band was staying and checked in. Then we decided to find something to eat. We rode around Cleveland in a taxi for an hour while our driver tried finding some decent food, not an easy task after midnight on a Sunday. Finally, as tired as we were hungry, we settled for a White Tower.

No sooner than Deb and I got comfy back at our room, the phone rang. We knew who it was. The Browns were the only people on the planet who knew where we were. Dee Dee said James was hungry and, since Danny Ray and Henry Stallings were nowhere to be found, would I mind bringing them some food. Disbelief spread across Deb's face as she snatched the blanket from under the note pad on which I was scratching out the Brown's breakfast order.

I threw on some clothes, found my way back to the White Tower, rode across town to James' hotel and rapped on the door of his suite. There was no answer. So I banged a little harder. Finally, Dee Dee cracked the door and whispered, "James fell asleep, but thanks anyway. Danny brought us some barbeque right after I spoke to you."

So much for our weekend "with the girls."

THE NEXT MORNING, James was off to New York, and Deb and I flew back to Cincinnati. I got to the office about two in the afternoon, just in time for Brown's first call of the day. He wanted to review the upcoming dates and decide where to augment the band—something he had hired arranger David Matthews to continue doing after the Latin Casino. I enjoyed having Matthews, a hippie jazz head, on the road with us. As the only white guys on the bus, we already stood out but, with Dave's shoulder-length hair, usually tangled in the collar of a musty, flowing cape, and my growing Jewfro and more trendy clothing, we really were the odd couple. On a more serious note, Matthews was a schooled musician with a unique hybrid of both classical and jazz credentials. Somewhere along the way, he developed an affinity for JB funk and became one of the few outside arrangers to grasp the knack of the James Brown sound. Dave also came in handy whenever the boss would guest on television programs without his own band. In such cases, Matthews would rehearse and conduct the TV studio bands that provided the accompaniment.

In the middle of August, James flew to Hollywood to tape such an appearance for the premiere episode of comedian Flip Wilson's new NBC-TV variety show. Earlier in the year, Flip had been Brown's support act for two weeks at the Flamingo Hotel in Las Vegas. On the day he arrived, James complained that the comic's name was too prominent on the hotel marquee. Truthfully, JB simply resented any attention the red-hot Wilson got, and he wasn't above using his headliner status as a bully pulpit. Every couple days, Wilson's name got smaller on the sign until it was gone completely, because so was Flip.

The rumor mill spread that JB had fired Wilson. The night before he flew to California, James told me, "People thought I ran Flip out of Vegas, but he ran himself out because I got all the press. NBC made him get me for this show. Flip knows he can't have a black show without me. I'm doing this so a brother can have a success on TV."

Revisionist history, i.e. bullshit? Absolutely. We all knew James had his eyes set on hosting a TV show and envied Wilson's opportunity.

Apparently, Brown brought his attitude to the show's rehearsal, where he was reported to have been critical of any and everything, chastising Flip for having "so many white technicians" on the crew. James balked at the script, the staging, the camera angles, and even got into it with one of the few blacks on the crew, all but calling him an Uncle Tom for being involved in the first place. According to Wilson's biographer, Kevin Cook, "The worst headache in the tense hours leading up to the first show was James Brown." Winston Moss, one of the show's writers, told Cook, "James made everybody nervous but Flip."

The drama peaked when Brown protested performing with the show's studio band, insisting he should have been accompanied by his own musicians. NBC execs refused to send for the J.B.'s. Stalemate.

To his credit, Wilson played down JB's tirade, calmed his crew, and cajoled James into performing three songs with the show's band. And, Flip got the last laugh when the show aired in September and Brown's segment had been edited to a brief, single tune.

OUR NEXT MAJOR DATE was at the Spectrum in Philadelphia. The show sold out, grossing over $100,000, a very impressive figure in the days of five- and seven-dollar tickets. Radio personality/promoter Jimmy Bishop had wisely insisted we add The Dells to the show, a wonderful vocal group who were at the peak of a five-year string of hits. As I strolled around the Spectrum's revolving stage, the Dells demonstrated why they were so popular. I thought about how they, like my boss, had many years of experience under their belts. We had a capacity crowd that was there to see two powerhouse acts, James Brown and the Dells, both of whose first hits had been recorded nearly fifteen years earlier.

I worked my way to the locker room serving as James' dressing room and found him ready for the stage, uncharacteristically pacing back and forth. It wasn't until he said something about Marvin Junior, The Dells' boisterous lead singer, not needing a microphone, that I realized, for once, James was concerned about something other than the box office. You could barely hear the show from the dressing room but hear it just enough to know The Dells were on fire—tenor Johnny Carter reaching for the sky and, JB was right, Marvin Junior's soulful baritone echoed all over Philadelphia. And we all knew the group's choreography was as silky smooth as their harmonies. The crowd was going crazy, and James was a wreck.

I was well aware of Brown's competitive nature, but I'd never seen this side of him. Maybe this was why he usually resisted hiring "A" level artists to support his shows—here were the mighty Dells on *his* show and they were bringing down the house. Chain smoking and stalking about, James finally burst out, "Listen to that. Fuckin' amateurs. They're amateurs! They had 'em in the palms of their hands, and now they blowin' it!"

Bobby Byrd, Danny Ray, Gertrude Sanders, and I looked at each other in silence as JB continued his rant. "They don't know when to come off," he yelled. "They stayin' on too long and blowin' it. Mr. Ray, you got to save the show. You got to get them off. NOW!"

Danny charged out and I soon followed. "What can I do about it?" Ray asked rhetorically. "If I take those brothas off that stage, we'll have a riot up in here."

We agreed that it was safer to just ride it out, which meant staying out of the boss' way until The Dells were finished. So, we wandered down an aisle towards the stage, which was set in the middle of the arena floor. My brother, Eric, was visiting from Pittsburgh and I found him perched in a makeshift photographer's loft, gleefully riding the revolving circular stage. But his spot was cramped between the edge of the stage and one of the drum kits—no room for me to squeeze in. I was still seeking a safe spot from which to watch the show when the Dells skipped off to ear-shattering applause. Sorry, boss, they *did* know when to get off. They had timed it perfectly, and the Spectrum was theirs!

After a brief intermission, the J.B.'s maneuvered their way down the access aisle through the audience and onto the stage. A few security guys and a weak velvet rope were all that stood between the audience and the artist's pathway. As I stood there, I felt scores of fans pressing against the rope as the aisle seemed to narrow. Then the house lights dimmed, and the band kicked off Danny Ray's trademark introduction, "Are you ready for star time?"

The aisle quickly clogged with additional security and hangers on. Then all hell broke loose. All hell under the guise of hurricane James. Suddenly, bodyguard "Baby James" Pearson charged out, Brown's head tucked under his arm like a football. Ignoring the rope and security folk, fans all but jumped on Pearson's back, half riding the two towards the stage. Brown made it in one piece but the same couldn't be said for his carefully styled appearance. He started the show almost as disheveled as he sometimes looked *after* a gig, his shirt ripped halfway down in front.

Then I witnessed the most intense James Brown performance I had seen all year. He was devastating. If The Dells got everyone up on their feet, "Sex Machine" had them dancing on top of the seats, and "Super Bad" had the whole building shaking. I honestly thought that the stage might come off its tracks. Afterwards, I considered getting James a copy of *Mad* magazine with Alfred E. Neuman's famous quote, "What? Me worry?"

After Labor Day, it was back to my old stomping grounds, Richmond's Mosque. It was no coincidence that Tom Mitchell and front man Allen Knight handled the date. JB and Knight had patched up their differences and, after two Mosque sellouts, James extolled Knight's virtues. "That Knight is finally learning. He's gonna be the biggest promoter down here soon, because he's into the new thang," the boss declared excitedly. "I'd been trying to teach him, and he finally listened. The old slick Allen Knight is gone. Now we got to work for him whenever it makes sense."

Then Brown turned in my direction before continuing. "Check out all his ideas. But check out the places carefully. He might be a new Knight, but he still got those same old places."

10

After Richmond, the bus parked in Cincinnati while James took the band in the studio to cut a radio commercial for S.S.S. Tonic, an iron enriched vitamin supplement. The track consisted of Brown singing the praises of S.S.S. to a funky version of "Cold Sweat." Leaning on my radio background, James asked me to do a ten-second voice-over that earned me a nice little check and the kick of hearing myself on a James Brown joint. The commercial ran for a year on just about every black radio station in the country, but I was tickled with the fact that I could now appear in any complete discography of Brown's recordings.

With time on his hands, James turned his attention to singer/ friend Leon "Lee" Austin, a childhood pal from Augusta who had come on the road as his mentor's personal assistant. Back home, Austin both operated a barbershop and led a popular local band, but Leon's main goal in life was to make it as a singer. The only drawback was his singing, which could best be described as that of a non-descript soul man. Of course, that didn't inhibit Brown's encouragement. Although he stopped short of allowing Austin a spot on the show, James periodically rewarded his loyalty by taking him into the studio. The tune JB had in mind was one that former Famous Flame Johnny Terry claimed to have written.

Since the Flames dissolved in 1968, Brown had generously employed Johnny on a couple of occasions, usually in capacities Terry wasn't really qualified for. To listen to Johnny, he had missed his calling. He fancied himself a tunesmith. After all, he had co-written Brown's first record, "Please, Please, Please." The new song was a ballad called "Who Am I." James convinced Leon that "Who Am I" was a hit—the record that could put him on the map.

"Who Am I" was a generic soul song but, even so, Austin couldn't sing it to Brown's liking. Thus resumed what was a common ritual when it came to JB producing his protégés—he'd find fault in their delivery and then insist on recording his own "demo" vocal version for them to study. "Learn to sing it just like this," James told a dejected Austin while handing him the demo as they left the studio—the lesson being, only Papa Brown knew how to do things right.

The easily forgotten recording session is only noteworthy because it inspired a twelve-month effort to produce a quality version of "Who Am I." A week later, James dropped by Henry Stone's T.K. Studios in Miami, where he was stunned to discover John MacArthur, a veteran of the Florida R&B scene, recording the very same "Who Am I." After a few questions, JB understood that MacArthur, better known as The Rootman, had actually written the song and sold it to Johnny Terry some months earlier. Then James unexpectedly took over the session and recorded it himself with T.K.'s studio band. The sloppy result of the spontaneous session was no better than Austin's Cincinnati version.

Some weeks later, Brown asked a Cincinnati vocal group called The Solars to over-dub vocals onto Austin's original track. This third version didn't impress anyone either and, for a while, "Who Am I" was forgotten. But, a few months later, James asked Dave Matthews to arrange and record another attempt.

Dave called an afternoon session, incorporating several of The J.B.'s into his usual studio band of crack Cincinnati musicians. James showed up an hour after the session, heard the track, and quickly dismissed it. Without any clear explanation of what he was looking for, he demanded that Matthews call another session and "do it right." Dave managed to reassemble most of the musicians, except for a drummer. "Never mind that," said Brown. "I'll play the drums myself." And so, still another approach to "Who Am I" found its way onto tape, complete with James' own drums *and* guide vocals—this time, as a demo for Roberta DuBois, a young lady who was part of a Cincinnati group called the Sisters of Righteous.

Roberta learned the song and returned the next day for another futile attempt at a release-worthy "Who Am I." Several days later, she tried it again. And again. James still wasn't satisfied. Then he sent for her to fly to Washington, D.C., where he and the J.B.'s cut "Soul Power" and still another crack at "Who Am I." DuBois added vocals and, this time, JB liked the results enough to schedule a release date. But it only took him a few days to have second thoughts. He cancelled the DuBois version in favor of the version by the Solars. Then he had third thoughts and stopped The Solars' release. (Although neither was officially released, both records were pressed and reached the collector marketplace when the King warehouse was liquidated in the 1970s).

"Who Am I" seemed like a thing of the past but, a month later, James dug out one of the earlier instrumental tracks, added his own vocals and inserted it into an otherwise live album recorded in Paris. That project was eventually scrapped when Brown signed with Polydor Records in July. The following year, James asked Matthews to revisit the song with the New York studio players they were using for some of their Polydor sessions. This final version was issued on Brown's *There It Is* album—two years after the initial recording of the song.

Score card time: five instrumental tracks, five different James Brown vocals, three by Roberta DuBois and one each by Leon Austin and the Solars. The latter was also released in 1972, with the artist credit inexplicably changed to The Famous Flames. If royalties were paid for rejected material, Johnny Terry would have died a rich man. As it was, the only people who saw a dime off of "Who Am I" were

Alan Leeds

Early to rise--Alan Leeds can even get the teenagers up and bouncing with his GO GO morning radio show--air time 7 a.m. to 10 a.m.

Alan graduated from Taylor Allderdice High School in Pittsburg, Pennsylvania, and then was introduced to the radio audience in New York City by his uncle.

He joined BIG WANT RADIO in 1965 and has been making the teenagers "rock" ever since. Alan is an ardent fan of "soul" music and of sports.

His experience is varied with the teenage market. Well versed as an emcee and promoter of show productions and record hops, Alan helps BIG WANT RADIO to remain Number I in this area.

BIG
WANT RADIO 99

BROAD-GRACE ARCADE, RICHMOND, VA. ● 23219 TELEPHONE 703-643-8368

(Top) The young author with his walkie-talkie "radio station."

(Left) WANT Radio sales brochure.

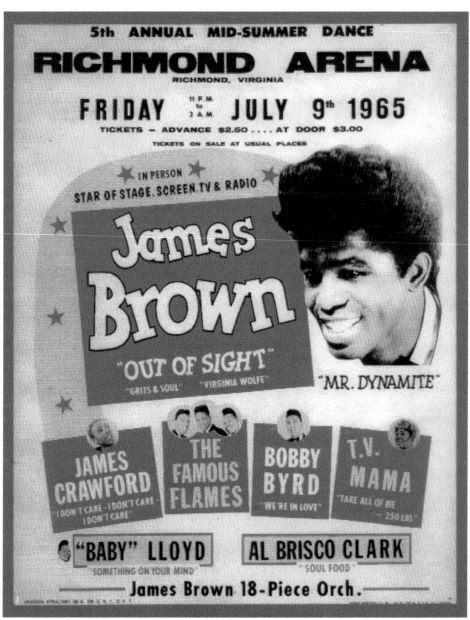

Poster for the show that led to the interview of JB.

(Above left) With singer Jerry Butler in 1966.

(Above right) The teenaged author meets his hero.

(Left) With Ray Charles in 1964.

(Right) With JB and Pittsburgh's Black Guerillas.

(Below) JB's first office in Augusta, Georgia (1971).

JB posing with the Model A Ford he impulsively bought off a gas station lot near the Cincinnati airport.

With Teddy Brown and Buddy Nolan hours before Teddy's fatal auto accident.

With Johnny Terry reviewing upcoming show promotions.

JB at his office desk in Cincinnati.

A posthumous JB seminar at the Apollo Theater. From left: Fred Thomas (JB's bassist), Danny Ray (JB's emcee), Leeds, Alfred "Pee Wee" Ellis, jazz star Christian McBride, Robert "Mousey" Thompson (JB's drummer), and Harry Weinger (Universal Music).

the recording studios and, quite properly, The Rootman, who was no fool for selling the song after all.

Around this time, Honey and the Bees joined the show, a quartet of cutie-pie singers from Philadelphia. To no one's surprise, JB already had his eye on one of them, and fellas in the band quickly staked out the others. In fact, trombonist Fred Wesley eventually married Gwen Oliver, who later enjoyed a few hits as part of the disco-era Ritchie Family.

There was another fresh female face aboard the bus, really the most intriguing of all, curvaceous super groupie Lithofayne Pridgon, fondly known in some circles as "Apollo Fayne." I'd never met anyone like Fayne; she was an avowed connoisseur of men, particularly entertainers and, most particularly, young ones. She did nothing to disguise her sexual appetite and, somehow, her forthright honesty discouraged anyone from taking her cheaply. In fact, there was nothing cheap about Fayne. Wise beyond her thirty years, she didn't hesitate to share her street wisdom, and she had plenty. None of which explains why she ended up on the bus.

Once upon a time, Fayne and a young Gertrude Sanders had run in the same Harlem party posse, familiar to James and just about every other entertainer who appeared at the Apollo. Most notably, in 1964, Fayne took Jimi Hendrix under her wings shortly after he moved to New York. Much has been written about their relationship and how Pridgeon hipped Hendrix to the Apple's fast ways and arranged his audition with the Isley Brothers. Jimi and Fayne were both free spirits, so monogamy wasn't in the cards, but they remained soulmates throughout his meteoric rise to stardom. When Hendrix died suddenly on September 18th, Fayne was understandably grief stricken. With Brown's permission, Gertrude invited Fayne to join her on the road for some sisterly support. Fayne's somber mood gradually changed into someone fun to have around—a life of the party, actually. I'm sure I wasn't the only one in the gang hoping to get closer to Ms. Pridgon, but I reluctantly accepted that I didn't stand a chance of being "chosen" when she started ogling my visiting baby-faced teenaged brother. Eric went home to Pittsburgh, unaware he was being coveted, but it wasn't long before Fayne was showing an even younger Bootsy Collins the ropes. Bootsy was barely eighteen years old, but he was a grown man by the time she was done with him.

11

The Twisting Parkettes might have been gone by the time I got on the bus, and I might have been too old for Fayne, but no matter; I had already figured out the sex part of "sex, drugs, and rock 'n' roll."

Music and sex (let's not worry about the drugs)—somehow, they've always gone together. I've never figured out why, but there's a certain kind of girl that is hopelessly attracted to anyone in the music business. Performers understandably get the pick of the litter, but a sub-set of groupies actually steer towards managers. Maybe it's an authority thing.

First, there were the proverbial small-town girls drawn to well-traveled guys. "Join the band and see the world." They usually seemed pretty pathetic to me, not very stimulating to have around. Then there were the gold diggers determined that the "right" relationship could turn into career opportunities, even an audition if they thought they had talent. If they proved "friendly" enough, these girls might actually get a shot.

None of these types caught my eye for long. I wasn't comfortable with exploiting their ambition or, conversely, the feeling of being used. My litmus test was whether I'd be interested had we met outside the music world.

You might think my seemingly altruistic attitude dealt me out of the action, but that doesn't account for a third type of girl you'd find near the band bus. That kind of girl had a self-assured *savoir faire* that the others lacked—she had a taste for adventure and just wanted to be around people she perceived as sexy or "hip," no strings attached. That last part was important because, unlike the others, these girls weren't looking for adventure THROUGH us, they were looking to share adventure WITH us. And that's what made them attractive to a guy like me. Of course, relationships are never simple and, as the new kid on the block, I had lessons to learn.

My first teacher was a go-go dancer in a club on Cincinnati's rowdy Walnut Street. In the early 1970s, before Queen City do-gooders convinced City Hall to calm things down, a downtown stretch of Walnut Street was full of action six nights a week. The anchors of the scene were the Playboy Club and the Hustler. Hugh Hefner's wannabe-elitist joint, complete with bunnies and jazz combos, was on one side of the street, while Larry Flynt's unabashedly seedy Hustler was on the other. Like several other bars on the block, the Hustler's attraction was gyrating bikini clad go-go girls. It was the precursor to the "titty bars" and upscale strip clubs that became common in later years, but in 1970, the only full nudity was at Flynt's private, after-hours shindigs. (There was no way any of us could have envisioned the notoriety, wealth, and influence that the obnoxious Flynt and his nascent Hustler empire would achieve in the coming years. Other than a four-page Hustler fanzine, there was nothing to separate the operation from any other sleazy local bar.)

As I mentioned earlier, I spent my first weeks in Cincinnati at Bob Patton's flat, which happened to be on Walnut Street, three floors above the Hustler. Bob's girlfriend worked at the Playboy, where they had strict rules about their bunnies fraternizing on the floor. But the Hustler thrived on their female employees living up to the club's name. Thankfully, our James Brown credentials carried a somewhat privileged status on the block. In other words, we didn't get watered down drinks, and the girls didn't work us like we were chumps. Just an elevator ride away, the Hustler should have been our Cheers. I did become friendly with a couple of the girls who worked there, but there was one huge problem. The Hustler wasn't very hospitable to black customers (unless they were entertainers or professional athletes). Larry Flynt and his redneck brother, Jimmy, tolerated me and Bob, but I was never comfortable there.

So, my nighttime hang became a third club on the block called Guys and Dolls. Guys and Dolls was Hustler-lite. The dancers in both clubs spent half their time flirting customers into buying them ten-dollar glasses of watered-down champagne. The glaring difference was that Guys and Dolls was racially diverse. In fact, the manager-hostess was a black chick we'll call Brenda, who also happened to be one of the hottest dancers on Walnut Street. It turned out that Brenda was the live-in girlfriend of the owner, who spent most nights running another club out in the burbs. But I didn't know all that when I spotted her in the club doorway on my first night in Cincinnati. I stopped in my tracks. "Who is THAT?" I asked, as she hollered a greeting Patton's way.

"Oh, that's Brenda," Bob answered. "Nice girl, good business head, but she's taken. Everybody on the block tries talking to her but she isn't going anywhere."

Oh, really? Life is nothing if not a challenge. In other words, I was too young and dumb to believe Bob. So Guys and Dolls became my hang. Once again, being "in the biz" bought me a pass. In "the life," there's no middle ground. You're either a sucker or you're not. If you're not, you get a respect that the wealthiest, best-looking customers could never buy, because THEY are the chumps that these kinds of clubs thrive on.

Brenda gradually became a friend. We spent hours talking about music, the bar business, and anything else that came to mind. Knowing what Patton had told me and what little Brenda shared of her private life, I started out as un-aggressive a friend as I knew how to be. My body language said something else. She knew I was interested in her. After a while, she seemed to miss me when I went on the road.

Once I mentioned I'd be away for a few days and she replied, "If you're flying back Sunday, that's my off day. You want me to pick you up at the airport? Maybe we could grab some dinner."

Bingo! Walnut Street couldn't keep secrets, so I spent about ten seconds worrying about what I might be getting into. But only ten seconds.

I should have given Brenda more credit. It was dinner and nothing else. That led to my next lesson in sex, drugs, and rock 'n' roll. When in doubt, import. Nothing closed a deal better than a plane ticket, a backstage pass, and a hotel room that was miles away from home. Before dropping me off that Sunday night, Brenda asked when I was going back on the road. "I could use a break," she continued. "Maybe I could meet you somewhere."

Brenda was a smart girl who wanted something more out of life than shaking her butt and keeping an eye on a boyfriend's cash registers. We saw each other for a while until my main girlfriend came to visit from Pittsburgh. We happened to bump into Brenda (and her boyfriend) in a restaurant. I innocently introduced everyone around and got a sneak elbow in my ribs for my trouble. The next day, it was Brenda on the phone, "How dare you show me up like that in public?"

Really? And what about your boyfriend? Go figure. Goodbye, Brenda.

My next adventure was on another level, a deeper step into the freak side of things courtesy of a talkative local promoter in Norfolk, Virginia. We were in the lobby of a Holiday Inn discussing an upcoming show, but I was tired and wishing he'd go home when he said, "Come out to my car. There's somebody you ought to meet."

Thinking I'd be guiding him closer to an exit, I followed him to the passenger side of a late model Buick Wildcat, where he addressed a young lady sitting on the front seat, "Lorraine, this here is Alan. He's James Brown's man."

With that, a doe-eyed, olive-skinned face without a blemish smiled and said, "That's one fine afro you got. What else has James Brown's man got to make me want to come in and have a drink?"

A drink was the last thing I wanted; I was thinking room service and a good night's sleep, but she didn't wait for an answer. Next thing I know, I'm standing next to a slender but curvaceous Lorraine. A tiny bit taller, and she could have been a model. In light of the come on, her conversation and her clean look were a no-compute. She had a wild, sexy 'fro of her own, wore little or no makeup, and dressed like a hippie with style. Nothing about her seemed cheap.

I started mumbling something about already having had enough to drink but she cut me off. "Man, I can tell you're not the drinking type. I won't waste your time but, if you're not busy later, I got a little weed I can bring by. I'm not sweating you. You just seem cool, that's all."

Agreed. See you later.

I really didn't know what to make of this chick. Was I being set up by Mr. local promoter? Or did he consider himself doing me a favor? Was Lorraine a pro? A drug dealer? Would she even show up? Meanwhile, room service and a nap after all.

Fast forward. Phone rings. "It's Lorraine, I'm downstairs. You still want some company?"

"Absolutely," I responded, although my radar was still up. Test time. "But it depends. Is there anything else I need to know? Any fine print in the deal?"

I waited to see if she felt insulted, or at least annoyed, but she kept her cool and calmly drawled, "If your time's that valuable…shoot, mine is too. I ain't got no game, man. I'm just lookin' for a little light sport. I just thought you were cool. No offense, Mr. James Brown's man."

What the hell. Sex, drugs, and rock 'n' roll. "My name is Alan, not James Brown's man, and I'm okay with sports. I don't know if I'm cool but, if you want to come up, we can try to figure it out."

Up she came. But my spirit dropped when I opened the door and discovered she wasn't alone. With her was another attractive lady. Not quite as attractive as Lorraine, I saw the friend as nothing but a roadblock.

I regrouped, deciding that Lorraine wasn't as bold as her conversation suggested. After all, she didn't know any more about me than I knew about her, so maybe she was leery too—too leery to come alone. I chose to give her points for that.

The three of us smoked a joint and discovered we knew some people in common. They both seemed to know a little something about the music business. Finally, her friend got up to use the bathroom. I suggested to Lorraine that she take her friend home and come back. She looked disappointed. After a few seconds of awkward silence, she said, "It's late. Once I leave, I'm not coming back. But I can come over tomorrow if you want me to."

Now I looked disappointed. My morning plan was a couple meetings and a hasty exit. But just maybe she was worth me changing to a later flight.

It turned out a much later flight. She arrived around noon. I suggested lunch. She suggested me.

"Tell me one thing," she asked as she kicked off her sandals. "Why'd you chase us out of here last night?"

"Chase you out?" I shot back. "If you wanted to stay, why didn't you just send your babysitter home?"

"Babysitter? I was just being neighborly. She wanted to be with us, fool." My jaw dropped as Lorraine continued, "She's a 'special' kind of friend. Sometimes we like sportin' together."

Oops! A whole term paper worth of oops.

I continued seeing Lorraine whenever I could get to Norfolk. She turned out to be the most liberated girl I'd ever known. She was quick-witted, had a sick sense of humor, always had great weed, and was clever in bed. Nothing made her lose her cool. Lorraine was too good to be true, a whole semester worth of lessons, and the tuition was free. Somehow, I knew better than to completely fall for her. Something told me that would have ended it. After all, she just wanted some light sport!

A few months later, I was in North Carolina where I decided to rent a car and drive to Norfolk for the weekend. I tried calling

Lorraine to give her a heads-up but couldn't reach her. I went to Norfolk anyway.

By then, I knew where she lived, and it wasn't far from the same old Holiday Inn. I dropped my bags at the hotel before driving to her crib. Passing through the lobby, I ran into Gary Johnson, a friend from New York who was the regional promotion rep for Atlantic Records. He was heading for the bar.

Gary smiled, "Hey, man, I've got an hour to kill before I go to the airport. Come have a drink and let's catch up."

I followed Johnson to a dimly lit corner. The table was covered with empty glasses. Snuggled up in the booth were two women looking like they had been there for a while. Before I could sit down, Gary started making introductions, "Lorraine, this is Alan. He's—"

Lorraine didn't miss a beat as she picked up his sentence, "...James Brown's man."

Small world this sex, drugs, and rock 'n' roll. Sometimes too small.

As the months on and off the road piled up, I grew more familiar with a variety of cities and towns. After a while, I had sought out enough late-night diners to realize that the leisure time world, or "the life" as hustlers called it, isn't much different wherever you go.

One place I visited more than I would have liked was sleepy Augusta, Georgia. After work, there wasn't much to do; most of the town shut down after dark, unless you knew where to look. In Augusta, the after-hours action was all on 9th Street. Besides the tattered pool hall, barber shop, shoe shine stand, and chop suey joint, there was the Amvets Club that served alcohol under the table and what record collectors now call "deep soul" on the stage. The Amvets jumped until the wee hours, after which the only places to go were home, jail, or the nearby twenty-four-hour soul food joint.

By default, the café was the hangout for everybody in "the life." Musicians, drug dealers, drag queens, and prostitutes comfortably mixed with more legitimate denizens of the midnight world like taxi drivers and delivery men. As small as Augusta was, the faces became familiar.

One of my many visits to Augusta happened to coincide with one of the city's periodic crackdowns on hookers. About 11:00 p.m. one night, Bobby Jackson, another James Brown crony, and I were cruising down 9th Street on the way home from dinner when we passed two squad cars pulled over to the side of the road, where the cops were rousting three or four ladies of the night. About two blocks later, we spotted two other young hotties on the stroll. Bobby and I had no reason to know them, but their faces (or behinds) looked vaguely familiar, probably from the Amvets or the café.

The cops would probably catch them next, so Bobby slowed down, and I rolled down the window to give them a heads up. As soon as our tip sunk in, the girls bolted towards the car and grabbed the door handle. They leaped into the back seat and one said, "Come on, man, drive away from here."

Jackson looked at me and we both shrugged as he pulled away from the curb. It turns out the girls knew our faces, too—there's that James Brown thing again. To Bobby's and my relief, the girls quickly made it clear they didn't see us as tricks. We drove a few blocks out of harm's way, and Bobby asked where he could drop them off. The talkative one said, "Hmmm, looks like we're off duty the rest of the night. What do you guys have in mind? Seems like we owe you a favor."

More free lessons. Bobby and I might not have BEEN tricks, but these girls definitely HAD tricks. Unfortunately, one of those tricks led to a doctor visit. Enough said. Class dismissed.

At the other end of this lusty spectrum is the idea of sex with a celebrity. Whenever one thinks of the sexism and the misogyny often associated with rock 'n' roll and groupies, it's about females with male stars. But what about the reverse? I'm not talking about a Jay-Z with Beyonce. I'm talking about an everyday guy. A guy like me. How does the male ego deal with being Mr. Patti Labelle, Mr. Aretha Franklin, or how about Mr. Vanity?

I was accustomed to being gawked at while accompanying celebrities, but that was in the course of my job. Off duty, I've always been a guy who liked rolling under the radar screen. When I moved to Minneapolis to work for Prince in 1983, Vanity a.k.a. Denise Matthews, was one of the few people in the camp I already knew. She was also a recent transplant to the Twin Cities, so we spent time together checking out restaurants and clubs. I couldn't pretend Vanity wasn't hot, but to me she was Denise, a fun girl to hang out with in Minneapolis while we both missed the cities and friends we had left elsewhere. I suppose the first few times we were out together, I couldn't resist a kind of "eat your heart out, buddy" attitude to any dude who recognized her and gazed a bit too long. But it got old very quickly. Male ego aside, I don't think I was ever really comfortable with the stares we (I mean, SHE) got every time we were out in public. I understood it. She was a star *and* she was gorgeous and provocative—if I didn't know her, I would have stared too.

In the early 1970s, I did have a brief fling with a sexy, talented young singer who shall remain nameless, a few years before she got a record deal and eventually became a star. I was attracted to her passion for fun of all kinds, but it didn't take long to discover she was awfully insecure. Despite deep self-esteem issues, her ambition knew no bounds, and I always wondered if my connections in the industry were the source of the attraction. We didn't see each other long enough for me to find out, because someone else's connections got her a gig in Florida.

When we next saw each other, it was in New York, several years and a few hit records later. I was eager to congratulate her success, but she barely acknowledged me. For a flash, I was insulted and hurt. But our lives had simply moved on from that harmless fling. It did give me pause to wonder what goes through the heads of those attracted to celebrity. Relationships are difficult enough without that kind of notoriety. (Fast forward: I am quite happy with my wife, Gwen, who also draws attention for her good looks—a non-celebrity but MY star, thank you very much).

By now, one may wonder whether I found anything unusual about my marriage to a black woman at a time when mixed couples in America were not yet "fashionable." First, let's lose the stereotype; as a young, single man, I was attracted to and enjoyed relationships with women of many colors. In a sense, "women of color" is a mis-leading term, unfairly throwing together so many different types of people under one umbrella. Color? What color? Which color? People come in so many shades and with so many varying characteristics.

Don't get it twisted. I'm not on some colonialist "oh, your beauty is so exotic" tip. But, as my career has sent me to far reaches of the globe, I have developed friendships, most platonic, a few not, with a wide variety of women ranging from a dark-skinned doctor from South Sudan, a tan East Indian from Trinidad, a dark-haired Italian-American from Queens, a brown-skinned six-foot model from Somalia, a lily-white blonde from Stockholm, a beige Nuyorican event planner, a redbone school crossing guard from Virginia, and a music-mad entrepreneur from UCLA, right up to my life's partner, my wife of thirty-one years from New Jersey.

I always chuckle when well-meaning (or not-so-well-meaning) whites claim they "don't see color." Maybe if they're blind! We all see color, and we should. The thing is, we need to see beyond color and not use it to characterize people. I know and adore every brown pigment in my wife's skin, but I didn't fall in love with those pigments because they're brown; I fell in love with them because they're Gwen's.

The good news is that, if I had been born fifty years later, I wouldn't be writing this sequence.

Next.

12

Beckley, West Virginia, is a modest mountain town with a small African-American community. Other than the fact that Bob Patton's wife was born there, I might have never heard of Beckley, except for the fact that Allen Knight booked our show there in October, 1970. Despite newfound confidence in Knight, James accepted the date with some skepticism, assigned it to Patton, and crossed his fingers. The night before the show, advance ticket sales languished between poor and worse.

The next day, James flew to Beckley, took one glance at the near empty arena, and cancelled the show. He screamed at Knight and Patton for even allowing him to fly down there, and then spent an hour visiting with a few disappointed fans before heading back to Cincinnati.

The date had been one of those few troublesome vacancies on our schedule until Knight offered to fill it in just two weeks out. With precious little time to mount a promotion campaign, I suppose Allen was gambling that he could quickly spread the word across such a small community. What we didn't know was that, once he was in Beckley, Knight passed himself off as a James Brown employee, rather than the independent promoter that he was. When the cancellation left a pile of unpaid advertising bills behind, Knight directed the creditors in our direction. Still, somehow his relationship with Brown survived the fiasco. Allen just hoped that he'd recoup his loss on future dates elsewhere.

The Beckley date became a turning point of sorts. While "Super Bad" was another smash hit, we were caught playing "B" and "C" markets to pad the schedule until November when we'd hit some bigger cities. It was frustrating that we weren't in a better position to benefit from the hit record, and even more frustrating that some weeks we struggled to make payroll.

It was crucial to eke out payroll on the road because James refused to dig in his pocket. If the shows lost money, payroll had to wait. He could be carrying around tens of thousands of dollars but, once the cash hit his briefcase, we knew we'd never see it again. In Brown's mind, it was our responsibility to keep the show self-sustaining. The few times it wasn't, payroll had to wait until we could pick up cash from the next date.

One of my fall dates was a Sunday show in Springfield, Massachusetts, and I made the grave mistake of staying home and trying to enjoy a weekend of girlfriend and football. Instead, I woke up to a frantic call from Danny Ray informing me that the boss was flat on his back in a New York hotel with a severe case of flu.

I need to take a minute to explain that James Brown hated sickness. He looked at illness as a weakness, and we were accustomed to him willing himself through any colds or viruses he might catch on the road. As I later learned, he even hated being around, almost seemed frightened of, anyone who was sick. Meanwhile, Danny warned me that JB probably couldn't perform that night and that I should remain on stand-by. The next call was from Bobby Byrd who reported that Brown was so dizzy that he couldn't walk from his bed to the bathroom. Full of fever, he couldn't hold down food or drink. A doctor had just visited, given JB an antibiotic, and ordered forty-eight hours of bed rest. Cautiously, I asked Bobby, "So you think I should cancel tonight's show in Springfield?"

"Absolutely. Don't worry about a thing," Byrd assured me. Dee Dee was on her way from Georgia to nurse the boss back to health, and Bobby was certain that there was no way in the world this man could get out of bed, let alone perform. With that, I began the arduous task of contacting road manager Freddie Holmes, our local promoter in Springfield, the venue manager, and radio and television stations advertising the gig. On my TV in the background, it was kick-off time, but football was the furthest thing from my mind, the only score I knew was how many people I was unable to reach. Mind you, this was before cell phones and business switchboards were closed on a Sunday. It took until about 3:00 p.m. to reach everyone. Soon, Springfield and Hartford radio stations were instructing ticket holders how to get refunds and the venue was sending home ushers, ticket takers, security, and concession personnel. Unsure when and where JB would resume our schedule, Freddie Holmes waited to determine where to take the bus.

After a deep breath, I decided to call New York and check on my ailing boss. Dee Dee answered the phone in his suite. I spoke softly, as if, somehow, my voice in the phone could have disturbed James. "Oh good, I'm glad you're there, Mrs. Brown," I whispered. "How is he?"

"How is he?" Dee Dee shouted back. "How would I know? He left for the gig before I even got here!"

I gasped, mumbled something and quickly hung up. Out of the corner of my eye, I glimpsed what would have been a game-winning field goal fall short of the goalposts and the Cincinnati Bengals walk dejectedly off the field. I envied them. At least they had another game a week later. I was convinced I would NEVER have another show. I pulled myself together and began calling Springfield to reverse the cancellation—assuring everyone that James Brown had left a sick bed rather than disappoint his fans. They must have thought I was insane. But I didn't really care what anyone in Springfield thought. I cared what JB thought. I told Deborah, "In about ninety minutes, I am going to get the ugliest call Cincinnati Bell ever carried on their wires."

Soon enough, the phone rang. The raspy voice was uncharacteristically monotone. "Mr. Leeds, are you a doctor?"

Not the question I expected. Without me answering, James continued. "Mr. Leeds, I know you're not a doctor. And you know you're not a doctor. Son, I love you for caring about me, but I already got a doctor and I don't listen to HIM!"

The voice began escalating. "SO WHY DO YOU THINK I'M GONNA LISTEN TO YOU? DON'T YOU EVER MAKE NO DECISION LIKE THAT UNLESS YOU HEAR IT FROM ME… AND ONLY ME!"

"But, Mr. Brown," I sheepishly responded. "Mr. Byrd said you couldn't even come to the phone—"

James cut me off. "Was Mr. Byrd sick? Is Mr. Byrd a doctor? If you were sick, are you gonna trust your life to Bobby Byrd? What's Byrd's hit record? Byrd's song is 'I Need Help.' Why you gonna trust a man who already admits he needs help? Now I got to do a show to a half-empty auditorium. THAT'S what makes me sick!"

Somehow, my job survived HIS sickness but, a few weeks hence, I came down with a cold that turned into what was probably pneumonia. I've never been as sick, before or since—fever, strep throat, couldn't eat or keep fluids down. By my second week in bed, too sick to even get to a doctor, James lost patience and told Charles Bobbit, "If Mr. Leeds is still too sick to come to work, he's too sick to get paid." It took another couple weeks in the penalty box before I had mended enough to confront JB. After a bit of humble pie and displaying enough energy to convince him I was a healthy horse to bet on, I got my job back.

Brown's icy-cold attitude towards sickness and health care was across the board. Bob Patton once missed a show when his wife was in a hospital about to deliver their daughter. Without knowing the circumstances, the boss got Patton on the phone and lit into him. "Where you at, Mr. Patton? Why aren't you here?"

Bob tried to explain, expecting James to sympathize. "I'm at the hospital with Vicki, Mr. Brown. She's going into labor and we're both very excited."

Without a pause, Brown snapped, "Excited? I'm excited too. I'm excited because you ain't where you're supposed to be. Mr. Patton, are you a doctor?"

There was that question again. A stunned Patton responded, "Of course not, Mr. Brown."

James continued, "Well, if Mrs. Patton is having a baby, she doesn't need you; she needs a doctor."

Before Bob could figure out what to say, the boss abruptly finished their conversation, "Your wife needs a doctor, but I need YOU. And, Mr. Patton, I ain't having no baby!"

13

As I approached my first anniversary in the world of James Brown, the office vibe was considerably calmer, primarily because the boss was spending many of his off days at his new home in Augusta. His moving back to Georgia was a statement, reversing a century of African Americans abandoning the harsh realities of their native South for job opportunities in the North. Those had been hard and fast realities until after the civil rights years, but the 1970s promised the dawn of a new South. After buying WRDW, an Augusta radio station, it was just a matter of time before James made the move. He sold his home in New York and bought a suburban, ranch-style house on Augusta's exclusive Walton Way Extension. Of course, he was only a phone call away from the office and, even when he was home with Dee Dee and their year-old daughter Deanna, the workdays were endless. He'd call in several times a day and got in the habit of frequently ringing me at home after hours. One such call was on the evening of October 22nd, but it wasn't for his usual nit-picking business conversation.

"Guess what I just did, man? Guess what I did?" Brown excitedly barked. It was the giddiest I'd heard him in a long time. "It's out of sight, man. Everything's mellow now, Jack. Best thing I ever did. You gotta be next. I'm telling you, everyone must do this."

Okay, I wondered. What now?

"I got married, man!" he explained. "It's a new day, Mr. Leeds. We men got to do the right thing. I had to make an honest woman out of Dee Dee. I'm telling you, Mr. Leeds, it's the only way. Marriage is what time it is, Jack. It's so hip, man. It's so hip that Bobby and Vicki are going to do it too!"

While congratulating him, I wondered what had him so excited. This really wasn't shocking news, considering he and Dee Dee had been living together for several years. It WAS spur of the moment, married by a white female justice of the peace in James' birthplace, Barnwell, South Carolina, with Bobby Byrd, Danny Ray, and JB's father as witnesses.

Maybe he had just needed to spice up an otherwise boring day, or maybe Dee Dee had been privately pressuring him. It was really none of my business, but wedlock was the topic of conversation for several days and, believe it or not, Bobby and Vicki Anderson did get married soon thereafter. Just to be safe, I made a point to keep my girlfriend as far away from these conversations as possible. Still, I was genuinely happy for the Browns. Dee Dee had been "Mrs. Brown" for so long that it was never questioned by anyone except, I suppose, Dee Dee.

Patton and I got our first opportunity to congratulate the couple face-to-face in New Orleans, where James was headlining an outdoor festival in the huge Tulane Stadium. Tagged the *Soul Bowl*, it was the largest black musical event until Wattstax in Los Angeles a few years later. The star-studded line-up included Isaac Hayes, Ike and Tina Turner, Junior Walker, Rare Earth, Pacific Gas and Electric Company, and our entire revue. *Jet* and *Soul* magazines sent reporters and photographers. *Downbeat* assigned a local stringer and London's *Melody Maker* was represented by an eager beaver who insisted on nothing less than an exclusive dressing-room interview with JB.

James wasn't due on stage until well after sundown, so, even though the marathon began at one o'clock, we didn't expect the boss to leave our hotel until five or six. Bob and I were lounging in the lobby around lunch time when we heard a commotion and spotted

JB, Dee Dee, and Danny Ray dashing out the front door. We quickly jumped in a taxi to follow. I should have known James wouldn't miss the opportunity to hold court with all those rival acts in one place. This was the same James Brown I had witnessed in Philadelphia with the Dells—the competitor. If the red-hot Isaac Hayes or perennial favorites Ike and Tina were going to pose a threat, he was going to be there to thwart it.

By the time JB settled into the musty football locker room that passed as a dressing room, Hayes was beginning his set. Over 30,000 fans were scattered throughout the sun-lit cement orb of a stadium. The stage stood at the center of the gridiron, so the audience tended to drift towards the side of the grandstand with the best view, but, soon, a blinding sunset neutralized Isaac's colorful garb. Lacking the intimacy that normally spellbound his audiences, Hayes' heavily orchestrated set flew over some folks' heads and he left the stage to surprisingly mild applause. It was simply too early in the day for a show to catch fire.

About the time Ike and Tina started the long walk across the football field to the stage, James joined me under the grandstand and softly said, "It won't be like that when we go out there."

The Turners fared much better than Hayes, thanks, in part, to the gradual darkness that had filled the Louisiana sky. Now it was our turn. First, The J.B.'s climbed on stage for their funky set of instrumentals. I had been in Brown's dressing room for a while, so, when I came out I was surprised to see that the crowd, swollen to over 40,000, had spilled onto the field, blanketing the entire turf. Security was no match for the throngs of avid youngsters who, by surrounding the stage hundreds deep, had closed off any path to and from the locker rooms. Getting James through the mob to the stage was going to be a real problem, and nobody had any immediate solutions.

First, we decided to drop our support acts. Putting Bobby Byrd and Vicki Anderson out there would just delay the inevitable. The only thing we could do was gather a ton of police and form a cocoon around the rental car that would carry James to the foot of the stage. Before we left the locker room, Brown, of all people, was the one to remind all of us to take off our jackets and jewelry, anything that might get torn or snatched in the crowd.

With Patton behind the wheel and JB riding shotgun, dancer Ann Norman and I squeezed into the back seat with bodyguard James Pearson. Cops surrounded the car and we began our crawl onto the field. The outer perimeter of the crowd quickly spotted us, the heavy police presence certifying who was in the car. The cops formed a wedge in front of us and pleaded over their shoulders for Patton to keep pace. But they were badly outnumbered, and fans closed in around us. Bob was scared shitless that he would run someone over.

Kids were leaning over the police, banging on the hood and the trunk of our car. As quickly as security could peel one off, two more youngsters would leap forward and cling to the windshield. Fisted black power salutes pounded on the windows. Inside the car, it sounded like a shell attack in a war movie. Pearson pointlessly shouted directions to Patton, Ann nervously clung to my arm, and James was cold silent. Gradually, Bob began to outrun the cops, so he hit the brakes just as two more fans jumped on the hood, their eager faces now blocking his view. Norman ducked her head in my lap and all I could do was sit there as the car rocked on its suspension. The boss never said a word, never displayed a hint of fear or concern. Somehow, after a terrorizing ten minutes that seemed a lot longer, Patton maneuvered us alongside the steep steps to the stage, where Bobby Byrd, Danny Ray, and another posse of police had opened a narrow path by lining up each side of the stairs. I pushed Ann out. JB followed. Then inertia shoved me halfway up the steps behind them. I turned around and the steps had already disappeared. With Brown safely on stage, the cops had relaxed, and the stairway was instantly jammed with fans. I was essentially trapped on stage for the entire show. Who cares? I had the best view in the stadium!

The crowd was ecstatic, but it was controlled delirium and Brown played them to a tee. It was an inspired performance but, when he was finished, he was really finished. No teasing cape routines, no crowd-baiting encores. He dashed towards the side of the stage, and his momentum pulled us down the steps and into the car below. The crawling departure was as agonizing as our arrival and, once we outran the crowd, JB directed Bob straight back to the hotel. Following a quickly organized motorcycle police escort, we sped out from under the stands and into traffic. Oops, what about my jacket, watch, and rings back in the dressing room? I was sure Gertrude wouldn't leave them behind, but they'd probably get packed with Brown's dressing room supplies. I envisioned chasing them across country for the next month. How DID we get along before cell phones?

Whatever shot in the arm the Soul Bowl provided was short lived. We all came abruptly crashing down to earth the next evening with a poorly attended throw-in date in Alexandria, Louisiana. Then, Monday night, we played Grambling University. During the performance, some off-campus thugs broke into the band's dressing room and made off with personal belongings and spare musical instruments, just as hundreds of fans without tickets ignored security and barged through the auditorium doors proclaiming the show a "free" event. Thank goodness, I got my watch and rings the night before in Alexandria.

BY THE END OF THE YEAR, our box office woes were beginning to confuse Mr. B. I was convinced our problem was overexposure; appearing in most areas once or twice a year took a toll. Stars that toured less frequently, such as Marvin Gaye, the Jackson Five, and Isaac Hayes, were doing solid business. But Brown kept insisting that our show was simply victim to the economy. "Don't be fooled by Motown and those other companies," he warned. "They give away tickets and paper the houses. Everybody knows that black folks ain't got money for entertainment."

The economy had always been Brown's go-to explanation for slow sales but, this time, he didn't stop there. His new conclusion was, "The only way we can make it now is go after the white crowd."

I've said it before and so has the boss: We always welcome new fans, of any color. But I was skeptical. There was a small, devout cult of white funk fans we could always count on, but James hadn't been making records with real pop appeal since the days of "I Got You (I Feel Good)" and "It's a Man's Man's Man's World." Maybe Ike Turner had been right. I don't think Soul Brother #1 had a clue about the pop market in 1970. He understood adult pop music, standards, and show tunes, but he really didn't comprehend the blues- and folk-inspired rock that made household names of people like Cream, James Taylor, and Bob Dylan.

It was totally out of character for Brown to cater to a white audience. I'm not forgetting that, years later, one of his biggest hits was called "Living in America" but, in the volatile era of the Vietnam war, nothing was riskier with youngsters than overt patriotism. As it turned out, at first JB wasn't courting the kids. He was gazing towards Las Vegas and the middle-aged night club crowd when he had an ill-advised brainstorm to perform "God Bless America" on NBC-TV's *Tonight Show*.

I was always afraid of anything that would take him too far from, or jeopardize the loyalty of, his base audience; ironically, something I learned from him! Sure, we could sell tickets in Vegas every year or two, but I knew his raw, funky music would never be anything but a novelty there. If we were going to expand our audience, I believed we had to do it on our own terms, the way James had always done things in the past. I felt we'd be better off going after rock clubs like the Fillmores, where music heads were known to support mixed genres and appreciate great artists of any kind. It had worked for Aretha Franklin, Otis Redding, and Ray Charles. Even Miles Davis had noticeably increased his record sales by appearing at Bill Graham's famous clubs alongside artists like Laura Nyro and the Grateful Dead. I went so far as to suggest that we could do away with the dated revue approach; 1970s audiences had no patience for comics, dancers, and mediocre support acts. All they needed was James and his band doing what they do best. But Brown's old-fashioned show biz DNA was in the way, and he didn't get it at all.

Thankfully, NBC brass nixed JB's plan but, in place of singing "God Bless America," James sat on the panel and spontaneously lit into three minutes of corny, patronizing flag-waving nonsense. The best thing that came out of it was realizing that James Brown's fan base obviously didn't watch the *Tonight Show*, because the feedback was negligible.

Brown didn't stay on the crossover tip very long. Three days after his *Tonight Show* appearance, King Records shipped "Get Up, Get Into It, Get Involved," a ferocious message song expressly directed towards James' young black audience. It was also his most political lyric in several years and didn't stand a chance at pop radio. Go figure.

14

We might have been struggling at the box office, but you wouldn't have known it at the record store. "Get Up, Get Into It, Get Involved" was another hit; its motivational message ringing true, even as the 1960s brand of social activism seemed on the wane. It also featured the returns to the band of Clyde "Funky Drummer" Stubblefield and veteran JB saxophonist St. Clair Pinckney. From the onset, the J.B.'s glaring weakness had been the absence of an exciting soloist—Robert McCullough, whom Brown inherited with the Collins brothers, couldn't hold a candle to the old band's familiar saxophonists, Pinckney, Alfred Ellis, and Maceo Parker. "Super Bad" was a song wanting for a Maceo-like solo and, after several aborted attempts, James flipped the script on the frustrated McCullough: "Hey, Robert, do your Coltrane thing, man." In Brown-speak, referencing the boundary breaking jazz legend John Coltrane meant Robert playing a series of atonal squeals and shrieks that passed for avant-garde. When he rejoined the band, St. Clair inherited the unusual solo and turned it into something more musical. What fans didn't pick up on was that the idea had been Brown's way of steering around McCullough's limitations. Soon after Pinckney showed up, Robert left the band.

Truthfully, I don't think James ever sensed any long-term commitment from most of the new band. As much as they idolized James, they were of another generation—one that lacked the patience and discipline of their predecessors. Furthermore, they had aspirations of their own. In fact, Brown missed the old band, even if he was too stubborn to admit it. Meanwhile, many of them were defiantly recording and touring as Maceo and All the Kings Men. James tried luring Alfred "Pee Wee" Ellis back to the fold, hoping he'd bring along trumpeter Waymon Reed, who was touring in Count Basie's band. Neither were interested. Then he reached out to trombonist-arranger Fred Wesley, deceiving him into thinking he'd be part of a reunion. In December, Wesley met The J.B.'s in New York. "I came back looking to find Pee Wee, Maceo, and Waymon," Fred remembers. "I didn't expect what I found, which was these young, untrained horn players."

A week later, Stubblefield was gone again, but Wesley still signed on as music director, determined to take The J.B.'s up a notch or two.

The James Brown Show traditionally closed the year on the West Coast. 1970 was different. Still a little gun-shy of the one-nighter circuit, James jumped at an offer from Africa. Two weeks in Nigeria and Zambia would be Brown's first appearances on the Motherland since an Ivory Coast one-off in 1968. It all sounded very exciting but, since Universal Attractions organized the tour, there were no reasons for me or Bob Patton to make the trip. Our time was better spent in the office concentrating on upcoming shows. Damnit.

By all accounts, the reception was astonishing—akin to the Beatles' first trip to America. Years later, Fela Kuti biographer Michael Veal wrote, "The excitement and anticipation generated by James Brown's Nigerian appearances equaled that usually reserved for religious or political leaders."

Entire townships stopped in their tracks to wave as Brown's caravan wound its way between airports, hotels, and stadiums. James was officially received by heads of state, spiritual leaders, and tribal dignitaries. I was anxious to hear his reaction when he called the office from Lagos. He spoke volumes about the liberating impact of seeing black men in every position of authority. Then, after deservedly boasting about his impact on African culture, he added, "I'll be glad to get home, though. The women ain't much to look at and the food is a drag—can't get no good ice cream."

So much for cultural exchange. When I next saw them, I learned that David Matthews, Bootsy Collins, and several of The J.B.'s hung out with Fela at his legendary Afro-Spot. While much has been written about the impact Brown's visit had on West African music, it went both ways. In a 1997 interview, Bootsy Collins remembered, "We were telling them, Fela and his band, they're the funkiest cats we ever heard, and they were replying, 'No, you cats are the ones!' I mean, this is the *James Brown Band*, but we were totally wiped out!"

Thanks to a slew of terrific pictures taken during the tour, I put on my publicist hat and mounted a very well received campaign. The lively photos illustrated the adoration felt for Brown. One shot captured a diminutive, elderly paraplegic stretched prone just to touch James' hands. There were pictures of Brown in African garb visiting hospitals and schools, socializing with royalty, and conferring with tribal elders. The publicity was thematically tied to Brown's upcoming single, "Soul Power," and inspired trade papers, fanzines, and African-American newspapers to run stories about the trip. The magic of the promotion was that the story couldn't be overstated. His visit was just that significant.

We closed the year with a brief run at the Apollo Theater, where Fred Wesley's influence on the band began to surface. In fact, by the onset of 1971, I was convinced that James, once again, had the hottest show on the circuit. He had worked his way back to the forefront of black popular music, and all the critics who had prematurely buried the "hardest working man in show business" had to eat their words.

Soul music was changing. Sly Stone's multi-racial, multi-sexual Family Stone had taken funk to a new level and a broad audience. Not to be left behind, the younger J.B.'s, particularly Bootsy and Phelps Collins, embraced the late Jimi Hendrix and welcomed George Clinton's exotic Funkadelic as a hint of things to come. They did their best to keep the boss in the know, but it wasn't easy. The hardest working man in show business was almost thirty-eight years old and really wasn't part of the cultural changes that informed the new black music. He wasn't vocally anti-war and certainly didn't view casual drug use as socially acceptable. But that's where Bootsy and the boys picked up the slack. They leaned on James to loosen up how The J.B.'s dressed on stage, frequently performed stoned, and smuggled Hendrix's "Power to Love" into the band's instrumental set. James might have thought they were out of their minds, but he sure did love how they played.

I thought we had every reason to enter 1971 with optimism. Since January was traditionally a slow month for one-nighters, we booked some club engagements, gigs that might attract fresh audiences, set the show in one place for a week at a time, and allow us time to comfortably set up a return to the concert trail.

Optimism aside, the new year would eventually prove that 1970 was no anomaly, that nothing in the world of James Brown was ever routine. In March, there would be another band upheaval, and July would mark the end of Brown's career-long relationship with King Records. But I'm getting ahead of myself, none of that had jumped off yet when we arrived at the Latin Casino. Our previous booking there had been a winner, even with the raggedy new band and, THIS time, the show was hot.

Gigs like the Latin Casino did make for a rather bizarre spectacle on stage, a portrait of the very generation gap that was playing out in black music. The ghetto-fashionable, young J.B.'s were spread across the stage; the guns-for-hire horn and string players, mostly middle-aged and white, sat behind them in off-the-rack black tuxedos; five scantily clad dancers gyrated on risers even further up stage; and conductor David Matthews stood in front wearing an Edwardian cut suit, his unruly pony tail flying down his back. Somehow, once Brown and the power of his music hit the stage, it all made sense. The week at the Latin was standing room only.

Our next stop on the club tour was the Sugar Shack in Boston. Catering to the black community, the Sugar Shack couldn't have been more different than the Latin Casino, which was a mainstream supper club that might follow James Brown with Bob Hope or Tom Jones. The Shack's owners also happened to be mobbed up. Besides the usual fans and music lovers, the Shack's clientele included night crawlers of all kinds. If you knew who to ask, there were more drugs around than at Walgreens, and it was a popular spot for colorfully dressed pimps to entertain and show off their stables.

Booking Brown was a coup, he was the biggest star to play the Sugar Shack. The club's capo, Rudy Guarino, celebrated the event with a huge banner over the stage: "Welcome James Brown." Since the club was accustomed to less expensive attractions, every seat was at a premium and the tight-fisted Guarino wasn't very hospitable to our guests, which included writer David Dalton, assigned to do a feature for *Rolling Stone*.

The influential magazine had never done a major piece about James, something that had disturbed me for a long time. So, I went to Boston primarily to chaperone the writer. Since the length of the article would depend on Brown's cooperation, I was determined to orchestrate the Brown-Dalton relationship as best I could.

James welcomed Dalton into his dressing room between shows on opening night. They talked for a while, and it became apparent that Brown was already counting their casual, get-acquainted conversation as part of the interview. Dalton explained that he appreciated this *tête-à-tête*, but he considered it preliminary and looked forward to their official sit down. To my dismay, James shrugged without picking up the hint to schedule their next meeting.

On stage, Brown milked the room's intimacy, assuming the role of a hero who'd "come home." By the finale, the frenzied crowd was on their feet and some were actually standing ON their chairs or dancing on tables.

After the show, I went backstage to gauge JB's reaction to Dalton. I was right. James had convinced himself that he had met his half of the bargain simply by receiving David in his dressing room and wondered why the writer hadn't taken any notes during their chat. He obviously didn't distinguish between a critic writing ABOUT him versus a profile in which he would actually play the lead role. As he changed to street clothes, Brown winked and told me, "He saw the show. He's got most of his story already."

Thankfully, James finally agreed to spend a couple hours with Dalton the next afternoon and the writer left Boston promising to stay in touch. But weeks went by without a word. Then David called explaining that *Rolling Stone* had decided it would be a major feature, perhaps a cover story. He asked when and where he could spend more time with his subject, preferably on Brown's home turf. The boss invited him to Augusta, where he really poured it on. He even flew him to Macon on the Learjet and let him tag along to a few more gigs.

And then we waited. And waited. What we didn't know was that *Rolling Stone* chief Jann Wenner was waiting too. It turned out that Dalton, who had written definitive profiles of Little Richard and Janis Joplin for the mag, had taken an abrupt leave of absence. Dalton had everyone under the impression that his JB piece would be his last before a hiatus to concentrate on a book project but, as deadlines passed, it became clear that he wasn't going to deliver the story. Finally, *Rolling Stone* offered to assign a new writer, but James understandably felt dissed and refused to start over. He had offered Dalton access no other reporter had ever enjoyed, all for naught. Nearly a year after the original interview, an angry series of letters ensued, eventually involving Polydor Records.

The magazine apologized but James angrily suggested that race might have been a factor and insisted that the magazine should have been able to persuade Dalton to deliver. He may or may not have believed all that, but JB was accustomed to adversaries buckling to such accusations. In that sense, he underestimated *Rolling Stone.*

The whole thing quieted until 1973 when, under pressure from Polydor, the magazine assigned writer Paul Gambaccini to meet the Brown show in London. This time, it was James who was underestimated. He decided that, if the only way he could get respect from *Rolling Stone* was through the efforts of a white-owned record company, he'd been right about the magazine all along. He refused to be interviewed and told a frustrated Gambaccini that, "Rolling Stone is finished in America."

Gambaccini fired off a hostile letter to Polydor President Jerry Schoenbaum blasting Brown with innuendo after innuendo. Finally, JB took it to the streets, responding through England's *New Musical Express*. James proclaimed that the American music press didn't accept him and that "*Rolling Stone* prayed for me to fail. (But) I made it without them!"

In retrospect, it was all very silly, a huge misunderstanding all the way around. But it was also another strike against us crossing over. It would be 1981 before *Rolling Stone* published a major piece on Brown.

OUR NEXT STOP WAS WASHINGTON, D.C. Throughout the 1960s, Brown had spent two weeks out of each year in residence at the Howard Theater in the heart of Washington's busiest African-American neighborhood. The Howard fell on hard times after the riots in 1968, so this week-long engagement was at the Loew's Palace Theater. JB felt at home in the nation's capital, where he had a long-standing circle of friends like Rufus "Catfish" Mayfield. A respected civil rights activist, Mayfield camped out backstage, patiently waiting for each opportunity to kick it with Soul Brother #1. On this particular occasion, though, the colorful and outspoken Catfish was upstaged by a visiting New Yorker, the equally loquacious Rev. Carlton "King" Coleman.

Coleman was a familiar presence on the Chitlin' Circuit in the 1960s—first, a radio disc jockey and recording artist, then a comic-emcee who had toured with Brown and many other entertainers. He left show business for the cloth in 1969, and dedicated much of his time to Harlem's drug abuse problem. Like Mayfield, Coleman stayed close to James, periodically soliciting support for his community programs. The two introduced themselves backstage while waiting for an audience with Brown, and the rhetoric started to flow. They were warming up, sparring as if expecting to compete for JB's attention while addressing anyone within earshot. But, really, everything they said was for each other's benefit. Eventually, the subject matter turned from inner city issues to how long each had known James. Finally, Coleman played his hole card, and began flaunting his years of camaraderie with veteran members of the band and crew as they happened by. Game, set, match. Mayfield was quiet for a while but became impatient and muttered, "Sure do miss the old days at the Howard." That set off round two, a loud debate over the post-riot problems facing America's urban communities.

I hadn't seen Coleman since his days as "the Mashed Potato Man," the nickname earned by his vocal on the JB-produced hit record "(Do The) Mashed Potatoes." He was bald, lanky, suave, and strikingly charismatic. History says Mayfield was a devoted and effective representative of his people, but his rap couldn't compete with the glib King Coleman. Mayfield dejectedly excused himself just minutes before James emerged from his dressing room and into the brotherly arms of the Rev. Mashed Potato Man. A couple weeks later, Brown produced a King Coleman comeback record, "Rock, Gospel, Mash." Mayfield hadn't stood a chance.

Well after midnight, Brown, Coleman, and an entourage that included *London Times* writer Philip Norman exited the Loew's stage door. Blustery winter weather had discouraged any fans from waiting around for autographs, except for one scruffy youngster holding a shoe shine box. He told James he'd been waiting in the cold to offer his hero a free shine. Brown surveyed the boy's poorly equipped, homemade kit and shivered. Then he reached in his pocket and peeled off a hundred-dollar bill, which he snuggled into the kid's hand. "Don't show this money to anybody. Not your mother or father—nobody," he said. "You go home and get warm and, tomorrow, go buy a new box and some fresh polish."

Sure enough, the next evening, the youngster was waiting in the alley alongside the stage door. He was wearing an obviously new overcoat and proudly displaying his new kit. "Thank you, Mr. Brown," he said. "Now can I give you that shine?"

When James hit the stage that night, the boy was in the front row, clutching his shoe shine gear to his chest as he rocked to the music. It was touching to watch, and I should have left it at that. But I'm ashamed to admit that I scurried around the theater in search of a photographer to document it, I envisioned a picture of JB and the boy on the cover of every magazine in the country. But, when I made the crass suggestion to Brown, he just smiled and told me to forget it. With unusual humility, James winked and added, "If this ever gets out, every kid in the world will be chasing me with a shoe shine box."

15

After D.C., the show worked its way South. Meanwhile, I got my first opportunity to visit the birthplace of my boss' career, Macon, Georgia, where Buddy Nolan was waiting to rejoin our team. Brown was coming to Macon to do some recording and had called a staff meeting. Buddy and I both arrived before James, who was driving over from Augusta, so Buddy suggested we visit Clint Brantley at the Two Spot.

Clinton Eugene Brantley had the distinction of having managed the early careers of both Little Richard and James Brown, TWO first ballot inductees to the Rock & Roll Hall of Fame. Brantley didn't share the kind of worldly ambitions that defined rock 'n' roll managers like Elvis Presley's Col. Tom Parker or even Macon's own Phil Walden. He was to Macon what a guy like Tom Mitchell was to Richmond, the main conduit between a community and the black music business. Brantley promoted concerts and dances, managed and booked bands, ran a bar and a restaurant; but knew his limitations, satisfied with being the proverbial big fish in a small pond. When Richard left him behind for Hollywood, Brantley simply turned his attention to James and The Famous Flames. After a year of regional bookings, Clint paid for their demo recording of "Please, Please, Please," and brokered their deal with King Records. Brantley remained their manager of record for several years until their growing success required Ben Bart's major league clout. James never turned his back on Brantley, supporting and caring for him until he died in 1980.

British writer and JB aficionado Cliff White visited the Two Spot a couple years after me and perfectly described what I encountered. White's fascination was no less than mine when he wrote:

> *Fifth Street, Macon, Georgia, is a tired aimless thoroughfare that lays quietly decaying. The focal point is a railroad station. The ageing heap of redstone and rusty steel stands by a roadside, a monument to bygone days when freight bays overflowed with the produce of intercity trade. On and around Fifth Street the faces are predominantly black. Opposite the station, supported on crutches, equally decrepit buildings lean forlornly shoulder to shoulder, still wearily housing the familiar establishments of such a street – a cheap hotel, a barber shop, a record store, a gas station and old shack that serves as a restaurant. Finally, as the street widens, an off-white single story building sits between two vacant lots. Brick archways frame battered doors and shutters. Inside an old man sweeps the wooden floor. The bar lies diagonally opposite the door, half hidden by a partition that divides the room into two halves. On one side the tables and chairs crowd the floor space, allowing just a narrow aisle across to a row of seats propped against the wall. In front of the bar the other section is clear except for a juke box and two pinball machines. At the front of the room the partition ends to form one large area stretching the width of the building where low platforms are laid, forming a stage.*

Buddy and I walked into the Two Spot and found Brantley, sure enough, sweeping the floor as a few regulars drifted to the bar for their first cold beer of the afternoon. Clint asked if he should expect James that evening but didn't really pay attention to our response—if Brown was in Macon, a stop at the Two Spot was automatic.

Macon's musical heritage is extraordinarily rich for an otherwise ordinary Southern town, dating back to Clint Brantley's first discovery,

Little Richard. In the soul era, the Macon scene also produced Otis Redding who, like Brown, often drafted local musicians for his bands. By the 1970s, the area was more recognized for the Allman Brothers and Capricorn Records, an outgrowth of the management-production company brothers Phil and Alan Walden built on Otis Redding's shoulders. Capricorn was Macon's studio of choice but, when it was tied up with in-house projects, James used Bobby Smith's modest facility. Smith was a white producer with a long-standing inside track to King Records. He had recorded both Redding and Wayne Cochran before their major label deals and countless regional soul singers. He treated Brown like royalty but never stopped pitching him a potential partnership that he was convinced could compete with the Waldens. James humored Smith enough to get a good rate in his studio, but had no intention of forming a business with him.

This time out, all Brown needed to do was lay down some quick vocals on tracks recorded earlier in Cincinnati. After the session, we all headed back to the Two Spot. No longer a lazy afternoon hang, now the Two Spot was jumping. The tiny dance floor was crammed with sweaty bodies gyrating to Brantley's latest protégé, soul singer Jimmy Braswell and his band.

Every eye in the club turned to watch when Brantley escorted us to a table in the back. An impromptu V.I.P. section, the table sat apart from other tables, but there was no velvet rope and no intimidating security goons surrounding us. Everyone in the Two Spot knew better than to bother Mr. Brown OR the long-respected Mr. Brantley.

The Fifth Street grapevine must have announced our arrival, because the Two Spot quickly turned into a fire hazard, fans and curiosity seekers appeared out of nowhere. The quintessential Southern juke joint, the Two Spot was unlike any place I'd accompanied my boss. He was a frequent visitor to Macon, a native in a sense, but still a fascination even to those who might have known him back when he was a nobody.

After a few drinks and some of Mrs. Brantley's trademark fried chicken, our attention turned towards the stage where the band was wrapping up their set. Instead of announcing an intermission, Braswell pleaded for "our special guest" to come up and do a tune or two. In any other club, JB might have begged off, but not at the Two Spot. He didn't dare—this was home. Truth be told, he wouldn't have missed this for the world.

A surprise walk-on by an international super star in a ramshackle backwoods club, this was not Brown's usual smooth, professional gig. The hometown crowd was only interested in the "real thing," down home soul. James worked his way to the stage where he briefly huddled with the band then suddenly spun around and tore into "Soul Power."

The forceful words of his anthem seemed more meaningful than ever, as the home folk energetically answered Brown's, "what we want?" with an ear-shattering cry of "Soul Power"! James strutted across the rickety stage, slid back on one foot, and fell to his knees. Quickly drenched in sweat, he condensed an entire concert's worth of emotion into ten exhausting minutes. When it was over, there was nothing left to say. Nothing left to give. The audience didn't dare ask for more. Brown returned to our table and sat down, but many in the club turned towards the exit—like leaving a prize fight that had ended in a stunning knockout.

Indeed, James *looked* like a victorious warrior, his cheeks stretched by a wide grin. Bobby Smith, who was well into his drink of choice, all but smothered James with a congratulatory hug. JB leaned back from Smith's alky breath and his expression changed instantly. Oblivious, Smith slurred, "Aw, James, we love you in Macon. Look at this. I'd never come here to drink if you weren't here. That shows how much I love you."

Wrong. James stood back on his heels and barked, "ONLY when I'M here? Something wrong with the rest of these folks, Mr. Smith? Then I'm afraid you can't be here at all."

Before anyone could say anything else, James wiggled further away from Bobby, as one of Brantley's staff hustled Smith out the door. Later, Brown asked Clint if he ever sees Smith in the Two Spot.

"Only when you're in town," was the expected reply. "That cracker wouldn't be caught dead down here any other time." That's why James never took Bobby seriously. He wasn't for real and, in Macon, that's all that mattered.

The next day, I flew to Cincinnati, leaving the boss in Georgia to prepare for his first European tour since 1967. The European promoters dealt directly with Universal Attractions so, just like with the African trip, there was no reason for any of the Cincinnati staff to make the trip. I lusted at the itinerary: Madrid, Brussels, Frankfurt, Berlin, Paris, London, Amsterdam, Rome, and Milan. My own schedule advancing future shows read: Dayton, Pittsburgh, Detroit, Cleveland, and Cincinnati. Oh, well.

It turned out to be his most successful European tour to date, documented by a red-hot live recording from the legendary Olympia Theatre in Paris. Another of the Paris shows was later telecast in Europe and eventually bootlegged, now familiar to many collectors and fans of YouTube. The J.B.'s were as impressed with Europe as audiences were with the show. "London blew our minds," Bootsy Collins told me. "Discos were everywhere, and the fashion was crazy. It was like we were discovering a whole new world we didn't know nothing about."

The European experience was an eye-opener for the band, prodding festering resentments to the surface. Many of the young musicians had grown to feel constrained, frustrated at how regimented the Brown band remained. They were also realizing what had driven their predecessors away. Collins told me, "Just like James was growing through our influence, we were growing too. It really began in Africa and continued through Europe. Suddenly, the band was rappin' about money all the time."

The European tour wrapped in Amsterdam and, two days later, Brown and the gang were in New York to open a two-week engagement at the infamous Copacabana, still the most important supper club in mainstream show biz. The booking was a trial of sorts. Success could mean lucrative return engagements and an open door to rooms that catered to similar audiences in Las Vegas, Reno, Atlantic City, and Miami Beach. The Copa's iconic front man Jules Podell recognized James' marquee value but was unsure whether raw soul would hit home with his highly critical, "downtown" (read: *white*) audiences. Healthy advance sales suggested otherwise.

I was excited. The idea of working the famous Copacabana was a personal "Big Willie" moment. This was the big time—where Frank Sinatra and Sammy Davis, Jr. played, where international celebrities and politicians competed for the best tables and gossip columnists hovered for scoops. AND it was known to be run by the mob. Not some small-time thug wannabes, the REAL mob! I flew to New York eager for a few days of courting media and V.I.P.s, not expecting the hornet's nest that lay waiting.

James seemed surprisingly fresh but a bit cocky from the regal treatment he'd received abroad. Of course, he flew first-class all over Europe and stayed in five-star hotel suites. As usual, the band and crew weren't so lucky. They came home weary and irritable from long bus rides, drab hotels, and countless delays at border crossings. When Fred Wesley and David Matthews called a rehearsal for The J.B.'s and the union musicians who would augment them at the Copa, Bootsy and Phelps Collins were deliberate no-shows. In our camp, that kind of willfulness was the ultimate sin. When the boss found out, he promptly cancelled the band's instrumental features in the show. No rehearsal? No spotlight!

I may have been the only one in our organization excited to be there. At least I had enough sense to recognize that the hardened Copa staff wasn't likely to view us as anything special. The first thing I did was stake out the head *maî·tre d'* and introduce myself. I knew he had long-time relationships with the mainstream media but suspected he was less likely to recognize reporters from the black press, so I gave him a hundred-dollar handshake along with a list of who we considered VIPs deserving of good tables.

Nightclubs, as such, were nothing new for us, but this was no Sugar Shack; this was an old-fashioned supper club popular with tourists. The dinner shows hosted some of the squarest audiences James ever played to. Opening night found Italian-American waiters scurrying about serving steaks and pasta to portly white businessmen and various high rollers, all wining and dining to "Sex Machine" and "Soul Power." The incongruous scene struck me as hysterically funny, but the cozy confines did offer a tantalizing opportunity to FEEL the James Brown Show up close and, by show's end, we had gained at least a few unlikely new fans. Whatever black clientele that patronized the club understandably favored the late shows.

No matter the audience, they didn't call James Brown "the hardest working man in show business" for nothing. Both opening night shows were standing room only and enthusiastically received. The influential syndicated columnist Earl Wilson wrote: "Soul singer James Brown opened screamingly and excitingly at the Copacabana in a show that packed the house." Rival writer Ed Sullivan referred to JB as a "smash Copa hit."

Unfortunately, the high didn't last long. By the third night, Brown was running out of gas from the two shows a day, and there'd be three on Saturday. Plus, he hadn't stopped bickering with the band, at one point chasing trumpeter Hassan Jamison from the stage for showing up wearing a new afro wig.

I wasn't spared James' prickly mood either, although it took a roundabout path to get me. Eric was on spring break, and he and our mother were in New York. James had known and treated Eric like a godson since he was thirteen years old, but had never met Mom. I hooked up a primo table down front for the dinner show and was touched by how many of our gang stopped by the table to pay respects. Eric was tickled by the idea of eating dinner to "Soul Power," and Mom was overwhelmed by the excitement and professionalism of our show. Shortly afterwards, I walked them up to the dressing room where James was at his most charming. He really laid it on thick, broke open a bottle of champagne, and complimented Mom on raising "two fine boys." After a warm visit, he asked if they had proper transportation back to their hotel. When Mom explained they would take a taxi, James would have none of it. Turning to me he said, "Mr. Leeds, you can't have your family looking for taxis in New York at night. You're excused for the second show. You make sure they get home safely."

It was a generous gesture, but I knew nothing is free in the world of James Brown. Not to say he didn't sincerely enjoy hosting my Mom and mean what he said. And not to say he was insincere about me taking them to their hotel. It wasn't any of that. It was that he wouldn't want ME to take his kindness for weakness. He wouldn't want me thinking his compliments meant I could relax. I arranged a car and did take them to their hotel, but I hightailed it right back to the Copa, arriving halfway through the second show.

Sure enough, the next morning James called me unusually early, insisting I come to his suite and bring my briefcase. I felt like I was going to court, and I was the one on trial. He spent the next hour grilling me about every detail of our upcoming dates, most of which was routine stuff that really required no conversation at all. His court didn't find me guilty, but I didn't feel innocent either. I guess it was a mistrial, but Brown proved his point—not to ever get too comfortable, even when my mother meets my godfather.

Without any off days to catch up on much-needed rest, James stayed on edge, and so did the band. The tension came to a head when we were due to make payroll and James sent me and Charles Bobbit to get a cash advance from Jules Podell.

Podell tersely refused us, citing his longstanding policy against advances. He pointed out that our contract called for draws on the seventh night of each week; we would have to wait. "Frank Sinatra and Sammy Davis don't get advances," he explained. "Why should James Brown?"

The club owner, famously protected by his well-publicized links to the mafia, assumed the matter was closed. But he'd never dealt with James Brown. Contract or no contract, mob or no mob, JB wanted some cash. Our marching orders were, "Go back and tell him we're selling out every show but, if he won't pay us, there won't be a second week."

I can't speak for Bobbit, but I felt like an ill-fated minion in *The Godfather*. Podell was so unaccustomed to being questioned that he was almost too stunned to respond. But, when he did, it was clear he wasn't about to be bluffed. He didn't give a damn whether we finished the second week or not. And we didn't.

I was pissed. The street talk had it that the Copa fired us because of light ticket sales but that was blatantly untrue. What *was* true was that, while nearly every show sold out, many of the high roller Copa regulars were nowhere to be found. After opening night, the clientele was about 75 percent diehard James Brown fans—frugal folks who wouldn't otherwise set foot in the stuffy Copa. Copa regulars were uncomfortable and waiters complained about low tabs and poor tips. Podell didn't spend one second trying to persuade us to stay. In fact, a recently surfaced document signed by both Brown and Podell indicates that the Copa bought out the second week—essentially paying Brown to NOT finish the engagement.

To Brown's credit, he left the club with his head held high. "Sometimes you just have to be a man, no matter what," he told me. "Mr. Podell will need to have us back one day, if he's still in business." James never played there again, but the club was sold a few years later, its prestige and fortunes a thing of the past.

The Copa cancellation turned out to be the least of our problems. Ignoring the humiliation of getting paid to not play, Brown claimed the unexpected week off was costly and sent the band and road crew home with only half-pay. It was the last straw for the already-restless Collins brothers, taking the hit for a situation that wasn't of their making. Bootsy later told me, "When James did that, I knew I had to leave." Several of the other J.B.'s walked with him. After a year and sixteen days, James Brown, once again, found himself without a band.

St. Clair Pinckney, Bobby Byrd, "Jabo" Starks, and a few others remained, but band leader Fred Wesley had his hands full breaking in a new trumpet section along with hastily recruited replacements for Bootsy and Phelps. Rhythm guitarist Hearlon "Cheese" Martin recommended bassist Fred Thomas and saxophonist Jimmy Parker from his old Brooklyn bar band. Meanwhile, Brown sent another guitarist from Macon, Robert Coleman, whose experience was limited to touring with Percy Sledge. In his wonderful autobiography, *Hit Me, Fred*, Wesley openly discusses his struggles honing this group of less than "A" level musicians into an acceptable band. "The musicians I ended up with were not the cream of the crop," Wesley wrote. "The best thing about Robert Coleman was his ability to play the blues and it turned out to be the total extent of his ability. He had no sense of funk or time. So I gave him all of the single string parts. 'Cheese' was forced to become the mainstay of the groove."

Fred has since confessed, "One of the most traumatic periods in my life was when I had to take that band, start from scratch, and put a whole show together."

But, by the time James got in front of the re-cast J.B.'s, Wesley had somehow shaped them into something worthy enough to move forward. Coincidentally, a week later, we played an Easter Sunday matinee in Cincinnati. Bootsy, Phelps, and trumpet player Clayton "Chicken" Gunnells showed up, pleasantly stoned, and dressed in a self-styled mix of Haight-Ashbury and London's Carnaby Street, the very fashion and culture that their ex-boss had determinedly repressed. They were obviously making a statement, causing a stir, as they worked their way to their seats and giggled throughout the show. Theirs weren't cruel laughs of contempt; they were simply amused watching a group of musicians struggle with the music they had so effortlessly performed for the past year.

(The musicologist in me might argue that the departure of the Collins brothers signaled the subtle beginning of Brown's ever-so-gradual artistic demise, but I'd be getting ahead of myself again. It is worth noting that, when JB finally fell from the charts in 1976, Bootsy's Rubber Band was enjoying their first of four smash albums and headlining many of the same arenas and coliseums they had first visited as J.B.'s.)

16

While Fred Wesley spent several off days fine-tuning the band, something else was brewing in our little orbit. Brown's recording contract was in its final months and the struggling Starday-King was unable to meet his terms for renewal. James was as attractive a free agent as the record industry had seen in years, and his attorney, Martin Machat, was fielding overtures from a host of record executives, including Columbia's Clive Davis. Brown had his eyes set on a sizeable signing bonus and creative autonomy would be paramount, but the shopping process was slow and wearing, and he wasn't about to let his limbo status effect his output.

With just three shows under their belts, the new band congregated at King Studios for a session intended for Bobby Byrd. James and Danny Ray burst in without greeting anyone. JB was in the midst of mercilessly taking Danny to task over a wide-brimmed "Super Fly" hat that was dwarfing his small head. "Mr. Ray, you know you cannot wear that hat no more. No, sir, not with me," he told his sidekick. "Ain't nothing happening with a man wearing a hat like that. No, no. Nobody can take you seriously with THAT hat. Nobody."

Like an admonished child, Danny dejectedly hung his head. Actually, with the hat sloped forward, I couldn't really see his head. Brown wasn't finished. "Bums and pimps wear those hats, jack. You know what that hat makes you? I can't have that. Not with me, oooooh, noooo!"

Ray slowly turned and slumped away. He spent the rest of the afternoon grumbling about the hat which had cost him a bundle and now lay in the trunk of their rental car.

During the warm-up for Byrd's "I Know You Got Soul," Brown had a light-bulb moment and began ad-libbing a different song. His excitement growing, James told Bobby, "You go and think on the words to your song. I'm gonna do this one."

James then explained to everyone present that a casual conversation with a lounge musician the night before had inspired him to use the term "escape-ism" as a song title. The lyrics were sparse, and the theme wore thin a minute or two into the song, so he cued the band to change keys and spontaneously began conversing with the musicians, rapping about their home towns and anything else that came to mind. The funky vamp went on and on until James ran out of things to say. I'm not sure if you call it genius or just good luck, but only James Brown, strolling around a studio familiarizing himself with his new musicians, could turn an off-the-cuff groove into a worthwhile track, much less a hit record. With an organ solo and St. Clair Pinckney's version of the squealing "Super Bad" solo, the marathon jam ran over nineteen minutes.

James charged into the control room and breathlessly addressed engineer Ron Lenhoff, "Whew, that's a long one. What was that, nine or ten minutes?"

Lenhoff smirked and replied, "That was nineteen minutes, Mr. Brown."

Brown's straight-faced response was, "Well, then that's enough for parts one, two, three, four, five, six, AND seven."

Carefully edited to just over six minutes, the TWO-part "Escape-ism" sold nearly a million singles. Then there was Bobby Byrd. Thankfully, the next jam they came up with proved just as exciting and fit Byrd's lyrics for "I Know You Got Soul" just fine.

The good news was that any fallout from the Copa debacle and the turnover in the band didn't affect the backbone of our business, the one-nighters. One of our next stops was back in Richmond, where promoter Allen Knight confronted us with a briefcase full of bills left over from Beckley. James wouldn't even look at them, but I knew we hadn't seen the last of Knight or his unpaid bills.

For some petty, long-forgotten reason, James fired Bob Patton and promoted me. The more-experienced Buddy Nolan was now my second in command—the same Buddy Nolan that had organized this very staff years earlier. It could have been awkward, but Buddy and I both knew our titles were just the product of Brown's impetuous whims, that we were really just a team of equals with shared goals. But, with Bob gone, I became solely responsible for a crucial weekend routed through Pittsburgh, Memphis, and Little Rock. Both Pittsburgh and Memphis were major dates in large arenas. James had even agreed to beef up the bill by adding the Detroit Emeralds and Tyrone Davis, both of whom had records on the charts.

As the dates approached, James urged that I spend the final week of the promotions commuting between the cities. I started in Pittsburgh where WAMO radio personality Brother Matt was finally our official local man. Matt and I spent a weekend plotting the final advertising and pushing JB's records onto turntables in the Steel City's hottest clubs.

Monday morning, I set foot in Memphis for the first time in my life. It was early summer in the "home of the blues," and its sprawling green and lazy pace were vastly different from Pittsburgh's familiar hills and asphalt. Other than its rich musical heritage, all I knew about Memphis was that the Holiday Inn chain had begun there and one of their premier properties was the Riverfront. Alas, it was sold out, so I opted for history and checked into what was lauded as the chain's first inn. I should have known better—located in a blighted part of the inner city, it LOOKED like the first Holiday Inn.

The saving grace was the hotel's lounge, whose fetchingly uniformed servers doubled as show girls. More accurately, the show girls doubled as servers. At various intervals, spotlights would suddenly focus on certain tables atop which the girls would sing and dance. No cheap sex show, it was a surprisingly professional revue, and some of the girls were damn talented.

What began as a lonely evening turned pleasant when I ran into Leroy Little, Jr., a record label promotion rep whom I'd known in Virginia. Leroy knew one of the show girls and we convinced her to join us after the lounge closed. It wasn't long before I discovered she also knew another local friend of mine, Funkadelic guitarist Harold Beane. We ended up at an after-hours club and, sure enough, there was Beane jamming with a funky house band led by legendary drummer Al Jackson, widely recognized for his recordings with Otis Redding, Al Green, and Booker T. & the M.G.'s.

Later on, Jackson introduced the "celebrities" in the house. I learned I was also in the company of writer-singer David Porter, members of the Bar-Kays, and many of the DJs from both R&B radio stations in Memphis. I had stumbled onto everyone in Memphis that I needed to know under one roof! Memphis mission accomplished.

After a day in Little Rock, I flew back to the 'burgh. The Steel City gig turned out even better than expected, a near sell-out in the 13,000-seat Civic Arena. As in many cities, James Brown shows there had become festive events, sprawling parties with much of the audience milling about the arena, settling only to appreciate the peaks of the show until Brown's own performance lured all attention to the stage. Even the local police, who had always vehemently discouraged unseated audiences, finally understood the atmosphere as a kind of indoor picnic. In fact, we introduced Pittsburgh to what became popularly known as "festival seating," which meant no seating at all—instead, an open floor sold on a general-admission ticket. Matt cleverly dubbed it a "boogie ticket," and the more restless, younger fans loved it.

Our show also marked the first time the Civic Arena's celebrated dome was opened for a black event. The circular arena was housed under a retractable roof that, through an elaborate system of cantilevers, folded apart, thrusting more than two-thirds of the audience under the stars and a plain view of Pittsburgh's skyline. It was a stunning effect but the arena's reluctance to showcase the treat had long been resented in the black community. Truthfully, it wasn't a race issue. All it took to open the dome was a promoter willing to cough up a substantial fee—supposedly justified by the additional union labor required. We could argue that point, but it still wasn't about race; it was about money. Matt and I convinced James the pre-show publicity justified the expense. It was a good look, and the black community credited Brown for "forcing" arena management into opening the dome.

Saturday night in Memphis was another winner, a sold-out Mid-South Coliseum jammin' to Tyrone Davis and JB at their best. After the gig, James was pleased, extolling my promotional virtues to anyone who would listen. I definitely wanted to celebrate, but that meant getting away from the boss who could be a real EOF (enemy of fun) unless it was HIS fun. Since we were at different hotels, once I left the Coliseum, I figured I'd seen the last of him until Little Rock. I figured wrong.

An hour later, I was standing in my hotel lobby waiting for Harold Beane and some local girls when James unexpectedly pulled up with a carload of folks, including one of Tyrone Davis' dancers. Turns out it was Tyrone's birthday. The girls in his group had cooked up a party and persuaded Brown to attend. Of course, once James spotted me, my recipe for fun was up in smoke. I ended up in his car, heading to the Riverfront and the birthday party. The dancers assured us that JB's surprise arrival would be the highlight of the night. Truer words were never spoken.

As soon as we approached the door to Davis' suite, I sensed something wrong. It was too quiet. If the party wasn't already over, it sure as hell was once the door opened. Sitting at a card table were the birthday boy with our Freddie Holmes, Henry Stallings, and Kenny Hull, engrossed in a serious poker game. A couple empty gin bottles lay on the floor.

I guess the money on the table had trumped any interest in a party. In order to appreciate this scenario, you need to understand how sensitive Brown was about his employee's behavior. Obviously, the last thing he needed was for three of his staff to get busted gambling in a hotel room, the same hotel in which James was staying. But how likely was that? These were grown men on their personal time but, like kids with their hands in the cookie jar, Freddie, Henry, and Kenny picked up their cash and sheepishly pitched their cards on the table.

On the other hand, a triumphant Davis had no such regrets. Well into his birthday gin, Tyrone begged James not to come down hard on the guys. "Look at this pile of money I won, James. They've had a tough enough time already," Davis laughed.

James just glared and shook his head. Enter the condescending boss who always knows best, a role Brown relished. "Pitiful. Y'all look stupid," he groaned. "Y'all ain't got no better sense than to sit here and let this man get you drunk and take your money."

Then Brown turned to Tyrone to make certain he wasn't offended. "I ain't got no problem with you, man. If somebody gonna take them fools, I'm glad it was you." As if that wasn't bad enough, James added, "I know what I pay these guys and they ain't got enough sense to admit they can't afford to gamble with you."

We stayed long enough for a birthday toast and then I broke away to meet Beane and his posse at a club. I was determined to be the one in our gang to salvage a decent night's fun. I can't remember her name but, suffice it to say, Memphis did me right.

Little Rock kept our victory streak intact and, Monday morning, I was back in the office, getting ready for the next round of gigs.

"Escape-ism" and the even newer "Hot Pants" were both on the charts and things remained pleasantly hassle-free until we booked a date in Chattanooga, Tennessee.

Just as I was about to kick-start our Chattanooga promotion, the last-minute cancellation of a Wilson Pickett show there caused a ruckus that exploded into five days of fiery, violent racial disturbances. Chattanooga was under temporary curfew. Our show was three weeks away, but the city fathers were apprehensive, threatening to cancel or postpone it. Of course, James wasn't hearing it and gave me carte blanche to put together a press release targeted at the Chattanooga media. He just said, "Do what you got to do to save the date." So, just as the unrest was tapering down, I ghost wrote a JB address to the citizens there that ended up on the front page of the Chattanooga Times. The timing was perfect. The paper's editor wrote:

> *Soul singer James Brown, one of the most popular black entertainers ever to perform here, has called for "peace and calm" for our streets. Brown said, "The economy is bad enough. I plead for my brothers and sisters to halt all violence and instead of attacking people and burning buildings, attack the economy and educational system. If the housing is bad and retailers unfair, don't terrorize, organize. Don't burn, learn. Don't hate, communicate. Don't tear down the community, build it up. The black community can be our biggest asset. We don't need integration, we need communication."*

Cheeky, perhaps, but I was pretty familiar with stock James Brown. Even if the "speech" was mine, at least the clichés were his. But I should have stopped there. The Times piece continued:

> *Brown was critical of the rock group which refused to perform at Memorial Auditorium last Friday, an action which resulted in the initial wave of violence here. "It's a shame when our entertainers can't take the responsibility to handle their audiences intelligently. I never fault my audience for bad promotion. There have been a few*

cases through the years when shady promoters have actually run off with the evening's earnings. But to refuse to perform after an audience has paid to see you is unfair. It's not their fault. They put faith in those they pay to see and we as entertainers owe it to them to conduct our appearances in a responsible fashion."

In getting a little carried away—I don't think I ever showed my piece to James for his approval—I had underestimated the impact my words would have. "Our" words ended up all over Tennessee TV and radio. National periodicals, even trade papers like *Cashbox*, *Variety*, and *Billboard* picked up the story.

I privately wondered how the Chattanooga city council could authorize another concert a mere three weeks after an ugly race riot, but I worked for James Brown, and he wanted to perform there. The decision was placed in the hands of a special jury composed of various city officials, including the auditorium director, Clyde Hawkins. To my surprise, after a day-long conference, the auditorium board announced a cosmetic plan for stricter booking procedures, but that "no action would be taken on the show planned by James Brown."

I later learned that Hawkins had voted against the show but was overruled by several commissioners, one of whom said, "Brown has been a good spokesman for 'responsible behavior' and had sent a message to young negroes here advising them to 'cool it' during our civic disorders. James will do our community more good than harm."

So off I went to Chattanooga. Dave Oliver, the program director of WNOO, Chattanooga's sole black radio station, picked me up at the airport and took me to their makeshift studios, inside a motor home parked in seclusion at the end of a narrow, muddy path. Their regular studios had been firebombed by whites, disturbed by what they deemed WNOO's "militant" news coverage. It sounded scary but, as the day progressed and I saw more of Chattanooga, I sensed that it was an exhausted community, worn and weary from its ordeal. Just maybe we would have an audience too emotionally crippled for anything except entertainment. Escape-ism, anyone? That is, if we could convince people it was safe to leave their homes. I was questioning myself whether I was trying to sell tickets against folks' best interests. But it occurred to me that, if we were going to stand behind our press release, we were obligated to go through with our show or face eating a lot of crow. My final stop was a tense meeting with Clyde Hawkins and some apprehensive police officials, discussing plans for what we all prayed would be a peaceful event.

It turned out to be just that, peaceful but a modest turnout, at best. The drained and fearful citizens of Chattanooga just weren't ready to face a large gathering. James rocked the house and addressed his fans, picking up where my press release left off. The Chattanooga Times reported:

> Brown told the applauding crowd that he did not like the large number of police cars and helmeted policemen ringing the Auditorium. "We can do our thing without that. I'm going to play for you and I'm going to the office AFTER I finish and get my money."
>
> Obviously referring to an incident in May when another entertainer refused to perform without being paid in advance, Brown said, "I'm not like some of the other people in the business. I am going to play for you; that's why I came here."

The footnote to the saga was Wilson Pickett's irate rebuttal in the music trades:

> "I bitterly resent Brown's remarks. What he's saying is that I was stupid in my actions and failed to live up to the show business credo of 'the show must go on'. He wasn't anywhere around at the time and for him to make ignorant remarks like that shows he lacks intelligence."

I understood Pickett's frustration at being called out. His Chattanooga show wasn't the first time an entertainer bolted rather than perform when a promoter defaulted. But I do believe said entertainer has a responsibility to gauge an audience's mood before making a decision that might put people at risk. And I always wondered who might have written his response because IT didn't really sound very intelligent. Maybe Pickett wrote it himself, but maybe, like Brown, Pickett didn't see "his words" in advance either. Either way, the issue was already old news in our camp. All that mattered to my boss was that he came off as the good guy.

In hindsight, I'm embarrassed by how casually I was willing to speak on James' behalf, which raises a broader issue. I was often asked what it was like working for a black man in a mostly black environment. Depending on who was doing the asking, it was a question that I usually found rude and annoying because those who asked it had already conjured up their own answer and were judging me, not my boss or my job.

For lack of a better definition, I considered myself a liberal, but I did recognize the patronization that was at the core of so much textbook liberalism as it pertained to race. I also realized that most blacks knew a lot more about whites than vice versa. I usually played past the job/boss questions but, despite what the liberal doctrine of blind equality would want us to believe, mine was hardly like most jobs held by young white men. In fact, the very question of it illustrated the difference.

Of course, there were countless other whites working in the black music business—from the condescending and exploitive to those who were viewed as fair minded—but, as I got to know many of them, I realized that even the most sincere and open-minded related to the black community on a very superficial basis. They might have loved, written, performed, or produced the music or even had black friends and lovers in their personal lives, but they didn't seem to have a clue about the diversity of professions, interests, styles, politics, morals, and philosophies among black Americans. Their perceptions were defined by only those within their immediate circle. It was as if their artists, friends, and lovers somehow represented all of Black America.

But I knew better. It seemed hit-over-the-head logical that the black community contained as wide a variety of people, informed by differing regional traditions, educational and economic levels, religions, political views, fashions, and musical tastes as any other group of people. But, somehow, that common-sense conclusion escaped most whites, leaving me to conclude that they lacked insight or interest or both. It was really as simple as the fact that my college friend, Clayton Brown, was nothing like my boss, James Brown, who was nothing like my girlfriend. That elementary perspective was still deplorably rare among whites in the early 1970s, who insisted on viewing blacks as all pretty much the same. As a result, I gradually developed a somewhat arrogant conviction that I better understood and empathized with the plight of Black America than just about anyone else whose view was through the lens of white privilege.

Loudmouth that I am, I also had to wrestle with how far I had the right to go as a spokesperson for a friend, lover, or boss who happened to be black. Lacking the credibility that only came from walking in black shoes, I still had a conceit from what I had learned in my experiences beyond the realm of most whites. It was a thin line that I would walk for a long time, until I tired of being defensive and decided to just do and say what I wanted to without feeling I owed anyone, black or white, any damn explanations. It's been quite liberating to simply live and love the life I live, but that was long after Chattanooga.

17

By early summer, the entire industry was aware that James was label shopping. James, his attorneys, and Hal Neely were going from one meeting to another, seeking a deal that would be mutually beneficial. There were several agendas at play, and Brown's loyalty to King and Hal Neely weighed heavily. As the company's only productive contemporary artist, Brown's departure would render Starday-King reliant on their rich back catalogue. In order to protect his own future, Neely's mission was to gain control of the company from Lin Broadcasting, its corporate sugar daddy. While negotiations continued, James teamed with Neely, who was seeking cash with which to buy out his partners to form People Records and a publishing entity called Crited Music, named after their sons Chris Neely and Teddy Brown. Of course, Starday-King would distribute the new label. Both "Escape-ism" and "Hot Pants" appeared on People, and were hits by the time Brown finally exited in July.

Of all the labels interested in Brown, Polydor Records surfaced as the company most willing to provide him the creative autonomy he was accustomed to at King. A giant in Europe but new to America, Polydor was determined to establish a base in contemporary black music, and what better way than signing a free agent superstar whose records they were already selling in many foreign markets under an old licensing deal with Starday-King? The multi-year deal was worth seven figures, plus the label agreed to pay Starday-King a handsome fee for Brown's entire back catalogue of masters, pick up the monthly payments on his jet, and provide James Brown Productions office space in their Manhattan headquarters.

The office space is what perked my attention most. Being based off the beaten path in Cincinnati had been the subject of good-natured teasing from industry friends on both coasts. I was thrilled to be going back to New York where we'd be "in the loop."

Naturally, after almost two years in the Queen City, there were things I would miss. I appreciated the "influence" James Brown Productions enjoyed at King, not to mention throughout the city—good tables at restaurants, tickets for Bengals and Reds games, free drinks in clubs. In the Big Apple, we'd just be one more music company. And nobody else in the entire industry could boast the novel convenience of working under the same roof as a studio, mastering lab, pressing plant, tape vault, art department, and shipping dock.

On a sentimental tip, there were Cincinnati memories that had more to do with James Brown the man than James Brown the boss. One night, James, Dee Dee, Deborah, and I were hungry for a late snack and decided to get some ribs. Brown's favorite rib joint, Ruby's, was in the middle of the 'hood. I got out to place our order and, to my surprise, JB jumped out behind me to play wingman. "You can't go in there alone," he warned. "These people don't know you. You go ahead and get the food, but I got your back."

I didn't dare ruin the fun by telling him I had bought food there many times without incident. I headed for the carry-out line as "bodyguard" Brown swaggered to the back of the room and ceremoniously draped himself over a chair, his "don't mess with me" expression all but daring folks to do just that. Other than a few quizzical "what is James Brown doing in here" glances, he was left alone. James didn't budge until our food was ready. Then he bolted to my side like a Brink's guard escorting a bank manager to a vault. Back in the car,

Deborah and Dee Dee had been watching the whole thing and were trying to smother their giggles. JB mumbled something about "silly women not knowing what we men go through" and drove off.

Speaking of driving, there was the day James impulsively bought an antique Model A Ford he had spotted at a gas station near the Cincinnati airport. The classic auto appeared to be in decent condition, so JB insisted on driving it to town himself with the ever-trusty Bobby Byrd as his co-pilot. With Danny Ray and Henry Stallings following in a station wagon, Brown got about a mile down the interstate before the Model A started sputtering. The car jerked its way another mile or two until it let out a belch and stopped dead.

James coasted onto the culvert, jumped out, and opened the old-fashioned folding hood. Danny pulled over behind him and offered to go get a tow truck, but Brown was determined to complete his trek. He tinkered with the engine and somehow got it started. Stallings, who had known James as kids in Augusta, whispered, "That's just how he used to start these things when we used to steal 'em back home."

Several miles later, there was a loud bang, the car jolted to one side and James and Bobby realized they now had a flat tire. JB nursed the car back to the side of the highway. Grateful there was a spare attached to the rear of the car, they changed the tire. But, once again, the car wouldn't turn over. Brown suggested a push. So Bobby, Danny, and Henry began shoving the old Ford forward with Soul Brother #1 sitting tall behind the wheel. Sure enough, the car eventually lurched forward on its own accord, and Byrd jumped in.

The thirty-minute drive from the airport to our office took them three hours. I just wish there had been a camera around when they pulled up and Byrd climbed out covered with soot and grease. Then JB insisted on taking me and Buddy Nolan on a see-and-be-seen cruise through downtown Cincinnati. Thankfully, the car kept running.

Most rides with Brown at the wheel weren't as leisurely as those in the Model A. One memorably hair-raising journey was from Dayton to Cincinnati. Byrd was riding shotgun and I was in the back. JB began the forty-mile trip at his usual pace, about thirty miles over the speed limit! A few miles before Cincinnati, James caught the eye of a young brother in the adjoining lane. He slowed to match the speed of the fella's souped-up Chevy and acknowledged him with a black power salute. I don't know if he recognized Brown, but he took the greeting as a challenge and roared ahead of us. Brown stomped on the gas pedal, and we were off—racing down the interstate. Bobby and I sat paralyzed as the speedometer strained towards a hundred. Suddenly, the Chevy leaped across us into an exit lane. James jerked behind him, careening down the exit ramp and across a major thoroughfare. Of course, we had no idea what kind of lunatic was in the other car. Maybe that's why JB stopped the chase and returned to the interstate at a slightly more civil pace. Just another night in Cincinnati with the hardest playing man in show business.

A FEW DAYS AFTER ANNOUNCING the Polydor agreement, James flew to Cincinnati for a sentimental meeting in our office at King. As expected, he explained that his recording operations would transfer to New York—he had already hired Jeannette Washington, one of his former dancers, to set up the new office. Ron Lenhoff was assigned to troll through the King vault to assemble the thousands of tapes that Polydor had purchased. Then he dropped the bomb. Aspiring to increase his hometown visibility, he had decided to move the tour business to Augusta! He had already incorporated a new business name, Man's World Enterprises, envisioning a full-service agency that would continue to promote his shows but also manage and book outside artists. He expressed his conviction that Buddy and I would love Augusta hospitality and then, almost as an after-thought, mentioned that he had installed Johnny Terry to head the agency.

I was devastated. Cincinnati was no New York, but at least it was a city. A city with major league sports teams and at least a modicum of cultural diversity. Augusta was a one-dimensional Southern hamlet, its night life mostly catering to the rough and tumble crowd of servicemen stationed at nearby Fort Gordon. The closest thing to what I considered civilization was Atlanta, over 150 miles away.

And was he telling us that Johnny Terry was now our boss? God bless Johnny but, other than the instincts of a street hustler, he had absolutely nothing to contribute. Worse yet, he thought he did; he had always been in denial about his limitations. What he *was* good at was staying in his boss' ear, and that too could be treacherous because he often misunderstood the nuances involved in what he was reporting. I concluded that hiring Terry was Brown's insurance in case Buddy or I declined to make the move and jumped ship.

Buddy didn't flinch. He just took the next thing smoking home to Philly. I too was considering quitting, although I tried to hide it. Evidently, JB picked up on it and, rather than let me have the last word, he conjured up a reason to fire me. I knew the door would stay open if I ever decided to kiss the ring, so, rather than sulk about being fired, I welcomed it as time off to regroup and make a thoughtful decision. I certainly never thought that my dismissal would stare back at me in the press. No, not the music press. *Hustler*, Cincinnatian Larry Flynt's porn mag!

A lot of male characters have been written about in *Hustler*, but I had no reason to think I'd be one of them. Since I moved to Cincinnati in 1970, the magazine had grown from a four-page Xeroxed bulletin distributed in the Flynt's titty bars into a national publication. One day, I was browsing through one of *Hustler*'s early editions hoping not to see any girls I knew, when my name jumped off the page. I paged back to find the writer's name and then it began to make sense. Shortly before we left Cincinnati, music critic Ed Ward was researching the history of King Records and dropped in our office where we chatted about the label's relationship with JB. Ward never published his King story but, with a freelancer's survival instinct, he sold *Hustler* on a story about the city of Cincinnati. His essay included a segment about the local music scene, which segued into his visit to King and James Brown Productions. It read:

We were joined by a young white with a red afro, who introduced himself as Alan Leeds, James Brown's tour manager. He stepped into his office, and I started to follow when a meaty black hand gripped my shoulder. "Hey," said a voice, "Who are you?" "He's cool," Leeds called, and I walked in. A man sat at a desk counting bills of large denomination. An amazingly beautiful black lady sat watching him. She had an emerald stud in her nose. Leeds gave me a couple of phone numbers and wished me luck. The next week he was fired, and James Brown Productions had moved, to Brown's hometown in Georgia.

I had no idea a typical day at the office could be so sensationalized. Buddy Nolan didn't routinely discourage visitors, and, if my attractive assistant was that "amazingly" beautiful, I would never have gotten any work done. And my ego bristled at how casually I was dismissed. I'm no prude but, given the Flynts' local reputation as bigoted rednecks and the magazine's tasteless cartoons, I didn't like the idea of being in there at all. But why worry? Nobody buys *Hustler* for the writing. If Ward had waited another month, he would have discovered that I had been rehired and had moved to Georgia.

18

I'd neither felt like I had been fired nor gotten the James Brown Show out of my system. Meanwhile, things in the Augusta office had been hectic from day one. The new local staff didn't understand music industry politics, and Johnny Terry grudgingly began hinting that he was in over his head. Forced to pinch-hit as an advance man on off days, road manager Freddie Holmes persuaded Buddy Nolan to temporarily return. But, even with Buddy's help, venue negotiations and advertising campaigns fell further behind. Pretty soon, Nolan was also reaching for help. When I finally confessed some interest, James called, and I was on my way to Augusta.

I suppose there were moments when I kind of romanticized the idea of living in Augusta. After all, it was James Brown's home and it could be argued that Georgia is to soul Music what New Orleans is to jazz—James, Ray Charles, Otis Redding, and Little Richard were all born there. But those moments were fleeting. I knew Augusta was just a small, non-descript Southern town—a tiny airport with few flights and just one or two first-run movie theaters. For goodness' sake, there were still railroad tracks running through the streets of downtown. You could be scarfing down a greasy burger at White Tower while right outside the window a mile-long freight train lumbered by, tying up crosstown traffic for ten or fifteen minutes. Nonetheless, there I was.

Johnny Terry had my old title of "tour director," so James re-hired me as a "consultant." I'm sure Johnny felt threatened, but I was determined to keep any drama to a minimum and went out of my way to be a team player. My loosely defined job description allowed me the time to revamp the show's promotion kits. The show hadn't received much press during my absence, so I hoped that, just maybe, James appreciated that all the old media coverage hadn't been an accident.

On the record front, James was exploiting his still nascent relationship with Polydor by deluging the market with releases on his People and BrownStone labels by Bobby Byrd, Lyn Collins, Hank Ballard, The J.B.'s, and several newly signed artists. It seemed like we had as much activity as some established labels, so I decided to begin a weekly "tip sheet" that compiled news about our records, artists, and road show. A precursor to today's blogs, the gossipy one-sheets found their way onto the desks of deejays, retailers, publications, and music critics. Before long *Billboard*, *Record World*, and *Cash Box* were running some blurbs from the sheet, *Rolling Stone* was clocking us in their Random Notes column, and *Amusement Business* was regularly reporting our itineraries and more successful box office grosses.

I kept myself busy during the work weeks, but the weekends were a different story. Newly recruited local friends only went so far—by my second or third weekend, I was climbing the walls. I was so eager to get out of Augusta that I spent a couple weekends driving up and down the highways with Bobby Jackson, whose modest job it was to deliver show placards to the towns on an upcoming run of dates in the Carolinas.

Bobby had been hired as Johnny Terry's assistant when he and his wife, JB's latest protégé, singer Lyn Collins, moved to Augusta a few months before I did. Back home in Abilene, Texas, Bobby had been a sometime concert promoter but an auto body expert by trade, proficient at customizing cars into the unique models that celebrities coveted. But then the show biz bug hit. Leery at the prospect of losing his wife to the world of Mr. Dynamite, Bobby hitched himself to Lyn's career the only way he could. Sadly, it only took a few months for Bobby's worst fears to come true. Lyn became Brown's latest "funky diva" in more ways than one, and Bobby quietly returned to Texas and, I hope, a lucrative auto business. We never heard from him again.

My day-to-day responsibilities soon included mentoring the overwhelmed Johnny Terry. During a staff meeting, James seized an opportunity to confront his befuddled tour director by making an example of my note taking.

"See, Mr. Terry. Mr. Leeds is a professional—he's taking notes. None of y'all have taken any notes since we moved from Cincinnati. An office must have notes! But you can't do what he's doing because you never learned how. I gave you a chance to better yourself and you're wasting it. Mr. Terry? If you gonna learn, you need to take notes too!"

This was another JB grade school sound-a-like, the type I found hysterically funny. But no one was laughing; everyone took it as seriously as Brown made it sound. It was awkward watching James belittle Johnny like that, particularly since his failures weren't for lack of trying. But, from that point on, Brown pretty much banished him to the smaller Southern markets and placed most of the "A" markets back in my hands. File that under "careful what you wish for." But I celebrated that I'd be spending more time on the road advancing my dates—time I wouldn't be stuck in Augusta.

Truth be told, I found Augusta pretty hospitable and eventually made the best of it. Johnny Terry had become the first black tenant in a stylish townhouse complex behind the Augusta National Country Club (renowned for the annual Masters golf tournament). I took that as a good omen and moved there too. Back in Cincinnati, girlfriend Deborah had protested my move South by putting our relationship on hiatus, so I made it my business to meet a couple young ladies willing to show me around. Augusta's night life wasn't very sophisticated but, thanks to nearby Fort Gordon's thousands of soldiers, the city supported a lively club scene.

I quickly learned that, even in Augusta, there was a currency in working for Soul Brother #1. The grapevine in such a small town was lightning fast. Before I could blink, I was recognized in restaurants and clubs as the new kid in town, the "Yankee white boy" working for Mr. Brown.

The attention was usually well intentioned, but it made me uncomfortable. One morning James' father, Joe Brown, strolled into the office direct from a friendly breakfast with Augusta's chief of police. Papa Joe told me the chief had casually asked, "how's that new boy with all that hair workin' out for Jimmy?"

First of all, I hadn't heard anyone dare refer to James as Jimmy since Ben Bart died. But, more importantly, as a sometime-weed-smoking carpetbagger, I was increasingly paranoid about my unexpected and unwanted visibility. Papa Joe saw that in my face and laughed, assuring me the chief meant no harm.

"Junior got his number—you don't have to worry 'bout the chief none," claimed Papa Joe. "It don't hurt for you to know him. He just likes knowin' what goes on in his city."

The irony didn't escape me. It was less than ten years since *In the Heat of the Night,* but how the script had flipped! Here was an elderly black American trying to comfort a young white man about a white Southern police chief. I humbly reminded myself that I could never imagine what it was like to be a black male in pre-civil rights Augusta. But then, not that it was at all the same thing, Joe Brown wasn't accustomed to outspoken, pot-smoking Yankees with Jew-fros in post-civil rights Augusta. Actually, no one was.

I PLANNED TO SPEND CHRISTMAS IN AUGUSTA and I was pleased that Deborah had decided to patch things up and come down from Cincinnati. My hopes for a decent holiday increased when James burst into the office excitedly announcing a company Christmas party. The theme of the party was "the workingman," and JB directed that everyone wear the appropriate garb, workingman's jeans or overalls. I was so happy to have a party to take Deborah to that my brain only registered "jeans." I didn't give wardrobe another thought.

On the day before the party, everyone in the office was talking about the overalls they were going to wear. Johnny Terry explained that old-school bibbed overalls were a staple in any Southern laborer's closet, and I had better get aboard. Hmm, jeans I had, but overalls? Oops, too late. It turned out there wasn't a pair available anywhere in town. As one store clerk put it, "The folks at James Brown's radio station bought them all."

So we had no choice but to improvise with some jeans and sweaters. The party resembled a farmer's market. And there was Farmer Brown in his perfectly tailored uniform of admittance, a floppy, denim engineer's cap perched atop his sagging Afro. Deb and I stuck out like sore thumbs.

James nodded a chilly greeting and then whispered something in Leon Austin's ear. Leon and JB had grown up together. And, since I'd been in Augusta, we had become good pals. Besides being part of Brown's road posse, Austin was a significant presence in Augusta's black community where he managed a local band and operated a popular barber shop where he periodically shaped my 'fro. Leon followed Deb and me across the dance floor and then apologetically explained that James was unhappy about our garb and "didn't we know it would be an insult to everyone who dressed right if he let us stay?"

I was embarrassed, exposed as the arrogant city slicker I tried not to be. But Deb took it differently. She wasn't thrilled about being in Augusta in the first place, and always had mixed feelings about my unpredictable boss. It was all I could do to restrain her from angrily confronting Brown as we worked our way out. Just as we neared the door, James intercepted us. He all but ignored me but stared at Deborah and said, "I'm sorry you didn't understand about the clothes. It's a respect thing. Our roots, you know. But y'all know you're always welcome at a James Brown party. Merry Christmas, Mrs. Leeds."

I had long ago stopped taking this kind of foolishness personally. Much of what James said and did was for effect, served some agenda. Sometimes we were all just interchangeable pawns in those games of his. It usually had nothing to do with how he really felt about us. So I was grateful that he chose to squash the tension. Deb and I stayed and enjoyed the party. But little did we know that Christmas with the boss was just beginning and that our "Santa" would soon transform from farmer to detective.

On Christmas Eve day, James did a free show for the soldiers at Fort Gordon. He seemed determined to have a positive community presence during his first holiday season home in Augusta. The expansive front yard of the Brown residence was elaborately decorated, including a black Santa sitting at the helm of a sleigh led by a pack of reindeer. Thanks to an open invitation delivered through the local media, streams of curious revilers filed down fancy Walton Way to gape at the brightly lit spectacle. Unfortunately, one TV station felt obligated to stir up controversy over Santa's blackness after which Brother Claus became the focal point for most visitors—everyone in Augusta wanted to see the Black Santa. What happened next was probably inevitable—Christmas Eve, a few vandals attacked the display, kicking over Santa and stealing a few of the huge wooden letters that spread across the lawn spelling out "Happy Holidays."

But Deb and I had no way of knowing what had happened when we decided to drive over to the Brown's with some holiday cheer.

There was a chilly drizzle in the air. When we pulled into the Brown driveway, we noticed that the guardhouse, normally brightly lit, stood in eerie darkness. I assumed the guard had the night off and drove towards the house and parked. When I opened my car door, I heard an urgent voice coming from the driveway behind.

"Hey! Quick—get back in the car!" It was Teddy, James' eldest son. He sounded serious and jumped in the back seat. Deborah and I stared at each other, wondering what kind of madness we had stumbled into.

Before I could ask Teddy anything, he rattled on. "The old man is upset. He thought he had them spotted but here y'all come, scaring them off. Daddy says you better stay in the car until we know what's happening out here."

We still had no clue, and Teddy couldn't answer our questions quickly enough. He gradually explained the vandalism and that James had spotted a couple teenagers scurrying off the property into the woods. I guess he had seen enough old detective movies to believe the crooks always return to the scene of the crime. At any rate, James was convinced the hooligans were coming back and he was going to be ready for them. He had summoned Leon Austin from the house and, together, they were on stake-out. In fact, Teddy explained, his Dad was on his knees in the pitch-dark guard house, pistol in hand, while Leon hid behind a nearby tree.

Deb, who had big sister affection for Teddy, noted the unlikeliness of anyone being foolish enough to return. "Teddy, you sound as crazy as your father right now. I'm going in the house and see Dee Dee."

In an uncharacteristic act of defiance, Teddy held up his hand and barked, "I can dig it. But Dad is gonna go crazy if they see you at the front door. All he's talking about is how he would have caught them if it wasn't for y'all. He wants you to turn off the car and stay still."

Deb had heard enough. "Stay still? I came to see Dee Dee on Christmas Eve and I bet she'll be glad to have somebody to laugh at you fools with. Think about it, Teddy. Your father—Soul Brother #1—spending Christmas Eve standing in the woods, in the rain, with a pistol in his hand, looking for somebody who ain't even here!"

With that, we all exhaled and cracked a grin. Teddy suggested that maybe we quietly follow him behind the garage to the back door. "I guess that should be okay. Daddy sent me to the house for more tapes and some fresh coffee anyway."

Now it was my turn. "Coffee? Tapes? You guys aren't on stake-out, you're having a damn picnic! He's worried about us moving around, a hundred yards from the street but he's sitting in that guard house playing music? You better believe we're going in the house!"

About thirty minutes later, James and his posse threw in the towel and joined us in the house. "A real man got to be prepared for anything, you know," Brown said as a greeting. "Got to protect my home and my family. On Christmas, Santa means a lot more than gold records!"

19

I spent the last week of December tightening up the rest of our holiday dates, the biggest of which was a New Year's Eve concert at the Scope, Norfolk's sparkling new arena. I also had to dig into Brown's ongoing saga with Allen Knight, which, in my absence, had turned into an outright debacle.

If you recall, Knight had a knack for filling in trouble spots on our tour schedule, but usually with some iffy scheme in an out-of-the-way town. James should have been leery, but he rationalized that these regions so rarely hosted first-class live entertainment that the shows would be easy sellouts. It seldom turned out that way. The dates were almost always booked as a last resort and invariably suffered from inadequate promotion. Then there was the matter of convincing people in a small town that a star of JB's caliber was even going to show up.

James had recently cancelled such a show in Wilmington, North Carolina, due to poor ticket sales. He and Knight hoped to make it up with shows in Danville, Virginia, on December 27th, and Lynchburg, Virginia, on the 29th. One might wonder why Knight continued dealing with Brown, what with the losses in Beckley and Wilmington. The answer was simple; he was just waiting for a date successful enough to recoup the unpaid bills. Our mistake was in assuming it would be one of *his* dates.

In Danville, we discovered that Knight had, once again, exaggerated the venue's seating capacity but the modest venue was sold out, so James played the show. Allen's plea to settle some of the expenses from his cancelled dates fell on deaf ears. JB muttered something about getting lucky in Lynchburg but, if I had been Knight, I wouldn't have held my breath.

As it turned out, Lynchburg wasn't lucky, and the boss refused to look at any old bills. Knight had committed a portion of the proceeds to a so-called charity in order to meet the leasing requirements of the "nonprofit" school auditorium that passed for a venue. It all sounded dubious; James insisted that the "charity" share was a promoter responsibility and then asked to be paid in full before taking the stage. When Knight declined, Brown angrily cancelled the gig. (Please don't tell anyone in Chattanooga.) As the saying goes, the third time's the charm. A third cancellation with both artist and promoter vowing it would be the last. This time, they were right.

I was happy Knight and his godforsaken little towns were out of our hair when I flew to Norfolk, where advance sales were booming. So there was a smile on my face as I strolled through the Norfolk airport searching for a pay phone to call the Scope for an update.

One thin dime—the price of a local call—is all it took to ruin my mood. Denzil Skinner, the Scope's director, said that their box office had just been served with a notice of attachment by the Norfolk Sheriff's Department. All the remote ticket locations had been similarly served. Every cent the show had generated was out of our hands.

Turns out Allen Knight had filed a lawsuit seeking the losses he suffered on his three cancelled shows. Since we were an out-of-state business, Virginia law provided the court with the authority to attach any materials of value that we might have within their jurisdiction, pending the results of the suit, which meant our money could be tied up for months—and that they might also take our bus, truck, and equipment, which could threaten our ability to perform.

I gasped and then paused to think things through. My instinct was to investigate our options before reporting to James—like any boss, he preferred hearing solutions than just problems. It was 5:00 p.m. on a Friday of a holiday weekend, so it was difficult to be optimistic about what we could accomplish before our show the next night. I quickly called Jack Pearl, one of Brown's attorneys in New York. I explained the situation and pointed out that Knight's claim was substantially less than what was attached. Shouldn't we be able to spring loose the excess? On the flip side, were our vehicles and gear at risk? Jack promised to dig into Virginia law and get back to me. I begged him not to tell James until we had a plan of action.

A few minutes later, Pearl referred me to Morris Fine, a Norfolk attorney said to have connections in all the right places. Jack had already briefed him, but I got the sense that Fine wasn't very familiar with James Brown. No matter—I didn't need a fan, I needed our money. Fine agreed that we should be able to recover all but the $6,000 that we were being sued for. He thought he would be able to get a judgment to that effect Saturday morning but that I shouldn't assume we'd have the cash before Monday or Tuesday. Since the court was already holding more than the claim, he assured me our gear would be safe.

Now I felt I could call the boss and tell him what was going on. Silence. Sixty agonizing seconds of cold silence. When he finally spoke, Brown's strained voice took a gradual upswing.

"Whaaaaaaattttt? Allen Knight did what?"

I cut him off, hoping to convince him I had everything under control, but he wasn't ready to hear that yet.

"That's it. Knight's a fool. He could have made a lot of money with us next year. But he's blowing it over some chump change. Who does he think he is, messing with our money? Where the…."

James abruptly stopped hollering. When he continued, his voice had regained a calm façade. "You're doing the right thing," he said. "You get the rest of the money tomorrow. In fact…."

Another sudden U-turn. Brown's voice jumped back up several octaves, "Hey, you're from Richmond. Rent you a car and drive up there and find some of those cats who hang out at that old hotel in the grease (JB's slang for the hood). Get a few of those cats and go find that damn Knight. Don't put your hands on him but scare him. You tell him to his face how much he stands to lose with all this. Tell him I'll see to it that no artist in the business will work for him. He got to be crazy! You tell him I said that, hear? You hear, Mr. Leeds? Go up there and tell him that!"

Click.

I didn't know whether to take James seriously or not, but I wasn't about to forsake the $50,000 I was trying to recover in Norfolk in favor of playing tough guy in Richmond. Knight was no thug, but I also knew he wouldn't be intimidated. Over the years, I had seen Allen connive his way out of many an ass kicking.

Word spread quickly on the JB grapevine. An unusually animated Charles Bobbit called from New York asking, "What in the world is going on down there with Allen Knight? Mr. Brown just called and all he kept saying was to be ready if he needs me to move. Need me for what?"

Before I could explain, the hotel operator interrupted with an emergency call from a Mr. Brown.

"Mr. Leeds, you better stay there in Norfolk and get our money in the morning. No telling what else Knight has up his sleeve, you need to stay there. Call me tomorrow soon as you got the money."

I met Morris Fine early the next morning. He was a pleasant man whose flapping arms were swallowed by the sleeves of a suit jacket at least a size too big. His polished wing tip shoes suggested the feet of a much larger man and I had a hard time keeping up with his brisk walk to a judge's chambers. The casually attired, friendly judge was obviously doing Fine a solid by coming in on a holiday weekend. He methodically processed the court order required to release the bulk of the attached funds. Next stop was the city clerk's office, where the lone person on duty added an official seal. Then we hustled to the sheriff's office where we were assured that the cash would be returned to the Scope box office later that afternoon.

I was impressed by Fine's effortless stroll through the legal maze; he had obviously pulled some strings to get all the players in place. Now I started worrying what his efforts were going to cost us, whether a $6,000 lawsuit was going to be worth the cost of Fine's efficiency. But no time for that. We had a show to do.

I got to the Scope around five in the afternoon. The marquee read "Tonight's Event—Sold Out," and scalpers were having a field day. Backstage the fellas in the band were unusually loose, determined to celebrate the new year despite a 2 a.m. bus call after the show. Meanwhile, up in Denzil Skinner's office, we got busy counting the very money that the sheriff had carried away just a day earlier.

After the gig, I waited backstage while Brown held court with the usual DJs, friends, and hangers-on. After what seemed like an eternity, James pulled me aside and slipped me a nice holiday bonus. A lot of people who worked for him loved complaining about his fines, but they seldom mention that he would sometime hit you with a bonus. The Lord giveth and the Lord taketh away.

It had been a crazy couple of days, and I was relieved to get back to the hotel, where a few of the J.B.'s had already converged on the lounge. The barmaid was trying to close down and go home; the poor woman had probably spent her New Year's Eve going through the motions for the handful of lonely sad sacks bringing in a new year in a Holiday Inn. She didn't know it yet but, as far as I was concerned, the party was just beginning. To cement the point, I hemmed her in a corner and explained that *she* was now the guest of honor. All she had to do was agree to keep the bar flowing until our bus got ready to pull out. She wanted to resist until I pulled out a couple hundred-dollar bills—one for her and one as a deposit on the bar tab. Her mood instantly brightened. Giddy musicians were flirting with the waitress, would-be partiers were stuffing quarters in the juke box, and there were still a handful of other guests whom the barmaid could rely on for additional tips. Then my friend Lorraine showed. It was the same lounge in which I had last seen her with my pal Gary Johnson. I bought two bottles of champagne, one for me and one for the barmaid to take home. It was her kind of party after all—and mine too. Happy New Year!

20

Ninteen-seventy-two promised to be an interesting year. Like a lot of things in 1970s America, music was changing. Some change is inevitable, a natural evolution, but the changes in black music seemed extra. The rock influence popularized by Sly and his Family Stone and Funkadelic was past the point of being a novelty, even to those who embraced groove-driven funk bands like Ohio Players and Kool and the Gang. Southern soul seemed dated to the youngsters watching Soul Train. As the sales of albums eclipsed singles, self-contained bands took much of the spotlight away from traditional soul men. Solo stars like Curtis Mayfield, Isaac Hayes, Marvin Gaye, and Stevie Wonder, survived only because concept albums afforded them a canvas on which their art and skills could grow.

What mainstream America had cast aside as "race music" just two decades earlier was growing up and diversifying and, for the first time in his career, James Brown had to work at remaining relevant. He was winning that battle thus far, if only because his unique appeal crossed generational boundaries—enough to justify a new nickname, Godfather of Soul. His first singles for Polydor, "Make It Funky" and "I'm a Greedy Man," didn't break any new ground, but any James Brown record dared you not to dance and still didn't sound like anything else on the radio.

James had outlived the career peaks of his soul era peers. Of course, Sam Cooke, Otis Redding, and Little Willie John all died tragically young, but Wilson Pickett, Solomon Burke, and Jackie Wilson were now viewed as oldies acts, their new records all but ignored. Somehow Brown remained contemporary, his stylized funk growing more personal and unique with each new recording. As always, his band played an important role. Fred Wesley's robust trombone solos had become a trademark, and their instrumental releases like "Pass the Peas" and "Gimme Some More" were well received. Only Bobby Byrd's status seemed in doubt.

Thanks to a handful of Brown-produced hit singles, Byrd was developing a marquee value of his own and he was growing anxious to test the waters. James reluctantly let Bobby put his own band together and accept a few solo dates, as long as he remained available to Brown when he needed him. It was no secret that the boss preferred Bobby close by, Byrd's vocal parts on Brown's own "Sex Machine," "Soul Power," and, most recently, "Talkin' Loud and Sayin' Nothing" were as familiar to fans as his own songs.

Bobby, talented and likeable, had been there for James through many years of ups and downs. Convinced the time was finally right for success on his own, the sporadic nature of his outside dates only added to his frustration. I knew the situation would blow up sooner or later.

Behind the scenes, I rooted for him. So did Freddie Holmes, Buddy Nolan, and Bob Patton. Nobody deserved his fifteen minutes of fame more than Bobby Byrd.

I STAYED IN CONTACT WITH MORRIS FINE, and James would periodically suggest that I call Allen Knight to encourage him to settle. Knight's response was always the same: "My lawyer says we sued for six thousand and we'll win six thousand. Why should I accept less?"

James never spoke directly with Fine but, one day, he asked me to send him an autographed copy of "King Heroin," his powerful new anti-drug record. When he was booked to perform the song on Johnny Carson's *Tonight Show*, James asked that I invite Fine to tune in. I guess he thought that demonstrating his humanitarian side might somehow influence the case or, at least, the attorney's efforts. If Morris was impressed, he kept it to himself.

Meanwhile, I was devoting way too much of my time to the case. In order to structure our defense, I had to question venue managers and the memories of our own crew. Then I spent two days in a New York accountant's office, rummaging through box after box of old road receipts. In March, we filed a counter claim, designed to encourage a settlement, but Knight held firm. Most of the original agreements had been personally negotiated between Allen and James, so, if the case went to court, our chances would depend on Brown's testimony. I knew that was a losing proposition. James didn't have patience for facts and figures and would likely be emotional under oath—not a recipe for success, so I kept postponing his appearance. Finally, an exasperated judge vowed the case would eventually be heard with or without Brown's participation. Fine reminded me that he was "somewhat at a loss without my client aiding in his defense."

While I played Johnny Cochran, life went on. The guys in the band got a thrill at the RKO Albee Theater in Brooklyn when jazz legend Miles Davis surfaced backstage. Miles had disappointed jazz purists by fusing rock and rhythm and blues into a hybrid all his own and made no secret of his fondness for Brown's approach to rhythms. During the J.B.'s' instrumental set, Miles got so absorbed in a hypnotic groove that he gradually edged from the wings onto the stage and began directing the band with animated hand movements. At the tune's conclusion, Davis stalked off stage past band leader Fred Wesley and without a greeting muttered, "That drummer was draggin'." Then he spun into James' waiting embrace and they strolled off towards the dressing room—two stubborn trendsetters, arguably the most influential figures in modern black music. Soon thereafter, Miles recorded *On the Corner*, his most R&B-informed music to date.

The winter schedule had offered its usual break from arenas and auditoriums with successful engagements in several theaters and clubs. But, come April, we were back on the one-nighter merry-go-round and our fortunes quickly turned. An Easter show in Houston was cancelled due to slow sales, and we struggled through lackluster gigs in Dallas and several "B" markets.

Brown was puzzled. He had always believed that box office paralleled record sales. But, this time, things were different, his strong record sales contrasted sharply with the diminished marquee value. As far as I was concerned, the enemy was always the same, overexposure—years of playing the same towns with a format that wasn't aging well. That's two strikes against us, which meant it was crucial that our promotion and publicity campaigns be aggressive and strategic, and that wasn't always the case.

Brown's road show was always a cash and carry business. He didn't even trust our office with a business bank account from which to pay operating costs. Instead, each week, we submitted lists of what expenses needed to be paid out of the road proceeds. The system worked as long as the shows were successful. But, if things were slow at the box office, James would arbitrarily refuse to fund certain items. The golden rule was that he would NEVER dig in his pocket to fund the shows. If we didn't earn a profit on the road, the bills didn't get paid.

With business dodgy again, the expense lists became a game of cat and mouse. Expecting delays, I tried anticipating our needs further in advance. Some weeks, Brown would only approve a handful of items, which left us juggling creditors like a bunch of deadbeats. Too often, we had to depend on whatever newspapers, radio, and television stations that would extend credit. What cash we could muster went towards posters, road trips, and the media that required advance payment. The results were predictable, sellouts in markets where we had good credit and problems where we failed to mount proper campaigns.

The boss didn't see our problem as plainly as I did. I begged James to re-think the structure of our business, but his solution was to assign his daughter Deanna's nanny to oversee the office and manage our financial needs! Ms. Sarah Mathis, the new office manager, did have some clerical background and the best of intentions, but she had no idea how to deal with the colorful personalities and politics of our industry. She didn't tolerate bullshit and, believe me, most of the promoters and disc jockeys we dealt with were full of bullshit. Hell, so were we—it was how the game was played and, if you couldn't think on your feet, you would get run over. The Ms. Mathis experiment didn't last too long.

Finally, Brown grudgingly opened a business checking account with Dee Dee as the sole signatory. Opening the account was one thing, but it was pointless without regular deposits from the road, which brings us back to square one, the weekly expense sheets. Mrs. Brown honestly tried to help, but it was a struggle to strike a balance between her new responsibilities and those to her volatile husband, so there were times when she understandably hesitated to press him about business expenses. When he got tired of me asking for cash, I could go home. But, when Dee Dee tried his patience, she already *was* at home, directly in the line of fire. The Browns' squabbles became the thorn in our new system. I couldn't exactly sweat Dee Dee for a check or two when JB had just punctuated an argument of theirs by burning her clothes in a driveway bonfire! Still, it was easier chasing down Dee Dee in Augusta than her husband on the road. I chose to view that as progress.

Our next important show was in Chicago. James got there early and, when he called into the office, I asked him to please review our latest expense sheet—the same expense sheet I'd given Mrs. Brown three weeks earlier. Suddenly, it dawned on James that the list included advertising for gigs less than three weeks away, and he went ballistic.

"What do you mean that advertising hasn't started yet? What am I paying you for? I'm out here working to make this payroll and you're not even promoting these shows? You ain't doin' nothin'! That's what you're doin', nothin'! Nobody told me about these bills."

I tried interrupting. I didn't want to throw Dee Dee under the bus, but I didn't know how else to defend myself. "Mr. Brown, we've been trying to talk to you about these bills and you always say talk to Mrs. Brown."

I barely got it out when I had to raise the phone and his scream-ing voice from my ear. "Mr. Leeds, don't start blaming anything on my wife. Did I hire my wife to promote our shows? Is her name Alan Leeds? Is she a tour director?"

It was a no-win, one of those tirades that just had to play itself out. He knew better, but he refused to take any blame for how we paid our bills. And my patience was wearing thin. I don't know if it was living in Augusta and working in a less-than-professional office, or whether I was simply tired of his drama. But it was getting harder to laugh things off. When Brown finally slammed the phone down, I was as angry as he was.

Not five minutes later, he was on the phone again. I composed myself for a minute before picking it up, but his mood had changed completely. "You know, I can't figure where we went wrong," he said calmly, as if we hadn't yet spoken. "But we know better. We're out here in a rough economy. Folks ain't got no money. That's what's hurting us. Mr. Bobbit is going to be in Chicago tonight, so you fly up here and we'll meet after the show. Bring along all the bills you need paid and let's get this mess back together."

Then, his voice revealing the rage he had been masquerading, he sternly barked, "You be up here tonight, you hear?"

Every direct flight to Chicago was sold out. I got a connection through Atlanta that left in two hours—no time to go home and pack. Flight; hectic connection; no time for food; another flight; pouring rain when I landed at O'Hare. I knocked on JB's dressing room door just minutes after he'd gotten off stage. After the obligatory visit with locals, he directed me and Charles Bobbit to follow him to his hotel, which was all the way back at O'Hare.

It was nearly 2 a.m. by the time we settled into Brown's suite. It had been a long day and I was apprehensive about how I'd handle another dose of his tyranny. He had seemed relaxed at the gig, but I wasn't about to lower my guard. I came prepared for a long, detailed meeting. Bobbit and I spread out calendars and worksheets for each upcoming date.

Then Dee Dee magically appeared with giant bowls of ice cream and sweating glasses of cold beer. James casually raised a few obscure questions about our advertising campaigns and then promised to handle the mounting list of expenses. Then he abruptly adjourned the meeting. No tantrums. No lectures. Not even a hint of frustration. Chicago had been a good show. His wife was here. And he had ice cream and beer. I guess that meant life was good after all. Then he asked if I wanted to fly with him to our St. Louis show the next afternoon.

That's when I realized that things had changed. Ordinarily, I would jump at any opportunity to fly with the boss in his Learjet, but the novelty had worn off. And I had no interest in getting stuck in St. Louis on a Saturday night. I stared him straight in the eye and calmly explained that I would do us both more good if I flew home and got some rest. Bobbit drove me to the Delta terminal and a red eye to Atlanta. With a lucky connection to Augusta, I was home by ten o'clock Saturday morning—WITH the money to pay our bills.

21

Augusta was wearing on me. There were some delightful people there, and I had my share of fun, but I'm a city boy. I missed major league sports, entertainment options, museums, window shopping, and a wide variety of restaurants. Most of all, I missed the energy and cultural diversity of a real city.

I knew James wouldn't understand or sympathize with me. In fact, he was spending MORE time in Augusta. He and Dee Dee seemed happy, he had radio station WRDW to look after and he had even discovered a local studio he could record in. On the other hand, idle time was not his friend. On any given evening, he was liable to tear into the office and collect the team for what turned into long showy dinners at one of his favorite restaurants. The interminable small talk was almost always about him. Sometimes he showed up earlier in the day to talk business. Or not.

One warm afternoon, James barged into the office and asked if I could break away for a couple hours. He didn't say why. I assumed he had business on his mind as I climbed into his new Mercedes. A few blocks from downtown, he jerked into a large indoor parking garage and motioned for me to get out of the car. Greeting the attendant by name, he asked that his El Dorado be brought down. Soon, a sparkling, black-on-black Cadillac cruised towards us. Moments later, we pulled back into traffic. As he toured the twenty or so blocks that make up Augusta's "Terry," the district in which he'd been raised, we made small talk until I realized he had made a circle and we were back at the garage. Five minutes later, we were back in the Terry, this time in his bright yellow, classic Excalibur. Arched behind the wheel with a hustler's lean, James waved to friends and strangers alike, many of whom had already recognized him in the El Dorado. Some were idling on corners, some waiting for buses, as we drove by, once again…and again…and again. A Model A, a Corvette, a Rolls Royce, all belonging to the Godfather of Soul. You name it, we rode in it.

It was harmless fun. James may have coveted their adoration, but he honestly loved his community and the people in it. And he was firmly convinced his visibility offered a positive inspiration, particularly to youngsters whose life decisions were still ahead of them. I don't doubt that he was right.

It was during another joyride in Augusta that I witnessed a different side of James that I hadn't seen before. We were in traffic on Broad Street, stopped at a red light alongside a telephone company truck. Without warning, Brown jumped out of the car and confronted the startled telephone man behind the wheel. "You might as well go home. I know what you're doin'," he yelled. "You tell your bosses they can't get me. I'm always going to be one step ahead of you."

Then James got back in the car and pulled off, leaving a stunned telephone repair man wondering what the hell had just happened. "You know they trying to get me," he told me. "Mr. Leeds, they got cameras everywhere. We must be very careful."

Brown's superstitions and phobias were well known inside our camp. I had once been instructed to evict a woman from backstage at a gig somewhere in South Carolina. It was apparent from her conversation that she had known James a long time. Whatever their history, Bobby Byrd told me she was a *Geechee*, and James was leery of Geechee women, that he feared she had put a spell on him.

Everyone who worked for JB got a kick out of his, shall we say, eccentricities. These were the kinds of stories we couldn't wait to share with each other, and we all had some. Ever since the IRS had come down on him for back taxes, Brown was convinced he was being spied on. It wasn't an outlandish concept, given how the media had uncovered the FBI's surveillance of just about any black man of influence, but I'm not sure Hoover's boys operated the way James pictured. A BellSouth truck?

Or, for that matter, a tooth? Once, he came into the office after getting a tooth filled. He was shaking his head and muttering that he could no longer trust his longtime dentist. "Mr. Leeds, I KNOW what they put in that tooth," he said convincingly. "That transmitter in my tooth will tell them everywhere I go and everything I'm thinking. Pretty soon, they're going to know what I'm doing before I do it!"

In May, I grabbed an opportunity to meet the show in Pittsburgh and spend a little time with old pal Brother Matt, who had the local promotion well under control. The only sour note at "Soul Bowl III" was a less-than-stellar performance by our comedian Clay Tyson. Tyson was a stoner, liked a toke or two (or three) before hitting the stage. And the sprawling Civic Arena had many quiet spots to light up some of the herb that finds its way backstage at every gig.

Halfway through his act, though, Clay began hesitating, then slightly staggering, as he tried untangling the microphone cord from his feet. When he started repeating jokes, emcee Danny Ray realized something was amiss and slid on stage. When Tyson started uncontrollably giggling at a punch line he hadn't even delivered yet, Danny reached and took his mic away. Then, in his deep, carnival barker monotone, he said, "Ahhhh, yes, ladies and gentlemen. Let's hear it for Brother Tyson. We can see he's a sick man tonight, but he still tried very hard for you. He just couldn't make it. You can see, he's a very sick man. Claaaaayyy Tyson, ladies and gentlemen. Give Brother Tyson a big hand for giving it a try!"

Drummer John Starks guided the confused comic off stage. There was concern because Tyson had a history of health issues, but it didn't take long to figure out that he was okay—just a little dizzy from his cocktail of Thai stick and stage lights.

Later on, I asked Matt whose weed got Tyson so stoned. He shrugged his shoulders pretending not to know, then pointed silently at a plastic baggie on the table in my hotel room. It was nice to be home.

In June, the show returned to Africa, including a first-time visit to Zaire. Once again, James left the Motherland on cloud nine. His receptions there never failed to massage his ego, and coming back to "reality" could be deflating. This time, Polydor took the brunt.

James had expected the label to rush out "Get on the Good Foot," the single he had recorded a few weeks earlier. When he got to New York and discovered the release had been bumped until July, JB went nuclear. Brown didn't hold Polydor President Jerry Schoenbaum responsible. Instead, he was under the impression (or chose to believe) that the decision had been made over Schoenbaum's head. So he directed an angry letter to the company seniors—the "Germans," as he usually referred to them. James wasn't about to let the label break their agreement that he schedule his own releases.

> *"You have failed as an r&b company. You don't know that part of the business. Mr. Schoenbaum knows the business, but he doesn't have a staff. He's a good man and a real brother but that's not enough in the record business. Unless we, James Brown Productions can set up our own singles and albums, control our own advertising, and control release dates, we are going to move all of James Brown Productions within twenty-four hours. From now on, I'll have to do it myself or I'll have to go see a couple of black lawyers."*

It may not have been wise to play Schoenbaum against his superiors, but I was amazed how quickly "Good Foot" shipped to radio, mere days after he got the letter.

I had met the gang in New York upon their return from Zaire and a stopover in Paris. Despite a jet-lagged and emotionally spent entourage, JB called a recording session their first night back. Though I sympathized with the band dreading one of Brown's sometimes-marathon studio visits, I always enjoyed them. The fan in me was still fascinated by his spontaneous creative process and there was always the possibility that I might witness something special, the next "Papa's Bag," "Cold Sweat," or "Sex Machine." I had also made it a personal mission to document his sessions, organizing data that wasn't properly preserved elsewhere due to his erratic and independent means of making records. There was no one place where anyone could research the dates, locations, and personnel of his countless recordings, so I was determined to fix that. Thus, I had dug in old files at King, interviewed musicians and engineers, past and present, Xeroxed musician union reports, chased down any and every bit of data I could find that related to any session Brown had ever been part of. As a result, whenever I was physically at a session, I didn't sit idly. I took notes.

The purpose of this session was to record new singles for the J.B.'s ("Giving Up Food for Funk") and a growingly restless Bobby Byrd ("Never Get Enough"). They had been rehearsing the tunes on tour, so both went down easily—easily enough that James had extra studio time on his hands.

The boss was in an unusually pensive mood and suddenly decided to record a new version of "Please, Please, Please." With Bobby Byrd at the organ, the J.B.'s kicked off a shuffle, a slower tempo than when they played it on the road. The exhausted band wasn't into it; I remember Jabo Starks sarcastically rolling his eyes, probably wondering why in the world they needed to cut "Please" for the umpteenth time. Then, about two minutes into the groove, James began ad-libbing a personal memoir about his and Byrd's early days in Georgia when they first sang the song, name checked all the original Famous Flames, and reminisced about their first trip to the Apollo. Maybe because he was tired, Brown's voice had an unusually rough hue, like a raspy gospel preacher. His startling tone sent chills to the few of us still hanging around A & R Studios in the wee hours of the Manhattan night.

It was common for James to embark on impromptu rants during recordings; sometimes they worked and sometimes they didn't. But this was different. He was in a zone and taking us to church, his phrasing and timing letter perfect. Those of us still hanging in the booth—Charles Bobbit, Bob Patton, Johnny Terry, and God knows who else—were captivated.

When Rev. Brown finished his sermon, he quickly called it a night. The track timed over twelve minutes and was released on the two-disc "Get on the Good Foot" album. Unfortunately, it was completely ignored. A rather polite mix failed to entirely capture the spirit in that studio, but it wasn't really about the band or even the old song itself. It was about James' uncanny, unplanned, and unexpected vocal performance—one of those perfect storms that best illustrated his innate genius.

WHILE BROWN WAS ABROAD, we had been able to work at our own calm pace and were confident that his first shows back would get us on our own good foot. Greensboro, Charlotte, and Richmond had always been dependable markets for the James Brown Show. Initially, I didn't think I'd have to worry about Greensboro because we had sold the date outright to an aspiring promoter from Norfolk.

Ever since our New Year's show, this fella had been pestering us about fronting some gigs. He wanted Richmond and Norfolk, but I explained that we had obligations to long-standing partnerships in those markets. Finally, I told him that, if he could find some financial backing, we could consider selling him a date outright. I really didn't think he had access to that kind of money, hoping it would end his annoying phone calls. But, to my surprise, the promoter hustled up a star-struck attorney friend with deep pockets and they offered to buy any date we had available in Virginia or the Carolinas. Greensboro was a logical choice, since we didn't have a regular front man there. We'd collect our fee in advance and advertising and ticket sales would be the promoter's responsibility.

I never could understand why some folks were so desperate to get into promoting shows. I suppose they assumed it was easy money. But, if it was that easy, we'd all be filthy rich. In the real world, promoting shows was based on a slender profit margin and a business model shaped by experience and relationships. It was also an industry viewed as somewhat of a closed shop. Venues and the advertising media would accept anyone's money, but there were intangibles that favored those of us who were regular players. For example, we always made sure there was some kind of incentive to motivate radio personalities to get behind our promotions and give extra exposure to our records. That usually translated to paying them to make stage appearances on our shows. Since we controlled our stage, that wasn't something an outside promoter could provide without our cooperation. In a sense, I felt it was insulting when an outsider thought they could just buy their way in. We worked hard at this game.

Of course, the only way for a promoter like the guy from Norfolk to learn that lesson was to roll the dice. Roll them he did, and, for whatever reason, his Greensboro date was soft, the leanest date we'd had there in years. When I arrived at the Greensboro Coliseum, Mr. Promoter started ranting about how I had intentionally sold him a show I knew would lose money. I couldn't believe my ears. I had all but begged him to leave well enough alone. HE was the one who chased me all the way to Augusta for an opportunity to buy a date.

He continued grumbling until I had enough and told him to shut up. The promoter jumped in my face, but I didn't blink. Before he could make another move, his lawyer partner grabbed him and sat him down like a little kid. Meanwhile, my peripheral vision caught Freddie Holmes in the corner with his hand inside his coat pocket. I knew what Freddie carried there—and it wasn't a water pistol. Another wannabe promoter bites the dust. It's always sad, but the industry is riddled with this kind of roadkill.

James had decided to spend the weekend commuting to and from Augusta, so I decided to fly back and forth with him. The next evening, our Charlotte show sold out and, on the flight home, we discussed Richmond. It was our first time in Virginia since New Year's and JB was a little leery. I assured him that Allen Knight had no grounds on which to tamper with another date. Unconvinced, he asked me to fly up first thing the next morning and keep my eyes open.

What the boss didn't know was that I had been urging Knight to come see us at the Coliseum. Six months had passed, and nobody had won anything except all the lawyers. I felt that, with all their history, if I could get Allen and James face to face, we stood a good chance of settling things, once and for all.

But, first, I had to get to Richmond from Augusta—the only way was a connection through Charlotte! The same Charlotte I had left with the boss just eight hours earlier. Then my flight was late out of Augusta and I missed the connection—the only flight that would get me to Richmond before the gig. I had no choice but to rent a car and dash the 300 miles to Richmond.

I made it—just made it—minutes before James arrived. It was our first time in Richmond's sparkling new coliseum, and there wasn't an empty seat. Sure enough, after the show, there was Allen Knight lurking around. I told the boss, who first pretended that he had no intention of seeing him. Knight kept waiting. And waiting. And waiting. After a point, I was surprised Allen stayed. Over an hour passed. Our bus and truck were loaded and gone. The semi-darkened coliseum was empty except for my old radio pal Ben Miles, a lone security guard, and our own entourage.

When James finally left his dressing room, Knight was right there to meet him. Without exchanging a word, JB ushered Allen into a nearby doorway that turned out to be a men's room. Danny Ray and Henry Stallings automatically fell in step behind the boss, but he waved them off. Henry looked at me wondering what this was all about. I simply put a finger to my lips and folded my arms. Five minutes passed, and then James leaned out and motioned for me to join them.

Inside the small bathroom, I found James and Allen standing around the single commode. Nobody had to tell me they had reached an agreement. I wedged myself into the tight cubicle, maneuvering my briefcase into a makeshift desk spread across our knees, propped up by three legs planted on the edge of the toilet. James dictated the terms of the impromptu settlement to which Knight nodded his approval. Allen was about to sign it when James suddenly reached across and grabbed the pen.

"Wait a minute. We need a witness," he barked in my direction. "Go get Ben Miles in here."

In the years I'd been gone from Richmond, Miles had risen from disc jockey to general manager of his station. And, of course, he had known all three of us for many years. Since he didn't have a horse in this race, Ben seemed a logical choice for a witness. But I knew better. Ben is cautious by nature, and I was afraid he'd think to get involved might jeopardize his position at his station. Before I found Miles, James got impatient and summoned the coliseum guard.

"He's almost the same as a cop. That's better," Brown offered as I ran back to his side.

But the guard, frustrated at the late hour, had other ideas. "I ain't signing nothing. I don't know you guys or what I'm signing. Wrap your business up, so we can all get the hell out of here."

At that point, we all decided I should just witness it myself and call it a night. Keep in mind, in those days six grand was still a nice piece of change. After six months of bickering, stress, legal maneuvers, and attorney costs, the dispute was settled in a toilet. I wasn't sure if that was a metaphor for anything, but both James and Allen seemed appropriately relieved.

I rode with James to the airport and, in the car, he slipped me a hundred-dollar bill and said, "Thanks for handling that. We really got the best of old Knight. Nobody will ever fool around with our money again once they hear what happened."

I wasn't sure how to take all of that; their agreement was to split the six thousand, hardly one-sided. And I don't think anyone else in the world was clocking this relatively minor case. But, on a personal note, a hundred dollars?

Brown must have sensed I was unhappy because he changed the subject, but not really. "You know, if Greensboro had gone into percentage, you would have had a helluva bonus this week."

THAT was when I almost wanted to throw the C-note back at him. I didn't ordinarily campaign for bonuses. My salary was fair—just pay me for what I do. But ever since Denzil Skinner told me our money in Norfolk was attached, I had been personally responsible for everything good that had happened in this case. Without my efforts, we would have defaulted months ago and lost a lot more than the $6K. And, if I hadn't lured Knight to the gig, that money would still be sitting in Virginia. And that's all my efforts were worth? A lousy hundred dollars?

I went home more disillusioned than angry. I still loved my gig, and I loved my stingy-ass boss, but I couldn't say the same for Augusta. I couldn't put my finger on it, but something about being in Augusta seemed to make James needier. There were too many phone calls at night and too many weekends he demanded I accompany him to gigs. My job was never intended to be a nine-to-five, but the infringement on my personal life was getting out of hand. I had no idea what was next, but I could feel my days in Augusta becoming numbered.

I did come back from Virginia to some good news. James told me he had made a deal with Bob Patton to help with some dates on a consultant basis. Patton wanted back but he didn't want Augusta. Just as I had rescued Bob in 1970, I knew he'd have my back now.

22

Bob Patton's first assignment was a string of West Coast shows. The dates were only mildly successful, and, by early August, James was back in Augusta and irritable. I had news for him: our upcoming shows weren't going to be much better. Once again, cash flow was an issue. Dee Dee was tired of getting caught in the middle and, as usual, JB didn't want to hear about it.

My concerns ran deeper than the immediate dates, long-range concerns I felt nobody shared, except maybe Patton. But, as a freelancer, he no longer shared my full-blown vested interest. It was clear to me that continued success on the road, let alone any growth, depended on revising our dated, formulaic approach to touring and recording. Since things had worked for so long, James and everyone else had become complacent. They didn't know anything else.

It still seemed like he could write funky dance hits forever, but they came so easily and frequently that most were quickly forgotten. Recent hits like "Make It Funky," "There It Is," and "I'm a Greedy Man" sold tons of singles but then disappeared, leaving little effect at the box office.

Furthermore, R&B record buyers had shifted their focus from singles to albums. JB's old-school devotion to singles meant little beyond radio and dance floors. Trying to attract more whites to our concerts

209

might help but, in 1972, pop radio was the least funky place in the world. I really didn't know how we could make a mark in that world without Brown willingly courting the rock media. My suggestion that we seek bookings on the rock circuit, once again, fell on deaf ears.

"How can we survive playing clubs like the Fillmore that only hold two thousand people?" James argued.

His numbers were right. We couldn't with our entourage and pay-roll. But, since it was so difficult getting his records on white radio, an occasional rock gig might be a smart investment—a loss leader, if you will. I even considered that we might explore an "alternative" show with a smaller, tighter, more economical production. It wasn't just about size or nickels and dimes. Obviously, I never forgot Brown was the artist and always supported Brown's creative vision; I just thought our business model was stagnant. Unfortunately, my thoughts were way too far outside the box for anyone in our camp to rally behind. It wasn't that I was only attached to my ideas; I just knew we had to do something different. Dwindling ticket sales already suggested it was just a matter of time before we'd be downsizing, whether we liked it or not. I just thought it was smarter to do so proactively, with a creative face, rather than out of necessity.

The fact that my concerns had no forum, no sympathetic ears, just increased my frustration. I shouldn't have felt that way. This wasn't about me; it was about James Brown, an amazingly gifted artist who stubbornly held to what he thought was best for himself, and he had every right to do so. The problem was that he couldn't see that it was going to stop working. My problem was how much I cared. Re-inventing the show could have been stimulating, but only if we were all on the same page. I wondered, if we had been outside of our cocoon, say, around industry peers in New York or L.A., whether James and some of the gang might have been more inspired. Our little provincial world in Augusta was just too far out of the loop.

There were other reasons I wasn't in love with living in Georgia—there were simply too many places where the "New South" wasn't so new. One gorgeous summer afternoon, Johnny Terry, Buddy Nolan, and I decided to drive to a gig we had in Savannah. Savannah is a delightful town—the ocean, great food, wonderful architecture—but it was still Georgia.

There was no interstate between Augusta and Savannah, just an old rural highway, U.S. 25. After a while, we stopped for some cold drinks at a rusty old gas station, the kind you see in episodes of *In the Heat of the Night*, set at a crossroads with no other buildings in sight. As we were paying the attendant, a rickety pickup truck pulled in with three rednecks in the cab and a couple more sitting in the back. The truck was bathed in decals, most of which seemed to include either a skull and crossbones or a Confederate flag. Sure enough, as soon as they spotted us, they spit out their toothpicks and the catcalls began. One whistled and said, "Ooh wee, ain't they a pretty bunch." Another noticed my Afro and hollered, "Hey, boy, how many birds live in that hair of yours?"

Up north, I knew how to defend myself, knew how to read an adversary. But I had read too many horror stories about the South. I was a duck out of water and scared shitless. I gritted my teeth and got in the car. We really had no way of determining whether these good ol' boys were really spoiling for a fight or just running their mouths, but we were three unarmed men in suits and ties, and this bunch of yahoos looked like they'd spent their lives doing chin-ups on their old oak trees. Johnny was said to be pretty deft with a switchblade, but the only one of us with any fighting credentials was Buddy. Back in the day, he was around boxing in Philly, sparred with some name fighters, and worked as corner man for welterweight contender Gil Turner. But Nolan was fifty-plus years old, overweight, and diabetic—not a resume for a bodyguard. And, by the way, Mr. Nolan and Mr. Terry were unusually quiet. I didn't like our odds—time to vamoose.

I got behind the wheel and hauled ass out of the dirt driveway and back onto Highway 25. The Johnny Rebels took off right behind us. Well, make your bed, then you gotta sleep in it. The chase was on. I was fairly certain their truck couldn't keep up with our El Dorado but, as we edged past 90 MPH, I began to worry about an accident. They did fall behind but were still in the rearview mirror when I spotted a state trooper ahead, idling in the lot of some backwoods barbeque joint. I hit the brakes and squealed in beside the cop car.

As I got out, the pickup truck slowed down and turned around. I thought just maybe the trooper would want to chase them, so I excitedly explained, "We were minding our own business, just going to Savannah and they threatened us, then they chased us for miles, at high speeds, could have caused accidents—"

The trooper calmly waved his hand in my face, cutting me off. "Hell, lookin' at you three, I woulda chased you too," he said. "Y'all just go ahead to Savannah. Them boys were just havin' fun. They ain't thinkin' 'bout you no more." So much for gorgeous afternoons.

Obviously, there is racism everywhere, and I couldn't deny that Augusta was pleasant in small doses, but I just wanted to breathe some different air. The question was how, without losing my job. I'd be happy with a deal like Patton's: work as a freelancer from wherever I decided to plant myself. But I knew James wanted me in the office, so I decided to resign—trusting that, after the dust settled, we could broker a compromise that would keep me involved. Writing the letter of resignation was difficult. I was gambling that Brown wouldn't just get angry and lose my number. Or, worse yet, feel abandoned and hold a grudge. I decided to keep it simple and as far from anything personal as possible. Rather than dissing Augusta, I argued that being away from the industry heartbeat was costing us. I left the door open for him to offer a solution.

I went into the office on a Monday morning and gave my letter to Mrs. Brown. I knew how James hated being broadsided, so I suspected he would ask me to immediately take my things and leave, but I assured Dee Dee that I would remain available and willing to aid in a transition, that everyone should feel free to call me any time they had questions about the upcoming dates. Sure enough, after Dee Dee read James my letter, he told her to collect my office keys and change the locks.

A few days later, he rehired Johnny Terry. I decided to hang around Augusta for a few weeks until James was home from a string of West Coast shows. One afternoon, when I knew he was scheduled to fly out for a gig, I drove to the airport and intercepted him as he was boarding his jet. He probably assumed I was there to beg for my job back—that's what I would have thought—but I just wanted to apologize for the suddenness of my resignation. I wanted to make sure he knew how much I valued his years of mentoring and the opportunities he had provided me, that my leaving was nothing personal and I was more than willing, even anxious to explore working some of his dates on a freelance basis. His face suggested more disappointment than the frustration that was in his voice. He knew me well enough to know, deep down, that living in Augusta was a no compute.

"You know I love you, son, but I'm sorry to hear that. You're making a big mistake. You're missing a chance to make a lot of money down here. Augusta is virgin territory and we're going to lock it up and produce every show that comes through here. And we're getting hot again. You should have seen the shows in California."

I loved his eternal optimism, but I couldn't help wondering how much of this stuff he actually believed. Did he really think we who worked for him were that gullible? And he wasn't nearly finished.

"I read your letter. You can't fool me. You're not a detail man; that's what the problem is. You've got creative ideas—too many ideas. But the detail work is too much for you. But that's what I need right now, leg work—someone like Mr. Terry who isn't afraid to get his hands dirty."

Then he suddenly flipped the script.

"You know, you might want to see a doctor. I feel like you're getting sick. Your face is drawn in—that's poison in your teeth. You must see a dentist. Remember what happened to Bud Hobgood? I'm telling you, I see it in your teeth. A man with poor teeth ain't got nothin'."

I have to admit I got a little emotional. Part of me felt I was leaving unfinished business, and I was stubborn (or foolish) enough to think that, under different circumstances, I could help change things for the better.

I thanked him for his concern and assured him there was nothing wrong with me or my teeth. Then I asked him if he was satisfied that I had left his office in good shape and if there was anything else he needed me to do.

"You talk to Mr. Bobbit about that. I need you for some of these dates we have coming up. Mr. Bobbit can help you and Mr. Patton sort it out."

Whew! I wasn't persona non grata after all; my plan had worked. But, of course, JB wasn't still wasn't finished.

"I got something else for you to do. I'm letting Bobby Byrd go. He's putting his own band together again. I know you always been soft for Bobby. In fact, you're probably part of why he thinks he can make it without me. But he don't know what he's doin'. You go over there and manage him. Since you both want to be big shots, you might as well go out there and learn something together. It ain't going to be what you think it is, Mr. Leeds. If I'm having trouble selling tickets, that means nobody is selling tickets!"

I guess he had forgotten about those California shows. Whatever. Helping Byrd would be fun. Mission accomplished.

23

James was right about Byrd's solo career being short-lived. He had a terrific band and his records were successful enough to get club bookings, but he needed a big hit to reach the next level, a level that could support his overhead. Of course, he was still signed to James Brown Productions, which meant his recordings were still at JB's whim. If Bobby had been a free agent, he probably could have gotten a deal with a label like Atlantic or Stax, whose stable of writers might have supplied him the kind of material that propelled the careers of artists like Wilson Pickett and Johnnie Taylor. That wasn't in the cards, but Bobby was determined to give it his all.

Universal got busy booking one-nighters for Byrd in Florida and the Carolinas. Then Jack Bart got Bobby a week in the Apollo co-starring with the "new" Miracles, their first appearance after Smokey Robinson went solo.

Motown's Edwin Starr was one of several support acts on the bill, but he couldn't afford to bring his own band. Always the team player, Bobby suggested that his band could play behind Starr. I wasn't crazy about the idea, preferring that the band's focus be 100 percent geared to Bobby, but quickly convinced Edwin's road manager to throw us a piece of change as gratitude. Byrd saw it as a win-win.

As luck would have it, James happened to be in New York. He sent word that he'd be coming to the evening show and asked me to make sure the Apollo management reserved some seats. The news spread quickly backstage: the Godfather was coming! In a sense, it was the last thing Bobby needed on the opening day of his most important booking. If James had been the type to simply lend moral support, it would have been fine, but Bobby and I knew only too well that our fearless leader's presence was bound to bring drama. We didn't need the stress.

Sure enough, shortly after the 7:30 show began, the opening act's turn was utterly disrupted by a commotion in the audience—James, Danny Ray, Leon Austin, and Lyn Collins ceremoniously storming down the aisle to the delight of everyone in the house. Once things calmed down, James worked his way back to Byrd's dressing room, where he quickly made a sarcastic remark to me about something trivial and then started interrogating Bobby about every detail of his act. He asked all the right questions, but the conversation belonged at a rehearsal, not minutes before show time. Finally, Bobby cut him off and asked if he'd be willing to join him on stage. "My fellas know 'Sex Machine,' so we can do that one, if you feel like it."

Bobby knew allowing James to get some "house" (audience appreciation) would be appealing. Brown nodded, slapped us five, and escorted his posse to their seats. Just then, Edwin Starr bounced on stage. JB spotted Bobby's band, made a U-turn, and raced backstage with a puzzled Danny Ray in tow. As irate as I've ever seen him, he lit into me. "How can you let that happen? That band is too good to play behind anybody else. I told you Bobby don't know what he's doing, but I expected you to look out for him. Go distract that emcee out of the way and tell Byrd to hurry and get dressed. Mr. Ray got to bring Bobby on."

JB mumbled something to Danny and stormed back to the house. I couldn't argue about the band, but Byrd wasn't worried. He trusted that his fellas wouldn't hit high gear until he got in front of them. The bottom line was that Bobby wanted the extra bucks we got for loaning them out.

I didn't move. Bobby was already dressed and stage-ready, and we all assumed that Starr had at least three more songs. But, just as Edwin finished his opening number, Danny strolled on stage and grabbed the nearest microphone.

"Let's hear it for Edwin Starr, ladies and gentlemen," Ray shouted to the confused audience. "Edwin Starr! He'll be back tomorrow with his own band and really turn it on for you. One more time, let's hear it for Edwin Starr!"

Bewildered, humiliated, then furious, Starr stalked off stage yelling to no one in particular, "Where is that fuckin' James Brown? I know that devil is behind this. They warned me about him. Where the hell is that James Brown?"

Meanwhile, the little Sammy Davis lookalike, the most familiar emcee in Apollo lore, began his ceremonious introduction. "Ladies and gentlemen, the Apollo Theater is proud to present a young man you all know and love from his many years with the James Brown show. This young man is internationally recognized as Soul Brother #2. You've heard him on 'Sex Machine,' 'Soul Power,' and his own hits 'Keep On Doin' and 'I Need Help.' Now he's got his very own revue, we know him as the man with the word, let's welcome BOBBY BYRD!!!"

Bobby was sensational, the finely tuned band kicking ass. Halfway through his act, he acknowledged his mentor, who was comfortably seated in the front row, Lyn Collins and the hulking Leon Austin flanking his sides. James climbed on stage and ad-libbed a long tribute to his life-long pal. Finally, he suggested they do "Sex Machine" but he couldn't leave well enough alone; he just had to throw Byrd a curveball. JB insisted they reverse their vocal roles, instructing Bobby to sing the lead. Bobby stumbled a bit with the lyrics, a part he'd never sung or rehearsed, but Brown jumped right in with the call and response and soon had the entire audience singing, "Get On Up."

It turned out to be a nice touch to a hot gig, perhaps the peak of Byrd's 1972 crack at fame and fortune. Tied hopelessly to James Brown Productions, Bobby wasn't able to muster another hit after "Keep On Doin'," and his marquee value soon faded. It wouldn't be until the late 1980s that his raw talent and well-earned legacy rewarded him with a successful solo career.

But, on that cool, fall night at the Apollo, Bobby killed. And James, who had gotten his propers, wasn't about to spoil things by going backstage and having to face a sulking Edwin Starr. At the end of "Sex Machine," he jumped back into the crowd, grabbed Lyn and Leon, and ran up the aisle, out into the Harlem night.

24

My arrangement with James continued throughout 1973, 1974, and into 1975. I would cherry pick cities in which to promote his shows on a percentage basis and, before long, I was making more money than I ever had on his payroll. I was also free to accept outside projects, such as when Buddy Nolan occasionally hired me to road manage the group he was now managing, Harold Melvin & the Blue Notes.

Working for Harold and the "Notes" was an adventure. The guys were smoothly professional on stage, but there was a soap opera behind the scenes. Harold owned the group and ruled with an iron fist. The four Notes were on modest salaries, so Harold prospered, even though he wasn't the sexy lead singer that had fans swooning to their records. That would have been young Theodore "Teddy" Pendergrass, the group's newest member. It doesn't take a genius to predict how show business egos would stir up that volatile set of circumstances. Harold and the other Notes, Lloyd, Bernie, and Larry, envied the attention Teddy was getting. Meanwhile, Teddy and the three Notes resented Harold taking home the bulk of the money. On top of all that, the group's real success was less than a year old, and all the fellas still had various hustles home in Philly. Not a recipe for a good outcome.

Despite the backstage drama, when I came aboard, the group was celebrating its burst of success every which way. Five tall, attractive guys who were real "players" anyway, the girls the Blue Notes attracted were top drawer, and there was plenty of spillover for our small entourage. Another perk was getting to know Harold's stunningly attractive wife. Ovelia Melvin ran his office in Philly, and I conjured up every possible excuse to do business there, just so I could look at her—I mean, she was THAT bad! Hell, every guy I knew in Philly was doing the same thing. Needless to say, it was always a very busy office.

The group's splashiest engagement while I was with them was a June week in the Copacabana. My brother, Eric, was in New York with me and so was Bob Patton. James was home in Augusta but, somehow, we all converged on Brown's offices at Polydor where we ran into his son, Teddy.

Everyone who worked for James loved Teddy; he was smart and personable beyond his years. In fact, he seemed to enjoy hanging with older guys, particularly those who worked for his Dad. I suppose we were all the uncles he didn't otherwise have. Teddy idolized his father, but it wasn't easy being the son of the Godfather of Soul. The young Mr. Brown certainly wasn't above escaping the uber discipline that ruled their Augusta home. In this case, Teddy and two pals were passing through Manhattan on their way to Montreal and a vacation from college.

It was a fun reunion; it had been a while since Teddy, Buddy, Bob, and I had been together under the same roof. Teddy and Eric were close in age and had known each other in Augusta, so young Brown tried persuading young Leeds to accompany him to Canada, promising a bunch of cute girls and a good time. Eric opted to stay in New York, so Teddy said so long and headed to Canada.

Later that night, long after I'd crawled into my hotel bed, the phone rang. I tried clearing the cobwebs to answer it—one of those times when you have no idea how long it's been ringing. It was Buddy, his voice strangely stammering.

"Have you, I mean, you got the, um, radio on? Have you heard?" he asked.

Rainman would have known something was wrong. Middle-of-the-night news is never good. Buddy's natural voice was boyish and when he was upset it squeaked like Mickey Mouse.

"Teddy's dead," he said, the words slow and separate.

It took me a minute, but my mind went to Teddy Pendergrass. He was rolling in the fast lane where, in the tragic tradition of Sam Cooke, it was easy to imagine something horrific. But, no. Buddy sighed, as it dawned on me that I had the wrong Teddy. My God, he meant Teddy Brown!

"They wrecked the Camaro. Upstate near the border. All three of them died instantly. Put on WBLS. They cryin' on the radio."

Teddy's half-brother Daryl, who played guitar in their Dad's band in the 1990s, has written that Teddy was mysteriously murdered, shot before the accident. But that's utter nonsense. Every bit of evidence supported that the driver had fallen asleep at the wheel.

I was in shock, the news so unimaginable it took me several minutes before I could digest it enough to cry. I pictured the happy, healthy, carefree Teddy I had been laughing with just hours earlier, full of the self-confidence and lust for life so typical of a youngster. A youngster just like my brother. Damn! Eric! My brother could have been in that car! I woke him and shared the grim news.

Next, I called Charles Bobbit to check in on the boss. Charles was also in New York and he too had seen Teddy earlier. His unenviable task was to wait for JB and his father to come north so they could go upstate and claim the body. Bobbit had to identify the remains—a duty so morbid, so demoralizing, so unjust that even Soul Brother #1 couldn't handle it.

I have no idea how James maintained his composure through the next few days, but he did. On June 21st, I met Patton and Hal Neely in Atlanta for the drive to the funeral in Toccoa, Georgia. If I had considered Macon and Augusta small towns, it was because I hadn't seen Toccoa. We got there early enough to grab a quick lunch at a greasy spoon where a bevy of local cops happened to share the counter with us. One stood up and asked us what time the funeral was. I suppose he couldn't fathom any other reason for three obvious strangers to be in town.

The Toccoa police had deputized a few locals to help manage the expected traffic. Bus after bus passed through the heart of town, packed with Teddy's friends and classmates from Paine College in Augusta. JB's staff, associates and friends, past and present, arrived from all over the country.

Sylvester Keels, one of the original Famous Flames and a life-long resident of Toccoa, conducted the music. The modest Mt. Zion Baptist Church was standing room only, and the service was piped into an adjoining annex for the overflow crowd. Scores more stood outside in the sun, straining to hear the ceremony through the open church doors. It was unbearably hot inside. Older women fanned themselves as James and his first wife, Teddy's mother, Velma, were led to their seats. As he neared the front of the church and spotted the coffin, JB finally broke down. He fell to his knees in the middle of the aisle, crying out loud, eerily reminiscent of what he did for a living, night after night. I cringed for him, certain that the irony had struck him as he struggled to regain his composure.

After the burial, Brown stoically held court. These were moments that belonged to James and the friends and family in Georgia that went back before this soul brother was #1. I leaned in, gave him a hug, and headed back to Atlanta. The next evening, James was on stage in Detroit, as scheduled.

The show didn't change much in 1973. James always added his latest singles to the set list, but there were nights when he was on automatic pilot. I even thought I sensed a trace of self-parody seeping into Brown's act—something the public and media didn't recognize yet. The set list wasn't the only thing that was stagnant. The J.B.'s under Fred Wesley were as tight as ever, but the caliber of musicians had diminished. They were no longer that cutting-edge outfit at the top of the heap. James had lowered the bar, and his reluctance to seek more accomplished musicians was puzzling, except to Wesley who once explained to me, "Having lost Pee Wee, Maceo, then Bootsy, James was more secure with a musician that wasn't liable to get hired elsewhere—a guy that was at the top of his career in the J.B.'s rather than just passing through."

Wesley always insisted that, "Because James Brown is such a great entertainer, whoever you put him in front of becomes a great band." And I had to admit that what the J.B.'s did, they did very well. Fred, knowing his players' strengths and weaknesses, was part of the secret; he never assigned them parts they weren't capable of playing. Wesley had also become the face of the band and its most exciting soloist, a role ordinarily reserved for a saxophonist.

Ever since Maceo and his Kingsmen broke up in 1972, James had been asking about his former sax star. What Wesley and very few others knew was that Parker had become so disillusioned with the music business that he had all but stopped playing. In January 1973, Maceo ended his sabbatical and accepted Brown's offer to rejoin the band. Parker provided The J.B.'s with a second exciting solo voice and a veteran stage personality. James quickly took the gang into International Studios in Augusta and recorded "Doing It To Death," a.k.a. "Gonna Have a Funky Good Time." The infectious party jam was issued under Fred Wesley and the J.B.'s but featured a Brown vocal, front and center.

A number one single, "Doing It To Death" turned out to be Brown's biggest hit in 1973, which said something about the records issued under his own name. "I Got Ants In My Pants" was mildly successful but hardly memorable. A re-make of "Think" with a New York studio band sounded dated. 1973 was also the year James jumped on the "easy money" movie soundtrack bandwagon. Scores for Blaxploitation films had become a cottage industry for high-level R&B

artists, providing new income opportunities and wider exposure for their music. Curtis Mayfield, Marvin Gaye, Isaac Hayes, and Bobby Womack had all struck pay dirt with Hollywood projects, often utilizing the forums to stretch their creative skill sets. Why not Soul Brother #1?

The problem was that James took the easy money more seriously than the music. He had no patience or interest in the tedious process of film scoring, telling Fred Wesley not to waste any time writing new music but to "use old tracks to go along with the scenes."

Thankfully, Wesley was more realistic about the job and tried his best to supply the film producers with what they needed. The soundtrack albums to *Black Caesar* and, soon thereafter, *Slaughter's Big Rip-off* were probably more successful than they deserved to be. One of the few hits to come out of the albums was "Sexy, Sexy, Sexy," a two-year-old track that was a thinly disguised reinvention of Brown's 1966 hit, "Money Won't Change You." Perhaps the most lasting accomplishment from the association with gangster films was his most recent nickname, which stuck for the rest of his life—the Godfather of Soul.

A third soundtrack deal was in the works for a film called *Hell Up In Harlem* when JB's casual attitude finally backfired. Film producer Larry Cohen told Fred Wesley a tune called "The Payback" wasn't "funky enough." Brown, understandably, exploded; his competitive juices stoked like they hadn't been in years. He withdrew from the film project and prepared to issue what had been intended as the soundtrack album.

I was in the New York office the day the album test pressings were delivered. James was more excited than I'd seen him about a record in a long time; he wanted to make a point to those who doubted the album's relevance. *The Payback* was Brown's first attempt at a "concept" album, so he asked me to write some liner notes that stressed the fact. The two-record set contained some of his best work in a long while, but I recognized that the concept he heralded in the title tune and the album artwork didn't really hold up through the balance of the album. That meant my notes had to be as obtuse as his themes. I lifted catch phrases or hooks from each song's lyrics and strung together a rather infantile essay. I stand by the punchline though. Thinking of Larry Cohen, I wrote: "It's time for even the Godfather to shoot his best shot, and payback is gonna be a mutha!"

Brown explained the record as the story of the workingman's plight in a changing America (remember the Christmas party?). Most of Brown's young fans happily embraced the "power to the people" theme. James would never admit it, but the title song's inspiration had nothing to do with common folk. Instead, it was quite personal. A young lady in Brown's camp was having an affair with Harold Melvin. JB had just caught wind of her broken loyalty before he was about to record "Revenge," a song Fred Wesley had sketched out for the opening scene in *Hell Up In Harlem*. James tossed Wesley's lyrics aside and began freestyling what quickly became "*The Payback*."

I don't remember if Harold ever knew the song's back story, but *The Payback* eventually became one of hip hop's favorite sides to sample. And a whole new generation misunderstood a lyric to the point of printing tee shirts reading "I don't know karate, but I know Ka-razy." JB had lifted the line from an old Clay Tyson comedy routine but the kids got it all wrong; it's actually "I don't know karate, but I know ka-razor."

With the title song a huge hit, Brown's biggest in two years, *The Payback* also became the Godfather's first official gold album. Strangely enough, several critics writing about the project referred to the "heavy" or, in one case, "strange" liner notes. For better or worse, it isn't often you see liner notes mentioned in reviews. And I suppose I can take the blame for the phrase "payback's gonna be a mutha" entering street vernacular. Needless to say, I didn't work with Harold Melvin any longer.

In the spirit of "if it isn't broken, don't fix it," James later asked me to write notes for his next album. This time, I was determined to submit something a bit more lucid, but *It's Hell* was an even less cohesive album than *The Payback*. It was the year of *The Exorcist*, so I called on my sci-fi-loving girlfriend to collaborate. We labored for hours over just a few paragraphs until we were satisfied, hoping our work wasn't too academic for the boss. When I saw the album cover proofs, our notes were conspicuously absent. Oh, well. I might add that the album failed to duplicate the success of *The Payback*. Do not underestimate the power of strong liner notes! (Little did I know that the next time my notes accompanied a James Brown album, I'd win a Grammy.)

The Payback spawned a new string of big hits, "My Thang," "Papa Don't Take No Mess," and "Funky President," that did give the road show a temporary boost, both musically and at the box office. It's noteworthy that two of those songs were recorded with studio bands instead of the J.B.'s. Fred Wesley remembers, "James thought using New York studio musicians was the way to move his music more into the mainstream."

The good fortune ended rather abruptly in 1975. Records like *Reality* and a tepid and pointless re-make of "Sex Machine" quietly came and went. Meanwhile, James stubbornly forged down the familiar one-nighter trail. Business was more erratic than ever. Lucrative trips to Europe, Japan, and Africa were like found money but, the rest of the time, the show precariously struggled week to week. Morale in the band deteriorated and, by the end of 1975, Fred Wesley and drummer John Starks, the J.B.'s' unflappable anchors, were both gone.

The worse things got, the more James tried persuading me to come back full time. I resisted, still making more money promoting isolated dates than I would have on his payroll. And, by the way, it didn't escape me that the payroll I was turning down now hosted the Shades of Soul, a trio of dancers from New York that included one Gloria Thompson, who had once been—you guessed it—a Twisting Parkette!

Don't get it twisted. I never doubted that James Brown would spend the rest of his life successfully entertaining audiences all over the world. The issue was how. The days of in-house promoting the barnstorming James Brown Show were drawing to a close. A month after my last promotion, a Pittsburgh Civic Arena gig that drew less than 3,000 people, Brown's fragile house of cards crumbled. Unable to make payroll, James stranded the band in California. Maceo Parker decided to join Bootsy's Rubber Band and the rest of the fellas found their way home.

James looked for blame. His employees blamed him. The media and fans debated about what went wrong. But, as usual, I didn't think it was complicated at all. As an artist, James had long ago defined himself, there wasn't much fresh in his arsenal. His records had become derivative and, worse yet, occasionally downright plagiaristic. "Hustle (Dead On It)" was blatantly lifted from an Afro-Beat jam he had heard in Cameroun. At least that one was obscure. Worse was "Hot (I Need To Be Loved, Loved, Loved, Loved)," an easily recognizable bite of David Bowie's popular "Fame." A disillusioned Fred Wesley says that, when he quit, he chastised Brown for, "copying people who are copying you."

James was always quick to call out those he felt were using too many of his tricks, but he didn't seem to mind getting caught copying anyone else. It was as if he felt the entire funk genre belonged to him and he was authorized to borrow anyone's licks he found attractive. That made me think that he didn't really care whether people understood the technical aspects of his innovations. I honestly don't think he gave it much thought. Maybe that was because a work ethic is what drove him rather than an artistic sensibility. He considered himself a businessman and entertainer first and a musician second— an entertainer whose vast repertoire and creativity provided him with options. The churchy doo-wop of his early years, the 1950s jump blues he covered so effortlessly, his textbook soul singing in the 1960s, his prototype funk in the 1970s, or his occasional forays into jazz and standards were all real parts of James Brown. So, whether he was recognized for his hugely important musical contributions or just his flashy dancing, so be it. It didn't appear to matter to him, as long as he was recognized, and people bought tickets to his shows.

1975's Payback tour was the James Brown Show's last hurrah as a contemporary, relevant creative entity. It was probably unfair to continue expecting anything cutting-edge from an artist who had been making records and touring non-stop for almost twenty years. In a business where "you're only new once," the Godfather of Soul had reinvented himself and his music many times over. It was difficult finding any music fan who hadn't seen the James Brown Show at least once. And we all know that the Godfather continued presenting wonderful shows with talented, professional bands, recreating his many hits to adoring audiences until his death in 2006.

25

It wasn't easy leaving my dream job. Just meeting, let alone working for James Brown had been a wild, unpredictable fantasy—the kind of lightning unlikely to strike twice. It had been a great introduction to the music business, and the lessons didn't end there. James Brown had taught me how to better appreciate the music I loved. He taught me about this country and its many faces. He demonstrated how to have hope when there is no hope, and he was living proof that, if you believe in yourself, sooner or later, someone else will believe in you too.

Part of my interest in a career change had to do with Deborah and finding out how we'd fare in a more normalized family situation. Through no fault of hers—not very well. The music biz and the life-style were in my blood, and I was too immature to even begin to know how to manage it with any balance. But, if everything happens for a reason, that reason was the birth of my son, Tristan Alan Leeds. His arrival may not have curbed my road addiction, but it sure convinced me that my life was about more than just me. I don't know if it was the best teaching experience but, as soon as he was old enough, Tristan was spending school holidays on tour with me and getting to know the stars I worked with. The good news is that he grew up with a very mature, balanced view of the celebrities that others foolishly obsess over. He appreciates the arts but hasn't got a TMZ bone is his body—I love that. More importantly, I love that in addition to being a son I can be proud of, he is also a partner and friend. To steal a line from Eddie Palmieri, he lives in my heart and pays no rent.

I have been very blessed. I've enjoyed a life-long career indulging in what essentially began as a hobby, my love of music and fascination with those who make it. I appreciate how that must sound to people who spend their lives bored by work or, worse yet, doing things they dislike. But they should know that nothing is free. Such a passionate career, particularly one in the arts, inevitably becomes a mistress. My life as a freelancer is one with erratic, unpredictable periods of employment and irregular hours. It's a lifestyle that discourages normalcy and can be terribly unfair to a family, thus causing one a ton of guilt. Having said that, I was fortunate enough to encounter a soulmate with a spirit as free as mine.

It was 1981 and I had just moved to Brooklyn Heights in my beloved New York. Soon, friends were trying to connect me with a girl—"You gotta meet her," claimed jazz drummer Philip Wilson, who had a project I was managing at the time. "She's the only girl I've ever known who is as crazy as you." Turns out Philip's wife had been telling her the same thing about me. Neither of us expressed any interest—until the Wilsons tricked us into both attending a Lester Bowie gig at Seventh Avenue South. Gwendolyn Gwyn, now Gwendolyn Leeds, and I became a couple soon thereafter.

She is definitely NOT crazy, but I'm still crazy—about her—and she is a self-secure, non-conformist who always marches to her own drumbeat. I'm sure there have been times that she was as glad to see me go on the road as I was glad to start a new tour. That's understandably less the case as we grow older, which has helped me really understand that my greatest blessing was not my career itself, but my life partner and my son who both supported it.

THERE WAS A TIME

As the years passed by, the Godfather was never too far away. Gwen had a chance to meet him on one of our first dates—a Brown gig at the Palladium in New York. A native of New Jersey who was then head of public relations for the prestigious Hayden Planetarium at the Museum of Natural History, Gwen's experiences with the South and Southern folk were pretty much limited to her college years at Tennessee State. I don't think she was prepared for what she considered a step back in time that reminded her of her days in Nashville. She wasn't far wrong. By 1981, the Brown crew's old-school soul show format and backstage ambiance may have been dated, but charmingly so. Mr. Brown's sincere but somewhat tasteless acknowledgement of Gwen, who happens to be black, was to point in the direction of his own companion, who happened to be white, laugh uproariously and bellow, "Ahhh, Mr. Leeds, I see you got the chitlin's while I got the bagels." Ms. Gwyn was unimpressed. At least until the Godfather told us about his 1980 shows in the state of Washington, where concerned promoters supposedly secluded him in a hyperbolic chamber, or "air bubble," as he described it, to protect him from any toxic fallout resulting from the recent eruption of nearby Mt. St. Helens. I don't know if Gwen appreciated the story itself or the balls it took to conjure it up. Welcome to my world, sweetheart.

By 1984, I was part of Prince's management team, and Gwen and I were based in Minneapolis. Just as the Purple Rain phenomenon was spreading worldwide, James came through town to play at First Avenue, the very club in which Prince shot the film's performance scenes. It didn't escape me that Brown was then relegated to the club circuit, while Prince had graduated into a bona fide stadium headliner. As we stood in the club's lighting booth watching the show, I asked the Purple One if he wanted to go backstage afterwards and meet one of his major heroes. In his inimitably understated fashion, Prince turned to me and simply said, "Why?" By the end of the show, he had quietly vanished rather than face the discomfort of meeting someone by whom he was utterly intimidated.

It was probably a smart move. The first thing James suggested to me was that our upcoming Purple Rain tour should coordinate its schedule to follow his performances, so he could plug our gigs in advance. I chose not to point out that the first month of our arena tour sold out in a day. Brown had already let it be known that he wasn't above attaching his wagon to the hottest record and tour of the year. Asked in an MTV interview how he felt about a youngster like Prince eclipsing his own record and ticket sales, James pointed out to a national television audience, "Well, Prince has some of my people over there, namely Alan Leeds."

Besides trying to glom some credit, it was also James' backhanded way of demonstrating pride that one of his professional family was part of Prince's success. I was fortunate. Unlike Buddy Nolan, Bob Patton, and many of my JB colleagues, I had been young enough to comfortably adapt to the "new" touring business, one more sophisticated and corporate than anything we had known in the '60s and early '70s. After the First Avenue show, Brown reiterated his fatherly pride when he interrupted a conversation I was having with Danny Ray to tell his long-time emcee, "Enjoy this rap, Mr. Ray. Mr. Leeds has come a long way. It ain't every day you can have this. You know, NOW you need an *appointment* to see Mr. Leeds. Mr. Leeds has become an appointment man." He was not being sarcastic. It was JB speak for giving me dap. Requiring an appointment was his metaphor for success.

After a lengthy dressing room visit, we hugged and pledged to stay in touch. Little did I know that our Minneapolis visit wasn't over. I naturally assumed that James quickly left town but, the next night, Gwen and I came in from dinner to a frantically blinking phone machine, three messages deep. I hit the play button and there was that unmistakable voice: "Alan, this is your godfather. Come to the Amfac Hotel and call me from the lobby."

The second message had urgency: "Alan, call me. It's your uncle, James Brown."

The third message was downright desperate. He was shouting: "Alan, I know you're there. This is James Brown, your uncle. Call me right away! Pick up! Pick up, Alan! Call me at the Amfac. Call me, right away!"

I wasn't sure what to make of it, but Gwen and I couldn't help but chuckle at the idea that he needed to identify himself in such detail. But I knew why—my JB radar was alive and well. I didn't know who, but I was sure he had an audience while making those calls and whatever he wanted had something to do with whoever was with him. I had a flight with Prince to New York the next morning, but that wasn't going to stop me from going to see what was up with the Godfather.

James had a two-level suite at the downtown hotel and, as I sat on the couch, I could hear a female voice coming from the bedroom above. Our conversation began casually, Brown asking me how I enjoyed living in Minneapolis. He thought I looked pale and decided that I needed the nutrients only found "back home." "Mr. Leeds, I'm going to save your life. Son, you need some red Georgia clay in your house. I don't care what you do with it, but you and Mrs. Leeds need to be breathing the same air as that clay. As soon as I get home, I'm sending you a box."

I knew better than to disagree—about my good health or the benefit of the clay. (I guess my teeth must have looked okay.) Then he reached for a small container of Vaseline from the coffee table. He stuck a finger in, took out a giant gob and ate it! "Son, I'm telling you, you're in the fast track now. You MUST watch your health. I'm telling you, you need me like never before." Then he offered me the jar of Vaseline and said, "Now, this will keep your system clean. That's where everything starts—keeping your insides clean as your outsides."

Remember, this was the 1980s. I was accustomed to musicians offering a wide variety of treats, some legal and some not, but Vaseline? He wasn't happy, but I passed.

Just then, a woman I recognized as Mr. Brown's current companion, Adrienne "Alfie" Rodriguez, descended from upstairs, and handed James a cordless phone. It was her mother, and James lit into telling her how happy Adrienne made him and how great they were together. Alfie went back upstairs, then James suddenly threw me the phone, "That's Adrienne's mother, she needs to know you—what a wonderful young man you are."

I had no idea what to say or any idea why I was talking to her in the first place. I adlibbed some nonsense about how nice it was to meet Ms. Rodriguez and how happy she and Mr. Brown seemed before James took the phone back and said goodnight. Only then did he reveal the reason for his calls. "Mr. Leeds, I need your help. I want to get married here tomorrow."

I was stunned. I told him about my early flight and began explaining that I had no idea what the requirements were for a Minnesota marriage license but, by then, he wasn't paying me any attention. He had gotten Rev. Al Sharpton on the phone and, after instructing him to catch the first flight to Minneapolis in the morning, he turned to me and said, "I'm sure Mrs. Leeds can contact your lawyer and figure out the details. Have her call me in the morning."

That's how we left it. When I got home, there was a message to call Rev. Al. "Alan," he said. "You know I love Mr. Brown, but he's stone-crazy. I ain't comin' to Minnesota tomorrow and I doubt he's getting married but do whatever you think you need to do."

I did just that, which meant catching my flight and asking Gwen to research the ins and outs of getting a marriage license. By the time she called Mr. Brown's hotel with her report, he had checked out and left town!

The mysterious exercise became clear a few days later during the flight back home from New York. I was reading a newspaper and came across an article about James Brown's home in South Carolina having been padlocked by the IRS. THAT's why he had to stay over in Minneapolis. He COULDN'T go home—not until his attorneys could work out a payment plan with the government and regain access to the estate. As for the marriage? I suspect he was afraid that the state of his affairs might frighten Adrienne away—that he better tie down the relationship while he could. Within a couple weeks, he had regained his property and he and Alfie did get married.

Throughout the next few years, there'd be an occasional phone call, and James and I would periodically cross paths on the road. I had been hearing tales of his drug use and volatile relationship with the latest Mrs. Brown, but I didn't experience it for myself until I took Sheila E to see his much-heralded return to the Apollo in 1987. She had never seen him perform and was excited at the opportunity. Once I got Sheila and her security settled into our seats, I dashed backstage for a quick pre-show hello. Rolling Stone Keith Richards and drummer/producer Steve Jordan were standing idly in front of James' dressing room door, through which I could hear Alfie hollering at Gertrude Sanders. "Gertie, I told you I don't care who it is; we're not seeing anybody right now."

I didn't know Jordan or Richards, but we all looked at each other—silently asking what to do next. Richards and I decided to wait and greet James on his way to the stage. About three minutes later, the door opened and JB came out. He saw us and stopped cold without a single word of greeting, a blank look on his face. It was painfully obvious he either couldn't recognize us or that he simply didn't understand why we were THERE. Whatever he saw was out of focus and out of place. Both Keith and I clumsily muttered something about it being nice to see him and "have a great show" before retreating.

St. Clair Pinckney and singer Martha High had warned me that he wasn't the man I used to know, but seeing it for myself was shattering. The show was awful. James cut off songs half-finished, left the stage to eternal Maceo Parker sax solo-stall tactics, and even repeated a song or two. I was hurt, embarrassed for James, and sorry for Sheila that THIS was the James Brown show she would remember.

In my day, Brown was NEVER out of control. He might have a drink or two in a club or a hotel bar after a show, but I never saw him tipsy. He was virulently anti-drug, his own substance use limited to an occasional joint late at night to unwind. Back then, he called weed "groove" and only after he was safely back in his suite at the end of an evening would he "get his groove on." But, by the 1980s, he had taken to lacing his joints with PCP (angel dust) and his drug use spiraled.

Worse yet, the drug problem didn't serve his other glaring weakness very well. James came from a long, ugly, backwoods tradition of men believing it was proper to control their women physically. The elephant in our tour bus was the rumor that he and his women, particularly his wives, frequently went a round or two. He tried his best to keep it under wraps but, on some level, we all knew there were times when Mrs. Brown, any Mrs. Brown, might be in for more than a casual slap. I have regrets that none of us who worked for him ever did or said anything about it, but it's not like we could have stopped it. And confronting James would have been a sure-fire pink slip. But knowing it went on was uncomfortable at best. And, from what the newspapers were saying, the PCP had taken his battle appetite to a new level. His numerous arrests and eventual prison term in 1988 were inevitable. Like many, I was relieved. He obviously needed the "time out."

After a 1991 pay-per-view comeback show, Brown's post-prison marquee value caught fire. Despite occasional drug relapses, his career stabilized and, throughout the 1990s, he toured regularly and profitably, an always-in-demand attraction across the far reaches of the globe. I was pleased to see the worldwide adoration he received as a performer, although I must admit it annoyed me that most people were unaware of the groundbreaking, razor sharp James Brown I knew back in the day.

In 1992, I had the honor of sharing a Grammy with Mr. Brown, Universal Music executive Harry Weinger, film producer-author Nelson George, and the late British writer Cliff White for our liner notes to *Star Time*, an elaborate four-C.D. career retrospective. It isn't often a non-performer gets nominated, much less wins a Grammy, so it was an exciting time. Brown was unable to attend the ceremonies, although Harry, Nelson, Cliff and I, non-performers all, were eager to get on the Radio City Music Hall stage to accept our trophies. But what means more to me than the Grammy is the booklet from *Star Time* that I had everyone—JB, the Famous Flames, the musicians, even the roadies, eventually sign like a high school yearbook. When it was his turn, James wrote, "Thanks for helping on <u>our</u> Grammy" (his under-score). I've often said that, if my house catches fire, after family, that booklet is the first thing I'd save.

A few months before his sudden death on Christmas, 2006, I saw the Godfather at the Palace in Hollywood. He was headlining an all-star benefit alongside contemporary stars like Usher, Justin Timberlake, the Black Eyed Peas, and my then-client, Raphael Saadiq. Since JB was only doing a cameo, it was a low-stress evening, and we had an opportunity for an uncharacteristically long hug and a warm, lengthy visit. I knew he had been battling prostate cancer and diabetes but, other than a noticeable weight loss, he looked good and I told him so. "Mr. Leeds," he said with a smile. "Look at us. A couple of old men but we're both still out here and lookin' good doing it!"

I worried that Saadiq felt ignored when I helped walk JB, entourage style, to the stage. But I'm glad I did—it was the last time I saw the Godfather alive.

My post-JB career has been an unending series of "coincidences," or simply being in the right place at the right time. In 1981, a friend dragged me to a Prince show against my will. But I left there in awe, dreaming of working with him some day. A year-and-a-half later, I was road managing a Kiss tour and a casual backstage conversation unexpectedly led to ten years as Prince's tour manager and the vice presidency of his Paisley Park Records—ten years that are worth a book unto themselves.

In 1988, Nelson George brought a young pal named Chris Rock to a Prince concert of mine in New York. Rock was a young comic, two years away from his stint on *Saturday Night Live*, but he excitedly told me, "One day, I'm gonna do a big tour and I want to work with you."

It was one of those, "Yeah, sure, kid" moments but we stayed in touch. Sure enough, once his career exploded, he hired me. I've now managed four Chris Rock tours, breaking down doors along the way by introducing his brilliant brand of comedy to Puerto Rico, England, Scotland, South Africa, Australia, and New Zealand.

I am fortunate in that I've met all of my musical heroes. I've known the always entertaining and ingenious George Clinton for several decades. Then there was every jazz fan's hero, Miles Davis. Prince was always reluctant to give out his phone number, so I became one of his conduits to others, notably including Miles. More than once, I came home to a blinking answering machine and then heard Davis' oft-mocked gravel voice growl, "Tell the little purple motherfucker to call me." Over a couple of years, we developed a rapport and I often visited him on his gigs. I last saw Miles in a Santa Monica hospital just weeks before he died. Representing Prince, I was honored to speak at Davis' memorial in New York, along-side Rev. Jesse Jackson, Quincy Jones, Bill Cosby, Herbie Hancock, Max Roach, Newport Jazz Festival founder George Wein, and New York Mayor David Dinkins—a most definite what-am-I-doing-here moment.

Jazz keyboard wizard Joe Zawinul was another long-time favorite of mine. I had followed his career since his early days with Cannonball Adderley's band, through his and Wayne Shorter's landmark band Weather Report. In 2001, producer-musician Bob Belden asked me to provide liner notes for a Weather Report retrospective CD package, which led to a fascinating visit-interview with Zawinul in his home.

Salsa/jazz legend Eddie Palmieri may be my favorite musician of them all. Once again, I'd been an obsessive fan since the 1960s and had known him since the 1990s. When *Wax Poetics* magazine scheduled a Latin issue in 2011, I volunteered to write the cover story on Eddie. A warmly hospitable Palmieri welcomed me into his New York apartment for an extended interview and brief private "piano recital." I was in heaven.

One of the gratifications of sticking around show business for so long has been the opportunity to "pass it on" to worthy protégés like Shawn Atkins, Cecilia Ramirez, and the queen of the tour managers, Tina Farris. Not to mention treasured friendships with contemporary musicians like Christian McBride and Ahmir "Questlove" Thompson, their talent exceeded only by their knowledge and curiosity about where their music comes from.

Nelson George once wrote a Billboard column about how I was one of the few that had successfully graduated from the mom-and-pop music biz into the modern era. To be sure, a lot changed. The joke was that a 1970s road manager's briefcase contained nothing but an ounce of weed and rolls of quarters for pay phones. Needless to say, today, we travel laden with a mandatory array of digital devices, connectors, and chargers. But the essence of what produces a great concert hasn't changed much. The wrappings may be high tech but, inside the package, it's still about exciting, creative artists with distinctive voices. In 1996, a friend gave me a demo pressing of *Urban Hang Suite*, soul singer Maxwell's debut album. I fell in love with its clever writing, savvy musicianship, and effortless vocals. Several months later, I got a call from Jeff Frasco, an agent at William Morris. Frasco asked if I was interested in taking on a new artist he described as "high maintenance" but one who "really has the goods." Guess who? Four Maxwell tours eventually led to D'Angelo, who has become family—a godson. Michael "D'Angelo" Archer is a pure artist—famously eccentric but extraordinarily gifted. A young man with an old soul, he has allowed me the most creative input I've ever enjoyed with an artist and helped this older man keep his soul young. By the way, to bring things fittingly full circle, D'Angelo grew up in Richmond, Virginia.

For what it's worth, I did nothing to provoke any encounter with the artists I've worked with. The only one I chased was James Brown and, at some moment in each of those relationships, I was still that starry-eyed kid meeting James Brown in his hotel room. I have no illusion that my life-long work has been any major contribution to the world—putting up concerts is hardly curing cancer. But I still get goosebumps when the house lights go out and an audience screams with joyous anticipation. It's gratifying to feel I am somehow contributing to their happiness, even if it's only for three hours.

In recent years, I was asked to consult on two James Brown film projects, *Mr. Dynamite*, an Alex Gibney produced documentary that aired on HBO, and the Hollywood bio-pic *Get On Up*. So, James Brown is still very much in my life.

A Grammy and fifty years later, I'm also proof that James was right when he said, "If you believe in yourself, sooner or later, someone else will believe in you too."

ACKNOWLEDGMENTS

THIS BOOK IS THE CULMINATION OF A NEARLY LIFE-LONG EFFORT. Many moons ago, the fan in me began collecting records, photos, and clippings about James Brown. I began interviewing Brown and his many cohorts, musicians, singers, and dancers the day I first met them. The entire time I worked for him, and for all the years after, I never stopped picking their memories and writing things down. In the 1970s, with Mr. Brown's urging, I rescued obsolete files full of recording session reports, publicity pictures, vinyl test pressings, and road itineraries that were otherwise destined for trash bins. I even own the only known pressing of Brown's primitive 1958 "demo" of "Try Me" and "Bewildered"—the recordings that convinced King Records to re-sign him and give his nascent career a second chance. Over the years, the archive has grown into five file cabinets and many shelves of records, videos, CDs, and posters.

This book began as a JB bio and gradually morphed into a diary of sorts. It became like a favorite toy that I would pull out and play with once or twice a year. Eventually, I shared a few pages here and there to friends who urged me to take it more seriously, no one more than my wife Gwen and my late mother, neither of whom really believed they would ever see a finished book. I hate that Mom was right, but she and my wife shared a special bond, so I'm sure Gwen will give her an update.

Gwen was listening when they said, "in sickness and in health." I owe her my life in more ways than many. She is a partner in every sense of the word, and gave me the large family I never had. We finish each other's sentences and view the world through the same crooked glasses.

I was blessed with parents who never encountered a son's obsession they wouldn't support. Without that unconditional indulgence, I wouldn't have had the career that I write about. Nor would my brother, Eric, the musician Leeds that I'm not. I can't write anything about James Brown without running it by Eric, whose uncanny memory and unerring attention to detail rivals my old diaries for accuracy. If anyone would ever mount an in-depth, scholarly study of James Brown's music, it should be Eric.

At this stage of my life, my son Tristan is my toughest critic but also my best promoter, suggesting everything from Dad bobbleheads to every sort of digital promotional platform imaginable. Tristan has no patience for bullshit and can read people like he has X-ray vision. In the 1980s, he was responsible for convincing my old-school ears that hip-hop was not a fad but a genre of Black music to be taken seriously. More importantly, he is an honest, quality man who expects the same from others—a pure soul and my pride.

Mutual support runs deep in the Leeds family, and it was Aunt Florence and Uncles Mel and Phil whose roles in the music business set the table for me. Now I have a bunch of much-loved nieces and nephews sitting there too. I'd give them all a shout-out, but that list would be long enough for another book.

Before I mention others, whose encouragement was special, I need to thank two people without whom this book wouldn't have happened. Minneapolis writer Steve Perry gave me tons of great ideas and helped shape and write portions of an early draft. Steve showed me what the book should be. Meanwhile, Nelson George, a cherished friend of over thirty years, taught me so much, including how to hurdle over writer's block.

Trolling through the complex, uber-dimensional James Brown story with others who share my obsession is crucial. Ahmir "Questlove" Thompson, Christian McBride, Harry Weinger, brother Eric, and I have an exclusive club in which we share all things JB. A week seldom goes by without us sending each other James Brown trivia, links to videos, internet stories, or simply opinions about JB recordings. Ahmir and Christian are today's hardest working men in show business—exemplary decency, work ethic, and ambition must run rampant in the Philadelphia Water Works. Weinger's caring work with legacy recordings has become the record industry's gold standard. In 1992, Harry became my first editor, immeasurably helped my writing and gave me the opportunity to work with the very catalogue of James Brown recordings that I adored all my life. A Grammy and a slew of CD reissues and compilations later, I feel like I get paid for a hobby.

Through my life's journey, I have been fortunate to cross paths with a rich group of people who offered an abundance of friendship, love, encouragement, and support. Deborah Thompson-Leeds lived through some of this story and always had my back; Mary Elizabeth Gwyn, my other mother who proves fam comes first—the Abernathys, the Gwyns, the Larsons, the Samuelsons, the Thompsons, and the Washingtons; Erin Sanders-Sigmon, and Lily Moon; Alan Buckman, best friend and running buddy from the very beginning; Ben Miles, who went on to rule Richmond radio for decades; Brother Matt Ledbetter, who did the same thing in Pittsburgh; Mark Adelman; Eothen Alapatt; Von Alexander; Khadra Ali; Michael Archer—the most soulful and purest artist I have ever known, who tutored me through Dilla 101; Marylou Badeaux; Harold Beane, Mathieu Bitton; Tony Blades; Dr. Stuart Bloom; Sharon Blynn; Jon Bream; Bug On The Rug; Jerry Butler; Jez and John-Henry Butterworth; Heinrich Buttler; Bob Cavallo; Dave Chappelle; George Clinton; Cheo Hodari Coker; Lisa Cortes; Frank Cuspard; Chuck D.; Sheila Escovedo; my sister, Tina Farris—the worst drum tech but best tour manager in the world; Blair Foster; Jeff Frasco; Shawn Gee; Peter Guralnick; Rob Hallet; Reggie Hudlin; Malcolm "Boots On The Ground" Kee; Josh Klein; Juli Knapp; Karen Krattinger; Sarah Lazin—who represents so many real writers but always had time for advice and encouragement—she made me feel like a writer before I deserved to; Spike Lee, who so wanted to do the JB biopic; Alan Light; Kevin Liles; George Livingston; Viveca Lowenhielm; Maxwell; Renee Neufville; Yvonne Orji—I'm framing the tee shirt; Rene Oudenhoven; Pino Palladino; Eddie Palmieri; Robbie Paster—the ultimate team player; Jim Payne; James Poyser; Billy Price;

Cecilia Ramirez; Bill Reeves—my road partner for so many years; David Ritz; Chris Rock; Maya Rudolph; Raphael Saadiq; Jeff Sharp; Rev. Al Sharpton; R.J. Smith; Billy Sparks; Therese Stoulil; Andre Torres; Touré; Ricky Vincent; Amy Wallace; Dyana Williams; Geof Wills; Aisha K. Staggers for caring and finding this book a home; Jacob Hoye, Heather King, and everyone at Post Hill Press.

Then there are those in the James Brown extended family, many of whom have generously indulged me whenever I needed to pick their memories. Deidre Jenkins; Deanna Brown-Thomas; Dr. Yamma Brown; Peter Afterman; Vicki Anderson-Byrd; Emma Austin; Bootsy Collins; Joe Davis; Fred Daviss; Alfred "Pee Wee" Ellis; Martha High; Keith Jenkins; Rock Laster; Lola Love; Anne Norman; Maceo Parker; Melvin Parker; Danny Ray; Henry Stallings; Fred Thomas; Ron Tooley; Frank Waddy; Fred Wesley, if you like this book you MUST get Wesley's book, *Hit Me Fred*; and Damon Wood.

The saddest thing about growing older is the mounting list of friends who are no longer here. I wish I could personally thank Clayton "C.P." Brown—my other best friend; Tiger Tom Mitchell—my very first mentor; Bill "Hoss" Allen; Leon Austin; Ben Bart; Bob Belden; Bobby Bennett; H.B. Bennett; Herferth "Tiny" Blue; Charles Bobbit; Joseph Brown; Teddy Brown; Bobby Byrd; Gregory "G.C." Coleman; Lyn Collins; Phelps Collins; James Crawford; Steven Fargnoli; Clayton Fillyua; Walter Foster; Luke Gonder; Kush Griffith; Johnny Griggs; Lewis Hamlin; Roy Hargrove; Freddie Holmes; Kenny Hull; Denise Matthews; Hal Neely; Prince Rogers Nelson; Buddy Nolan and Bob Patton who showed me the ropes; Jimmy Nolen; Irwin Pate; St. Clair Pinckney; Gertrude Saunders; Lloyd Stallworth; John Starks; Henry Stone; Clyde Stubblefield; Johnny Terry; Dominique Trenier; Teddy Washington; Cliff White; and Marva Whitney.

Finally—to Soul Brother #1, for letting a fan have a career. Fifty-eight years and a long career later, I'm still a fan!